T0361928

Ably examining the interactions between trade and foreign investment 'liberalisation' and other industrial policies, and their implications for Indian industrial restructuring, Smitha Francis critically considers Indian participation in global value chains, especially electronics, and with plurilateral 'free trade' agreements.
    – **Jomo Kwame Sundaram**, *former UN Assistant Secretary General for Economic Development*

India's economy is delicately poised in the context of today's globalisation. Smitha Francis's theme that India urgently needs firm-level industrial policy is well argued, convincing, timely and relevant beyond India.
    – **Pasuk Phongpaichit**, *Professor Emeritus in Political Economy, Chulalongkorn University, Bangkok, Thailand*

A path-breaking book, which undertakes a critical look at the interactions between trade, FDI, global value chains and manufacturing sector in India. A highly recommended book for researchers and policymakers.
    – **Abhijit Das**, *Professor and Head, Centre for WTO Studies, New Delhi, India*

Global production networks have changed forever the way in which cross-border transactions in goods and services are conducted. Smitha Francis has provided a remarkable account of this complex phenomenon with considerable deftness. This volume is a must-read for all students of international economics.
    – **Biswajit Dhar**, *Professor, Centre for Economic Studies and Planning, Jawaharlal Nehru University, New Delhi, India*

Industrial Policy Challenges for India

This book looks at the debates on global value chains (GVCs) and free trade agreements (FTAs) as springboards for industrial development in developing countries, especially India. It connects the outcomes in GVC-led industrial restructuring and upgrading to industrial policy choices in trade and foreign direct investment (FDI) liberalisation, in particular those through FTAs.

With the share of manufacturing in GDP stagnant at around 15–16 per cent since the 1980s, India's policymakers have pinned their hopes on greater integration into GVCs to revitalise the manufacturing sector. The multiple FTAs the country has signed over the last few years, specifically the ones with the Association of Southeast Asian Nations (ASEAN), South Korea, Malaysia and Japan, have been sought to be rationalised using the same argument. The book argues that failing to factor in the industrial policy causalities involved in sustainable indigenous technology development, structural barriers to the entry into GVCs, the assessments of the available evidence on the adverse impact of trade and FDI liberalisation as well as existing FTAs on firm-level incentives for undertaking domestic production, and the industrial policy constraints imposed by FTAs can prove costly for the trajectories of developing country economies, including India.

Rich in data, this book will be useful to scholars and researchers of development economics, economics in general, development studies and public policy as well as government bodies, industry experts and policymakers.

Smitha Francis is a Consultant with the Institute for Studies in Industrial Development (ISID), New Delhi, India. Her research interests cover the interfaces between different processes of trade and FDI liberalisation, industrial policy, digital transformations and manufacturing sector development. Previously, she has worked at Economic Research Foundation (ERF), New Delhi, the Secretariat for International Development Economics Associates (IDEAs); and Research and Information Systems for Developing Countries (RIS), New Delhi. She has also served as a Visiting Faculty member at the South Asian University, New Delhi, and Ambedkar University Delhi. In addition, she has been a consultant in projects sponsored by the Department of Commerce, Government of India; the Indian Council for Social Science Research (ICSSR); the Rosa Luxemburg Foundation, Brussels; the Centre for WTO Studies, New Delhi; the Frederick S. Pardee Centre for the Study of the Longer-Range Future, Boston University; the United Nations Office of the United Nations High Commissioner for Human Rights (UN OHCHR); and the United Nations International Children's Emergency Fund (UNICEF).

Critical Political Economy of South Asia

Series editors
C. P. Chandrasekhar and Jayati Ghosh
both at the Centre for Economic Studies and Planning,
Jawaharlal Nehru University, New Delhi, India

At a time when countries of the South Asian region are in a state of flux, reflected in far-reaching economic, political and social changes, this series aims to showcase critical analyses of some of the central questions relating to the direction and implications of those changes. Volumes in the series focus on economic issues and integrate these with incisive insights into historical, political and social contexts. Drawing on work by established scholars as well as younger researchers, they examine different aspects of political economy that are essential for understanding the present and have an important bearing on the future. The series will provide fresh analytical perspectives and empirical assessments that will be useful for students, researchers, policy makers and concerned citizens.

The first books in the series cover themes such as the economic impact of new regimes of intellectual property rights, the trajectory of financial development in India, changing patterns of consumption expenditure and trends in poverty, health and human development in India, and land relations. Future volumes will deal with varying facets of economic processes and their consequences for the countries of South Asia.

Global Players and the Indian Car Industry
Trade, Technology and Structural Change
Jatinder Singh

Industrial Policy Challenges for India
Global Value Chains and Free Trade Agreements
Smitha Francis

For more information about this series, please visit: www.routledge.com/Critical-Political-Economy-of-South-Asia/book-series/CRPE

Industrial Policy Challenges for India

Global Value Chains and
Free Trade Agreements

Smitha Francis

Routledge
Taylor & Francis Group

LONDON AND NEW YORK

First published 2019
by Routledge
2 Park Square, Milton Park, Abingdon, Oxon OX14 4RN

and by Routledge
605 Third Avenue, New York, NY 10017

First issued in paperback 2020

Routledge is an imprint of the Taylor & Francis Group, an informa business

© 2019 Smitha Francis

The right of Smitha Francis to be identified as author of this work
has been asserted by her in accordance with sections 77 and 78
of the Copyright, Designs and Patents Act 1988.

All rights reserved. No part of this book may be reprinted
or reproduced or utilised in any form or by any electronic,
mechanical, or other means, now known or hereafter invented,
including photocopying and recording, or in any information
storage or retrieval system, without permission in writing from
the publishers.

Trademark notice: Product or corporate names may be trademarks
or registered trademarks, and are used only for identification and
explanation without intent to infringe.

British Library Cataloguing-in-Publication Data
A catalogue record for this book is available from the British Library

Library of Congress Cataloging-in-Publication Data
Names: Francis, Smitha, author.
Title: Industrial policy challenges for India : global value chains and
    free trade agreements / Smitha Francis.
Description: Abingdon, Oxon ; New York, NY : Routledge, 2019. |
    Includes bibliographical references.
Identifiers: LCCN 2018056793 | ISBN 9780815366058 (hardback : alk.
    paper) | ISBN 9780429244209 (e-book)
Subjects: LCSH: Industrial policy—India. | Free trade—India. |
    India—Commercial policy.
Classification: LCC HD3616.I43 F73 2019 | DDC 338.954—dc23
LC record available at https://lccn.loc.gov/2018056793

ISBN 13: 978-0-367-73137-3 (pbk)
ISBN 13: 978-0-8153-6605-8 (hbk)

Typeset in Sabon
by Apex CoVantage, LLC

In memory of my father, K. K. Francis,
mother, Leela Philip, and
brother, Shaji K. Francis.
But most of all for Ammachi, the bravest of all.

Contents

Illustrations

Figures

Tables

Acknowledgements

This book project was conceived in the beginning of 2017, subsequent to the completion of a study commissioned by the Rosa Luxemburg Foundation (RLS), Brussels, to examine the interactions that I had grappled with for some time by then—challenges posed by global value chains (GVCs) and free trade agreements (FTAs) to the industrialisation efforts of developing countries. I am grateful to Dr. Roland Kulke and Dr. Claus-Dieter König of RLS for commissioning the study, which subsequently became the inspiration for this book. I am also thankful to Dr. Cedric Durand, University of Paris, and Dr. Roland Kulke for their very constructive comments on the original paper.

I am deeply thankful to Jayati Ghosh, Professor at Jawaharlal Nehru University, for all her support since my time as a doctoral student with her in the late nineties. I am also fortunate to have been able to work with her as well as C. P. Chandrasekhar, Professor, Jawaharlal Nehru University, and to have received their guidance and personal support through life's many twists and turns. Whatever I may have achieved as an academic also owes in no small measure to the long years of learning at the Economic Research Foundation (ERF) and the exposure to some of the best minds in economics I received from being a part of the International Development Economics Associates (IDEAs) network. Apart from a vantage point to understand global policymaking and different development experiences, IDEAs also gave me the privilege to know and learn from such luminaries as Prof. Korkut Boratav, Prof. Jomo Kwame Sundaram, Prof. Prabhat Patnaik, Prof. Jan Kregel and Prof. Utsa Patnaik, among many others.

I am equally fortunate to have been associated with the Institute for Studies in Industrial Development (ISID), an ICSSR-affiliated institute with a legacy of in-depth research on industrial development issues in India, including on the role of foreign capital, going back to the 1970s. I am very grateful to S. K. Goyal, Founder Director and Professor Emeritus, ISID, and Prof. M. R. Murthy, Director, ISID, for the opportunities I have gained at ISID for further learning. The fourth chapter in this book originated from the research project "Understanding India's Industrial Development Puzzle through the Interactions between Industrial Policy and Trade Liberalisation: A case study of the Electronics Industry" supported by ISID while I was a Consultant during 2014–16. I'm also thankful to the ISID librarian Amitava Dey, Usha Joshi in the ISID office and Dhanunjai Kumar in the media and publication division for all their support.

I am very grateful to the *Economic and Political Weekly* (EPW) and the Oxford University Press, India, for granting me permission to use material from the papers earlier published with them. I am also thankful to Shoma Choudhury and Rimina Mohapatra with Routledge India for their immense support with this book project, and all the people at Routledge London for their excellent editorial assistance.

I would also like to acknowledge my sincere gratitude to the two anonymous reviewers of my book proposal and especially to my manuscript reviewer, all of whose discerning comments became partly influential in the way the arguments were framed and helped to significantly improve them.

I am very thankful to Chalapati Rao, Emeritus Professor at ISID, who has been a source of inspiration and support. I also owe intellectual debt to him and Biswajit Dhar, Professor at Jawaharlal Nehru University, as evidence building for some of the arguments in this book has benefited from the painstaking and exceptional research they have undertaken on India's FDI inflows over the last several years.

I would also like to thank Prof. Abhijit Das, Head of the Centre for WTO Studies, who deemed it fit to commission a study on the evolution of digital technologies in 2017, which immensely helped me to understand the emerging all-enveloping nature of the digital economy we have entered into.

Needless to say, none of the above mentioned persons can be held responsible for the infirmities in the analyses or arguments presented in this book. I am solely and entirely responsible for all deficiencies, omissions and commissions therein.

My doctoral research experience in the late 1990s to early 2000s of Thailand's FDI-led industrial restructuring efforts has immensely influenced my learning and exploration of the Indian industrialisation experience. I am very thankful to Pasuk Phongpaichit, Emeritus Professor at Chulalongkorn University, Bangkok, for her continuing support all these years. I also remain grateful to Prof. Suwattana Thadaniti, then Director of the Chulalongkorn University Social Research Institute (CUSRI), who was like a local guardian to me during my long stay as a CUSRI Visiting Fellow.

I am very thankful to my friends Shalini Misra, Gayatri Balagopal, Sarah Nial, Rajeswari Raina, Surajit Majumdar, Balakrishnan and Sita, Anirban Dasgupta, Geetha Prakash, Shiji K. Francis, Sindhu Francis, Sumangala Damodaran, Anil and Saumya, Anandita Sharma, Resmi and Ravi, Jitha, Anu and Tom, Gopakumar, Pushparaj, Hasheem Mannan and Swarabji, for being there for me in one way or another, in various phases. I would also like to acknowledge my gratitude to Dr. K. Sudarshan and Dr. A. J. John for all their support and to Dr. Alok Sarin for his blind faith in me. I am also thankful to Annie Auntie, Devaki Ma'am and the Tenderfeet family, Kunjumol Auntie, Mother Marykutty FDSHJ, Fr. Mathew Edayanal and Prof. M. P. Philip, as well as Ikkamma chechi and Joychayan, my cousins, my mother's friends and Chechi, for their support at various times.

I'd very much like to thank my co-traveller Murali for giving me immense encouragement and confidence, which I have sometimes taken for granted. I am also thankful to him for his timely support on issues related to data analysis whenever I needed it. I cannot wind up without mentioning Achu, who has often surprised me with his love and understanding. I'm also very thankful for the loving support from Murali's parents, Rameshettan and Anithechi, as well as the extended family.

I'd like to remember with love and gratitude Kunjappachayan and Annamma Elemma, my late paternal uncle and aunt, whose support saw me through many troubled years. Last, but not least, I am deeply indebted to Animma Auntie and Aju, Joy uncle and Sicily auntie, Avirachan and Bindu, Jojo, Shiney chechi and Gracy auntie, and all their respective families, for being a part of my life. I would not have reached this point without all of them.

Chapter 1

Introduction

India has seen much discourse on manufacturing sector revival strategies in academic and policymaking circles in recent years. This has followed widespread recognition that the stagnant manufacturing sector, and its growing import dependence and lacklustre export performance after more than 25 years of liberal reforms, reflects the limited extent of structural diversification that should have accompanied economic development.[1] With the manufacturing sector's share in India's GDP stagnating at about 15–16 per cent since the mid-1990s despite extensive and intensive trade and financial liberalisation, India's policymakers have pinned their hopes on greater integration into global value chains (GVCs) to help revitalise the manufacturing sector. The multiple free trade agreements (FTAs) the country has signed over the last few years, particularly the ones with ASEAN, South Korea, Malaysia and Japan, have also been sought to be rationalised using the same argument. India is currently involved in more FTA negotiations, including one with the EU, as well as a mega regional FTA, the Regional Comprehensive Economic Partnership (RCEP).

Meanwhile, in a silent admission of growing concerns about Indian industrial performance, and in a reflection of the fact that the popular opprobrium attached to industrial policy has 'waned' after the resurgence in industrial policy discussions globally, the Department of Industrial Policy and Promotion (DIPP) under the Ministry of Commerce and Industry came out with a Discussion Paper on a new Industrial Policy in August 2017. With an explicit focus on increasing "global strategic linkages", the stated objective of the new policy is to provide "an overarching umbrella policy framework" (Government of India 2017: 7, 8). However, the document considers foreign direct investment (FDI), exports, domestic value generation, technological development, employment, etc. in a piecemeal manner, raising the question as to whether there will be any fundamental break from the past in the expected new industrial policy in terms of the underlying analytical model.

Indeed, most of the ongoing academic and policy discussions surrounding India's manufacturing sector revival strategies take place without acknowledging the following: that the analytical framework underlying the changed national policy framework since 1991[2] has imposed serious constraints on successive governments in dealing with the structural diversification challenges facing a lower middle-income economy like India under globalisation and rapid technological changes. This has been a framework that – after realising the 'limits' of the state-led import-substitution strategy – has perceived liberalisation of trade and FDI flows as policy objectives rather than as policy tools in achieving industrial development. This fundamentally owes to the fact that the theory underlying this framework equated 'inefficiency' of the import substitution industrialisation (ISI) strategy with industrial policy itself. The consequence has been that trade strategies, foreign investment policies, science and technology policies, labour policies, SME development policies, financial sector policies, fiscal policy, etc. have been considered in silos, divorced from a coherent industrial development framework.

It will be incorrect to say that this has been a singularly Indian problem. The export-led growth strategy that has been the preferred development model for successive Indian governments since the drastic and comprehensive policy shift in 1991, the accompanying progressive liberalisation of FDI and the tendency to shun industrial policy (by encapsulating it within the state-versus-market debate) have all been part of a global trend.

Global industrial policy debates: the underlying currents

From the beginning, trade policy has been one of the principal issues surrounding development strategy, and as such, it has been an integral part of industrial policy. Intense debates related to trade strategies associated with the development of then late industrialisers, the United States, Germany, France, etc. in comparison with the trade strategies that enabled Britain to develop its industry and progress have gone on since the 18th century. These debates continued after the US became the dominant economic and political power in the early 20th century and afterwards, as a number of former colonies became independent. Subsequently, it was widely recognised that the financing of developing country growth through primary product exports would come up against constraints to development in the form of undiversified production structure and net financial outflows leading to financial fragility. This was based on critical observations by early development theorists contrasting the way Britain, the US and other countries had developed their underdeveloped economies by promoting manufactured goods, while Latin America (dependent on its primary exports) had continued to be underdeveloped. Consequently, active policies for the targeting, promotion and protection of domestic production in increasing return activities, in particular, manufacturing, were designed by developing countries too. These were aimed at promoting diversification, away from activities based on natural (or static) comparative advantage and existing endowments of labour and capital, towards new sectors offering higher productivity potential for the whole economy (see Dutt 2005; Kattel et al. 2009; Reinert and Kattel 2010).

This development framework, which integrates state policies with the need for strategic protection and promotion of national increasing return activities through their import substitution *and* export-led market expansion phases, squarely places trade policy as a tool within the larger industrial policy framework – with the goal of advancing specific sectors that bring economy-wide productivity gains required to sustain a dynamic development process (detailed discussion follows in Chapter 2).

The post-World War II policies relating to foreign capital were also integrally linked to these industrial policy goals. It was recognised that, to harness foreign capital's role in the development process, it must be channelled mostly to savings and investment rather than to an increase in import-dependent consumption. The latter could lead to displacement of whatever little domestic industrial production exists in a developing country and prevent further industrial development, as well as lead to adverse balance of payments situations. Once again, this in turn requires that these strategies to utilise FDI must be used in tandem with the targeting of increasing returns activities (see Chapter 2).

Subsequently though, as several scholars have shown, debates on development strategies became dichotomised in terms of state-led versus market-led growth models. While industrial growth had accelerated throughout much of the developing world at varying rates after World War II, a number of internal and external factors got manifested in different medium-term outcomes in Africa, Latin America and Asia. The particularly contrasting industrial growth experiences of a selective few Latin American and East Asian economies were interpreted by neoclassical development economics as proof that, while developing country governments that intervened strongly in markets suffered from gross inefficiencies (like in Latin America and India), those relying on competitive markets operating broadly on neoclassical principles could foster high levels of economic efficiency and rapid self-sustained growth (as in East Asia) (see Ghosh 2009; Reinert and Kattel 2010). 'Misguided' state activism and development planning which had been pushing industrialisation for the domestic market in defiance of static comparative advantage were attacked by the neoclassical economists (Storm 2015). Gradually this interpretation came under increasing attack, especially in terms of the crucial role of government intervention in the market-oriented economies in East Asia (in particular, the first-tier newly industrialised countries or NICs of South Korea, Taiwan and Singapore) in building their productive capacities ("the developmental state") (see Amsden 1989, 2001; Wade 1990; Sridharan 1996; the literature cited in Fine and Jomo 2006; etc.).

However, one critical element that mainstream economists have continued to highlight is the apparent openness of these economies in terms of trade and FDI that facilitated their rapid economic restructuring. Particularly in Asia, this emerged in the form of the 'flying geese' paradigm, as a type of catching-up industrial development strategy to be led by FDI (see Francis 2003). This is despite the fact that several scholars showed empirically through case studies (indeed the only way in which debates about the role of FDI in technology transfer and industrial catching-up can be settled) that the dominant forms of interaction with transnational firms by late industrialisers (starting with Japan, followed by South Korea, Taiwan and Singapore) involved 'unpackaged' forms for technology transfer – such as licensing arrangements, franchising, management contracts, turnkey contracts, production-sharing contracts, international subcontracting, etc. (see Helleiner 1989; Sridharan 1996; Lall 1992, 1996; see also the extensive literature cited in Francis 2003).

While there were definite domestic and external factors behind India's 1991 balance of payments crisis,[3] the dramatic shift in Indian economic policy framework from the early 1990s was a part of this global shift with the ideological ascendance of neoliberalism. The tragedy in Indian economic policymaking, as elsewhere, has been that arguments against state intervention – such as the danger of corruption and rent-seeking, inefficiency and misguided economic incentives leading to distorted resource allocation – became equated with industrial policy itself. Arguably, this has been a major factor preventing the development of intelligent economic policymaking in India, unlike, say, in China. Rather than tweaking policy interventions for overcoming the observed causes of state failure under the varied ISI experiences in Latin America and Asia, the industrial policy baby was thrown out with the bath water of import-substituting industrialisation.

Thus industrial policy – of the selective or 'active' kind, as understood in the early development literature – was shunned in international policy discussions with the advent of structural adjustment programmes from the mid-1980s onwards. *Ex post*, it is evident that it was always a part of the Washington Consensus and post-Washington Consensus of the late 1990s (and into the 2000s), albeit in a different form. Accordingly, the policy prescriptions by international financial institutions like the International Monetary Fund (IMF) and the World Bank shifted to 'passive' or horizontal industrial policies (Francis 2017), supposedly of the non-price-distortive kind of state intervention.

As described in UNCTAD (2016: XIV, 185–188), a horizontal industrial policy framework (also called a functional industrial policy; see Lall 1996: 126) essentially accepts existing factor endowment-based static comparative advantages and mainly aims to reduce the costs of doing business, while carrying out hands-off trade and financial liberalisation to allow greater play of market forces.[4] The reduction in the costs of doing business ('ease of doing business') is achieved through policy measures aimed at removing inefficiencies and 'dead-weight losses' by improving infrastructure, business entry and exit regulations, taxation, customs and other administrative procedures, investment promotion and facilitation, labour market 'flexibility', trade facilitation, etc. (Low and Tijaja 2013: 4; see also Lall 1996).

Quite evidently, lagging infrastructure development (including energy supply) is an important supply-side factor impacting firm-level competitiveness, just as it impacts the overall development of a country (Francis 2015a). Cumbersome administration of tax and customs is also efficiency reducing. However, other horizontal policies that are advocated such as economy-wide labour market 'flexibility' (meant to address the so-called 'rigidities' in the labour market) and reduction in corporate tax rates have critical development implications, quite apart from the fact that the rationale underlying these have been seriously contested. Their development implications include adverse impacts in terms of inadequate demand, loss of government revenues and the generation of significant inequalities, all of which lead to unsustainable growth trajectories.[5] In fact, all talk about 'inclusive development' (a misnomer in itself) becomes vacuous in the backdrop of implementing such policies.

'Active' or vertical or selective industrial policies that were practised by the first-tier newly industrialised countries in East Asia (South Korea, Taiwan and Singapore) during their 20th century catching-up decades and continue to be practised by them and some of the other late industrialisers such as China, Brazil, etc. are quite in contrast to 'passive' industrial policies (UNCTAD 2016: XIV; Lall 1996; Gallagher and Shafaeddin 2009; Yu et al. 2015; Kasahara and Botelho 2016; etc.). Vertical industrial policies seek to influence the pattern of national industrial development by policy interventions that guide and promote investment domestically towards new activities and sectors with higher productivity, better-paid jobs and greater technological potential (UNCTAD 2016: XIV) – i.e., increasing returns activities. Indeed, policies adopted by most developed countries – including the US, Japan and the EU as well as others like Israel, Ireland and Taiwan – have also continued to make important departures from the rhetoric on 'non-price-distortive' industrial policy, as, for example, documented in the several papers cited in UNCTAD's Trade and Development Report (2014, 2016, 2017); Breznitz (2006); Wade (2012, 2016, 2018); Mathews (2010); and Brandt and Whitford (2017).

From the mid-1990s onwards, along with the spread of an export-led economic growth paradigm, the developing world saw a much wider shift towards passive industrial policies. This was driven primarily by their commitments on tariff liberalisation, along with the restrictions on national policies deemed as trade-related investment measures (TRIMs) and trade-related intellectual property rights (TRIPs) under the World Trade Organization (WTO) from 1995 onwards.

However, by the mid- to late-2000s, after nearly two decades of trade and financial liberalisation, there was recognition that the

Washington Consensus policies had not led to the desired effect in developing countries (Rodrik 2008). Soon, research began to emerge discussing industrial stagnation, deindustrialisation and middle-income traps in developing countries (Wade 2006, 2012; Felipe et al. 2012).[6] Meanwhile, renewed interest in industry's role as a dynamic instrument of growth in the developed economies after the global financial crisis has coincided with a renewed concern for industrialisation and structural change in the mainstream of development economics (Storm 2015). Ironically, around the same time, the policy discourse on developing countries saw a broad shift from trade liberalisation as the panacea for underdevelopment to participation in global production networks (GPNs) and global value chains.

Globally, the post-global financial crisis resurgence of industrial policy discussions has been followed recently by increased focus on the state's role amidst rapid advances in advanced manufacturing technologies and digital disruptions (and increased public attention around Germany's 'Industrie 4.0'). Thus the developed world has been debating the evolving role of the state as observed in practice and 'in effect' (Mathews 2010; Wade 2012, 2018; Fine et al. 2013; Low and Tijaja 2013; Nawrot 2014; etc.),[7] which have included discussions around 'the networking state', 'the entrepreneurial state' and re-visiting the role of the public sector (Kattel and Lember 2010; Mazzuccato 2013, 2017; Lember, Kattel and Kalvet 2013; Brandt and Whitford 2017; Kattel 2018). On the contrary, the global development literature and mainstream economists in developing countries have been advocating that simply easing investment and business regulatory policies for participation in global value chains (GVCs) and entering into free trade agreements (FTAs) will offer springboards for industrial development for developing countries, through greater access to export markets and increased foreign investments (see UNESCAP 2011; OECD 2013; WTO et al. 2013; etc.).[8]

Industrial policy evolution in India: an overview

It is widely known that import liberalisation was initialised in India in the 1980s in response to the realisation that the planned form of state-led import-substituting industrialisation (ISI) development strategy – with extensive controls on production, prices, investment, trade and foreign collaboration – subscribed to in the post-independence decades had *in effect* led to stifling competition and the eventual establishment of an inefficient industrial sector (Mani 2000a; Nagaraj 2003).[9] Despite having a broad-based industrial base, inadequate indigenous technological development meant that import liberalisation raised the import intensity of domestic production (see Ghosh 2013; Sridharan 1996; Nayyar 1994; Chandrasekhar 1994a; etc.). The increase in current account deficits following increased imports was financed by an increase in foreign borrowing from the IMF, the international commercial banking system and non-resident Indians (Ghosh 2013: 177).

One of the major objectives of the liberalisation process was to raise the growth performance of the industrial sector by removing various constraints (on entry and expansion of firms) and especially the requirement for an industrial licence (Mani 2000a: 63). The initiation of the 1991 economic reforms also saw the dilution or dismantling of a large variety of other industrial policy instruments, which had been used to help improve domestic manufacturing capabilities and create the conditions for the development of technologies in the post-independence decades. Apart from the mechanism of industrial licensing and import protection linked to the coordination of plans/strategies, public sector manufacturing, directed credit, etc., industrial policy measures under the ISI regime had included an elaborate FDI regulatory policy, which was coordinated with small-scale industrial policy, patent protection, strong indigenisation policies, etc. in a number of sectors (Chaudhuri 2010).

These FDI regulatory policies had been put in place because of the awareness among policymakers in the immediate post-independence years that, rather than the financial capital invested by MNCs, technology transfer is the essence of 'the FDI package' along with the export market access enabled through the MNC parent firms (Francis 2003, 2010; Rao and Dhar 2018). Given the ownership advantages linked to their proprietary assets and lasting interest, foreign direct investors often maintain tight control over operations of their affiliated companies (Francis 2010), and therefore regulations were a must for ensuring the faster technology development that is expected to occur through technology transfer by MNCs. As we will see in the discussions in Chapters 2 and 3, the coordination of FDI regulations with the other industrial policies mentioned above was thus very important.

Simultaneously, during the first period of state-led ISI, India had also actively pursued the development of indigenous technological capabilities through government policy. As observed in Mani (2001: 23), economic growth with technological self-reliance had been one of the avowed objectives of the planned form of development to which India subscribed. Considerable investments and effort were directed at building a substantial technological infrastructure, with the aim of avoiding dependence on foreign technology. All these policy efforts were successful in a broad range of industries and particularly in textiles and garments, pharmaceuticals, automobiles, iron and steel and other metal-based industries, light and heavy electrical machinery, etc., while they did not lead to successful outcomes in other industries like electronics.

The observed gap between policy intentions and actual outcomes surely called for the appropriate tweaking of trade and FDI regulatory policies as well as other industrial policies to remove the identified excesses of the ISI regime,[10] along with a change in macroeconomic policies. However, Indian policy establishment was swept off by the currents of the changed global outlook on ISI with the rise of neoliberalism and was weighed down by the critique of the 'licence raj' that became overwhelming from the late 1980s.

On the trade front, drastic tariff liberalisation was carried out in the 1990s, initially under the IMF's structural adjustment programme and subsequently as part of India's WTO commitments. Trade liberalisation included import liberalisation in the form of moving from import quotas to tariffs and reducing tariffs (and eliminating them in some cases)[11] and reduction or removal of export controls, etc. (see Banga and Das 2012; Dastidar 2015; Veeramani and Nagaraj 2016 also). But trade liberalisation went far beyond that was required to meet her multilateral commitments at the WTO. As a result of the autonomous (unilateral) tariff liberalisation carried out by India since 1995, India's average applied tariff for all non-agricultural tariff lines stood at around 11 per cent in 2015, while average bound tariff was actually at 34 per cent (Dhar and Das 2015). Despite the gap offered by the higher average bound tariffs, India went on reducing tariffs on manufactured goods during the 1990s.

On the FDI front, in principle, the 1991 Industrial Policy Statement kept true to the earlier intention that India "will . . . welcome foreign investment which is in the interest of the country's industrial development" due to its attendant advantages of technology transfer, managerial techniques, marketing expertise and export potential (Rao and Dhar 2018: 3). Indeed, in order to attract foreign investment in high priority industries requiring large capital and advanced technology, the restrictive approach towards FDI under the ISI regime was relaxed, and approval for direct foreign investment up to 51 per cent of equity in high priority sectors was provided. However, successive governments since then have continuously liberalised the FDI regulatory framework in ambitious drives towards attracting FDI presumably for achieving *East Asian-like growth*, which was perceived as *FDI-driven export-led growth under passive industrial policies* – we call this 'the flying geese syndrome'.[12]

Continuous liberalisation of regulatory policies related to FDI and technology import since 1991 have included the following:

- reducing or eliminating restrictions like limits on which sectors FDI can enter; relaxing rules about extent and nature of ownership (such as caps on foreign equity in various sectors, joint venture requirement), lock-in periods for original investment, divestment requirements in case of foreign subsidiaries in sectors with foreign equity ceilings, etc.;
- relaxing and eliminating rules related to technology transfer, local content, export performance, foreign exchange balancing, etc.; and
- elimination of constraints on repatriation of outflows associated with inflows (such as capital, interest, dividends, technology payments and others); etc.

While FDI was freely allowed in all sectors,[13] including the services sector (except where notified sectors policy did not permit FDI beyond a ceiling), these sectoral caps were all removed during the 2000s. Around 90 per cent of total FDI inflows are now through the automatic route. Only a few sectors such as publishing and printing, satellite, food product trading, mining and mineral exploration, titanium-based minerals and ores require government approval (Government of India 2017: 3).

While automatic permission was given for foreign technology agreements in high priority industries in 1991 itself, and all foreign technology collaboration agreements became permitted on an automatic basis from 1998, the latter was still subject to certain conditions on technology payments (see Mani 2000b: 63). However, the 'Foreign Technology Agreement Policy' in 2009 removed all previous ceilings on technology-related payments for facilitating the inflow of FDI and technology transfer (see Verma and Ranganathan 2016). The expectation of the policymakers guiding such liberalisation was that dismantling all constraints on these payments would encourage better sourcing and transfer of technology. Thus government policy in recent decades has been focusing on creating a facilitating environment for foreign investment in the hope that FDI would bring technological know-how that would automatically spill over into the broader economy. This, despite the fact that, as emphasised by Rao and Dhar (2011, 2016, 2018), there has been "a wide gap between what is meant by FDI and what is measured and reported as FDI" (Rao and Dhar 2018: 5).[14] In reality, the FDI policy liberalisation tended to reflect the need to finance current account deficits.

The debate on foreign technology acquisition has been reduced to how together with improving the overall 'ease of doing business' and adopting export promotion measures, liberalisation of FDI regulatory policies will accelerate foreign investments. Simultaneously, export processing zones (that later became special economic zones or SEZs), infrastructure development and FDI promotion became the policy buzz words.

In the recent years, the focus of FDI liberalisation has shifted to putting an even greater proportion of FDI proposals through the automatic route without requiring government approval.[15] The announcements associated with the 'Make in India' programme initiated by the present government in September 2014 to transform India into a manufacturing power has also placed major reliance on FDI calling them to 'make in India for the world' – in an obvious emphasis on export-oriented FDI. But as we will see below, despite the liberalisation of FDI policies, India did not see large or consistent inflows through the FDI channel.

It must be remembered that since 1991 India has been relying on private capital flows to cover the deficit in foreign exchange needed to finance its increasing current account deficit (Ghosh 2013: 178). Typically, foreign exchange earned through exports or received as remittances used to fall substantially short of payments for imports, interest and dividends. Thus financial deregulation and liberalisation was carried out to allow more capital flows in the forms of especially portfolio investment and external commercial borrowing (Ghosh 2013),[16] while substantial financial flows became possible through the FDI route itself as we will see below.

The rationale behind the liberalisation of capital flows was summed up in Ghosh (2013):

> Ever since India opted for its first big IMF loan in 1981 in the aftermath of the second oil shock, increased dependence on foreign capital inflows has been justified on the grounds that they provide the economy the wherewithal to transform its economic structure and redress its long-term weakness: poor export performance. It was argued that capital flows would allow the country to liberalise trade and subject domestic economic agents to efficiency-enhancing international competition; permit Indian firms to access the foreign exchange needed to import capital and technology required to modernise their equipment and establish internationally competitive capacities that would allow them to compete in export markets; bring with them international producers intent on using India as a base and source for production for the world market; and finance any 'interim' deficit resulting from an import surge that might follow trade liberalisation, but precede India's transformation into a successful exporter.
>
> (Ghosh 2013: 180)

But studies examining the impact of capital flows on India's export productivity and growth in the late 1990s and mid-2000s concluded that capital flows – including FDI – did not contribute to export growth or productivity (see the literature cited in Mazumdar 2005: 278). Now, more recent empirical analysis clearly proves that even after more than a quarter century of trade and foreign investment liberalisation policies, India has not been able to attract significant amounts of FDI into the manufacturing sector or benefit from FDI to meet any of the stated policy objectives.

In-depth studies carried out at the Institute for Studies in Industrial Development (ISID) by Chalapati Rao and Biswajit Dhar (see Rao and Dhar 2016, 2018) at the level of individual FDI inflows during 2004–2014 and October 2014–March 2016 established the following:

- Out of the reported FDI inflows during 2004–2014, *only about half* (53.5 per cent) could be termed as realistic FDI (RFDI), that is, investments "by foreign investors investing in their respective lines of activities who can thus be expected to possess the attributes associated with FDI".[17] This share showed a marginal increase to 58 per cent in the second period.[18]

- In the first period, about 15 per cent of the inflows were by India-related investors, and the remaining was by various types of financial investors. In the second period, foreign portfolio investors accounted for nearly 27 per cent.
- Within RFDI, what was targeted at the manufacturing sector was a little less than half during 2004–2014, and this declined to 26.2 per cent in the second period.

India's open-door FDI policy together with the quirkiness of its liberal definition of FDI has meant that a significant part of 'FDI' inflow has been by private equity, venture capital and hedge funds, etc., which by definition do not represent long-term productive investments. Within the manufacturing sector, transport equipment, expectedly, turned out to be the most important FDI recipient segment. (While transport equipment alone accounted for 30 per cent of the inflows into the manufacturing sector, together with other closely associated industries, like automotive tyres, its share reached 34.5 per cent.) As underlined by Rao and Dhar (2018: 41), the emergence of the automobile sector – a case of classic industrial policy – as the largest 'real FDI' recipient is notable.[19]

On the other side, the lack of coherence in FDI policies and industrial development objectives that ensued as part of reforms has resulted in an increase in FDI inflows through the brownfield route. Rao and Dhar (2018) has shown that FDI through the foreign equity inflow route was itself sustained mainly by a substantial increase in acquisitions of Indian companies/displacing existing shareholders (that is, brownfield FDI). During 2016–2017, acquisitions accounted for practically the entire increase in equity inflows over the previous year (*ibid.*: 32).

It has been found that FDI through the acquisition route has led to increased acquisition by foreign firms of several competent domestic firms – especially in industries such as pharmaceuticals, food and beverages, automobiles and chemicals – to expand their Indian operations and to exploit the capabilities built by domestic firms through years of effort (see the pattern of foreign acquisitions presented in Saraswathy 2016; Rao and Dhar 2018). These are some of the very same industries, in particular, pharmaceuticals and automobiles, which had built up significant indigenous capabilities with the support of industrial policy measures until around the early- to mid-2000s (see Khan 2010; Chaudhuri 2013; Felipe et al. 2010b; Abrol 2014; Jha and Jha 2015; etc.).[20] Ironically, detailed analysis of FDI inflows into the pharmaceutical sector by Joseph and Ranganathan (2016) found that it was in fact those Indian companies which were doing better in terms of exports and R&D, which got converted into FDI companies through the brownfield route. The study also found that FDI did not result in further percolation of widely acknowledged benefits of FDI – promotion of exports and transfer and development of new technologies. In the case of the largest FDI-recipient manufacturing industry (automobiles), a study by Verma and Ranganathan (2016) on listed and unlisted foreign-invested Indian automobile firms found that very few of the foreign-invested firms in the Indian auto sector engaged in any local R&D and that many cases showed perpetual technological dependence.

Another crucial trend that has been observed is that a significant part of the FDI inflows into the manufacturing sector were neutralised by large outflows on account of repatriations/disinvestments. Consequently, the net contribution of the inflows to new capacity creation in manufacturing would have been quite small relatively (Rao and Dhar 2018: 31–32). Thus FDI has also not offered current account support, except in a transient manner.[21] The government's Industrial Policy Discussion Paper has also acknowledged that there have been minimal positive externalities from FDI and significantly low value addition done in India, apart from raising concerns about the brand value of Indian products (GoI 2017: 8).

All these recent findings raise significant questions about the quality of FDI in Indian manufacturing after more than two and a half decades of liberalisation.

On the export growth front, the slowdown in India's export growth since 2009 clearly indicates that Indian exporters have been unable to compete globally in spite of the import liberalisation that has been carried out premised on improving India's export competitiveness (Francis 2015a). Despite any apparent short-term productivity growth that could have materialised from the increased use of imported intermediates, there is no evidence that trade and FDI liberalisation and increased global competition have induced Indian firms to become more globally competitive or technologically innovative in a broad range of industries or in a sustainable manner (see Mani 2009, 2016; Kallummal and Bugalya 2012; Ranganathan and Murthy 2013; Abrol 2014; Kallummal 2014; Jha and Jha 2015; Francis 2015a; etc.).[22]

India's share in global merchandise exports has remained low – it inched up from 0.5 per cent in 1990 to 1 per cent finally in 2006 and reached 1.8 per cent in 2013. But subsequently, it fell and stood at 1.5 per cent in 2015. India has been unable to garner significant global export market shares in manufactured products (defined as global share above 5 per cent), except in the gems and jewellery industry (Francis 2015a). But its share too had declined steadily from the peak in 2010 and stood at 5.1 per cent in 2013. Among the other major sectors, the increase in India's global export share has been amongst the most consistent for organic chemicals and pharmaceuticals, though India's global shares stood at 3.1 and 2.2 per cent in 2013. Once again, these are industries that benefited from industrial policy support during the pre-reform decades. India's shares in global exports in none of the other major exports of India constituted even 2 per cent of global exports. In iron and steel, its share stood at 1.8 per cent in 2013. In the two sectors of non-electrical and electrical machineries, usually considered technologically advanced, India's global export shares in 2013 stood at only 0.6 and 0.5 per cent respectively. In vehicles and parts, India's global share stood at 0.7 per cent in 2013, which was a drop from the 1 per cent share it had reached in 2011 (see the in-depth analysis in Francis 2015a). India's poor export performance across the major manufacturing sectors and its lack of momentum reveal that, in a highly competitive global economy dynamics based on technology-centred competition, export promotion policies such as tax holidays and allowing duty-free imports for export-oriented firms will only go thus far.

Meanwhile, at 2.5 per cent in 2013, India's share in global merchandise imports stands higher than its share in global exports, reflecting the rising import dependence of the economy that has led to the growing trade deficit in the recent past (Francis 2015a). The import to domestic output ratio has gone up significantly in most industries (Chaudhuri 2013; see also Banga and Das 2012: 25). There is also evidence that India's manufactured exports have been import-led – that is, exports have grown mostly on the basis of the productivity gains obtained through easier access to competitive imported inputs following trade liberalisation in the 1990s that accelerated in the 2000s (Francis 2015a; Banga and Das 2012; Ghosh 2013).[23] Against this backdrop, the proliferation in the use of non-tariff measures – such as sanitary and phyto-sanitary standards (SPS) and technical barriers to trade (TBT) – by both developed and developing countries (Kallummal 2006) further increase the concerns about India's ability to increase exports in highly competitive and increasingly protective global markets.

Moreover, as several studies have shown, the record on the fronts of industrial growth and its stability as well as structural changes has not been better under liberalisation than under the interventionist regime (see Nagaraj 2003, 2018; Papola 2006; Majumdar 2013; Chandrasekhar and Ghosh 2017; etc.). It has been acknowledged that industrial production has diversified with perceptible improvements in the quality and variety of goods produced with growing domestic competition (Nagaraj 2018: 169). However, as mentioned earlier, the manufacturing sector's share in India's GDP has been stagnating at about 15–16 per cent since the mid-1990s. It was taking cognisance of this stagnant manufacturing sector that the 2011 National Manufacturing Policy announced the policy objective to increase the share of manufacturing in GDP from 17 per cent in 2005 to 25 per cent by 2022. The 'Make in India' campaign of the current government seeks to raise the manufacturing sector share in GDP to 25 per cent by 2025.

The lack of continued momentum in export performance in many major export sectors, and the absence of evidence that FDI has helped India in achieving either new capacity creation, sustained export growth or technological prowess for its manufacturing sector, all point to the dire need to formulate strategic policies to enable further industrial upgrading, building on the capabilities and capacities built up over the earlier decades. However, the successive Indian governments have been quicker to follow the shift in global development literature, which began advocating that participation in global value chains (GVCs) and entering into free trade agreements (FTAs) will offer springboards for industrial development for developing countries. This seems to have been a boon for the Indian policy establishment under different governments,[24] which has perceived pursuit of trade and FDI liberalisation as an end in itself.

GVCs and FTAs: partners in development?

Global value chains (GVCs) are hardly a new phenomenon that emerged suddenly on the global scene in the 2000s.[25] Production networks in East Asia go back to the 1960s, especially in textiles and electronics. Further, the fact that vertical fragmentation associated with production networks has been an important driving force behind deepening international specialisation in East Asia, particularly after the mid-1980s, has been well acknowledged by scholars of East and Southeast Asian economies (Francis 2010; also see the literature cited in Francis 2003; Menon 2013). However, Indian academia and policymakers began to 'discover' GVCs around the mid-2000s – roughly around the same time India's Look East Policy began assuming increased significance. GVCs have since been the new *lingua franca* of development agenda both among economists and policymakers, with research and policy questions centring on the question of how India's integration into GVCs can be facilitated in order to advance India's industrial development.

GVCs are considered as offering an opportunity for developing countries to integrate faster into the global economy and achieve rapid export growth and industrial upgrading as supplier firms learn from the association with the MNCs. Based on this rationale, getting inducted into and increasing participation in GVCs has become a much-loved agenda driving recent trade and industry-related research (see Baldwin 2012; Baldwin and Lopez-Gonzalez 2013, etc.). For instance, Suh and Kim (2014: 118) observed: "plugging into East Asian IPNs (international production networks) for manufacturing may seem attractive for other Asian countries to get on sustainable development paths". This has also become a clichéd policy advice in the reports of multinational development organisations (e.g., OECD 2013; WTO et al. 2013; UNIDO 2016; World Bank 2017, etc.) and industrial development programmes of governments. As observed by Milberg and Winkler (2013: 238), "the expansion of GVCs amidst a global push to trade liberalisation and export orientation has rendered the goal of 'industrial upgrading' within GVCs to be nearly synonymous with economic development itself". As observed in UNCTAD (2016: 119), the argument is persuasive: rather than having to develop new products or break into extremely competitive markets entirely on their own, such networks enable participating developing country firms to specialise in specific segments of the production process or segments of a multitude of value chains, starting at the relatively accessible bottom.

But as increasingly acknowledged in the literature, international production networks are driven by firm-level decisions regarding the organisation and location of their production units. Mainstream scholars consider MNC location decisions to be determined first and foremost by factor-cost advantages of a particular location in relation to offshoring costs. The latter includes costs of coordination and management as well as direct shipping costs (Baldwin and Venables 2010; Anukoonwattaka 2011; Suh and Kim 2014; World Bank 2017). As pointed out in Anukoonwattaka (2011) based on a literature survey, a general conclusion from the offshoring literature is that MNCs determine the division of labour or vertical specialisation between countries on the basis of the factor intensity of different production stages and the differences in factor prices between countries. When factor-cost savings are large relative to the costs of fragmenting business activities across countries (that is, offshoring costs), a multinational firm will decide whether or not to fragment the production into stages as well as where to locate those fragmented units (Anukoonwattaka 2011: 11–12). For Baldwin and Venables (2010) also, fragmentation of its production process by a firm is determined by the trade-off it faces between international cost differences that create the incentive to 'unbundle' and the centripetal forces of agglomeration benefits (of co-location of related stages).

However, the mainstream literature addresses GVC-related issues within the framework of the 'cost minimisation problem' that confronts MNCs in their production fragmentation decision. These understandings do not factor in the consideration that technology capabilities are endogenous to the determination of cost competitiveness of different locations for a particular production/process segment, as argued in Francis and Kallummal (2013). The mainstream analyses also eschew the broader framework in Milberg and Winkler (2013), Gereffi (2014), etc., which considers how the business model underlying GVCs is built on asymmetric governance relations created with oligopolistic lead firms at the top and highly competitive suppliers at the lower tiers. Thus the balance of power within GVCs is always tilted in favour of, and therefore maximum rents accrue to, firms which maintain technological leadership (see Nathan and Sarkar 2011; Milberg and Winkler 2013; Gereffi 2014; Banga 2013, etc.; detailed discussion follows in Chapter 3).

Because of their focus on relative factor-cost advantages without incorporating technology, the ongoing mainstream discussion in developing (and developed) countries, typically, focuses on how developing countries can rely on their comparative advantage based on existing factor endowments and undertake trade and FDI liberalisation along with passive industrial policies to facilitate new foreign investments and exports. Liberalisation of FDI norms will attract FDI and enable developing countries to participate in GVCs, while trade liberalisation will provide greater flexibility to these MNCs to source components from or undertake tasks in partner countries at different stages of development and increase intra-firm trade within the GVCs. Both together will help increase exports from the host developing countries and lead to dynamic gains from trade that accompany industrial upgrading. It is therefore argued that there would be a sizable benefit for late-comer countries like India if and when they were to increase their presence in existing international production networks of Asian manufacturing industries (Anukoonwattaka 2011: 2).

Thus GVCs have provided yet another framework for trade and FDI liberalisation in the continuing saga of economic growth tied to export performance. While there have been some cautionary sounds (Francis 2011a, 2015b, 2017; Banga 2013; Menon 2013; Francis and Kallummal 2013; Banga 2016; Gupta 2016; and Das and Hussain 2017 are some examples in the Indian context), the overall thrust of arguments usually tends to move in the above manner. The focus is typically on horizontal industrial policies to reduce the costs of doing business together with trade and investment liberalisation (see, for instance, Anukoonwattaka 2011; Athukorala 2016)[26]. The latest study on GVCs by the World Bank also concludes that trade facilitation and infrastructure are obvious places to start for countries that want to get more involved in GVCs (World Bank 2017: 8). The study did not address the issue of capabilities that have been proven to be necessary for developing country firms to participate in GVC segments (detailed discussion follows in Chapter 3).

In Asia, trade liberalisation through free trade agreements (FTAs), in particular, has been argued to enable rapid and 'efficient industrial restructuring' by allowing countries to participate in GVCs (see Kumar and Joseph 2004; Kumar 2007a,b; Batra 2006; Francois et al. 2009; Das 2009; Park et al. cited in Francis and Kallummal 2013; Anukoonwattaka 2011; Suh and Kim 2014, etc.). Anukoonwattaka (2011) argued that FTAs with important players in Asian/ international production networks may provide a stepping stone for India to increase its integration into the Asian IPNs. Another study by Suh and Kim (2014) analysed the structural disadvantages that confront late-follower countries like India to participate in pre-existing East Asian production networks. They found that, while a typically relative labour abundant country like India should have broken into labour-intensive manufacturing exports, India faces disadvantages due to its low level of agglomeration (proxied by the level of industrialisation)[27] and weak alignment with downstream and upstream production processes as compared with her counterparts already active within the East Asian production networks. The underlying logic given is that "multinational firms invest in a country that has the capacity to perform a certain role within their production networks. The level of industrialisation in a country offers clues about that potential" (Suh and Kim 2014: 137). Thus, after beginning by arguing that plugging into East Asian IPNs for manufacturing would be attractive for other Asian countries to get on sustainable development paths (*ibid.* 118), they arrived at the above finding that it is the existing level of industrialisation in a country that determines the potential of a country to plug into any particular segment of a GVC (*ibid.* 137). Yet, based on the argument that an MNC will incur offshoring costs if it decides to incorporate a new region in its existing production chain where every stage of production takes place in a single region (as in East Asia apparently), the policy recommendation is that "having additional or deeper FTAs with countries in the network will help latecomers to overcome this type of disadvantage by reducing the offshoring cost" (see Suh and Kim 2014: 140–141).

One underlying argument in this stream of thinking has been that, through the multiplier effect of tariff reductions on production fragmentation trade, reduction or elimination of tariffs within the free trade area may make it more profitable for goods that were previously produced entirely in one country to become vertically specialised, exploiting differences in cost competitiveness across members of the FTA. It follows from this argument that the proliferation of FTAs has supported the spread of production networks (as reflected in an increase in intra-regional trade), and therefore the continued growth in production networks will be enhanced by expanding or increasing the number of FTAs (see Yi 2003; Suh and Kim 2014 and the literature cited therein). The associated second rationale for FTAs' role has been linked to their ability to attract vertical FDI, which will enable 'efficient industrial restructuring' across the countries participating in GVCs (see Kumar 2007b).[28]

It is important to note that the shift to bilateral and regional preferential/free trade agreements has occurred after developing countries have already seen their policy space significantly constrained under the WTO regime. The WTO sought the disciplining of national industrial policies through the harmonisation of several policies and regulations at the multilateral level that go beyond the ambit of trade policies (see Akyuz 2005, 2007). While countries like Brazil and China have been using the remaining policy space available under the WTO ingeniously, many other countries, including India, have entered into a complex web of bilateral and regional FTAs. Particularly since 2000, trade policy in the region has come to be dominated by the proliferation of FTAs (Menon 2013: 3). In fact, the term 'noodle bowl' was developed by Findlay and Pangestu (2001) to reflect the simultaneous participation of multiple countries in crisscrossing and often overlapping FTAs (see Mikic 2007 cited in Francis 2015b).

From the mid-2000s, increased engagement in free trade agreements has been one of the most striking aspects of India's changing trade policy strategy also (Francis 2015b). India is currently involved in about 18 bilateral and regional FTAs. Like in the case of 'the flying geese syndrome', the misconceptions tied to the causalities behind ASEAN and China's GVC participation as running from their trade and FDI liberalisation have significantly influenced India's policy approach towards FTAs. As mentioned, the much smaller East and Southeast Asian economies – starting with Singapore's electronics industry in the mid-1960s and subsequently, Hong Kong, Taiwan, South Korea followed mainly by Malaysia, Thailand and the Philippines – had been already integrated into GVCs. The latter has been due to historical economic factors (going back to the political economy of the 1960s, and later on, the 1985 Plaza Accord that led to the yen revaluation) and critical domestic policy initiatives for building capabilities. Thus *de facto* regional integration was already relatively high in East and Southeast Asia by the late 1980s due to their involvement in MNC-driven production networks in several industries (Francis 2011a). While the policy frameworks had differential outcomes in terms of the depth of industrialisation in these first and second-tier newly industrialised economies, all the above factors came together to create entrenched capacities (including clusters) and interests which have increased the attraction of MNCs to invest in and export from some of those economies. On the other side, as observed by Menon (2013: 13), despite being a 'latecomer' to the Asian production networks and one of the least active in pursuing FTAs in this region, Vietnam has become an example of a new entrant successfully joining production networks.

Despite its huge domestic market, India looked at and drew incorrect lessons from the first- and second-tier NICs in East and

Southeast Asia. However, except for a couple of papers like Francis (2011a: 46), Menon (2013: 3), the literature has ignored the fact that these countries' engagement in production networks pre-dates the formation of FTAs. In India, mainstream economists and analysts have typically argued that India's participation in FTAs, especially with the East and Southeast Asian economies, offer mutually beneficial linkages through dynamic industrial restructuring within the region leading to greater competition and improved efficiency, as well as gains from greater inter- and intra-industry specialisation, economies of scale and learning-by-doing (see Kumar 2007b; ADB 2008; and other literature cited in Francis and Kallummal 2013; see also Anukoonwattaka 2011; Suh and Kim 2014).

It must be remembered that more than 31 per cent of the India's NAMA tariff lines were unbound at the multilateral level at the commencement of the WTO's Doha Round in 2001 (Department of Commerce Annual Report 2009–2010). Even though the country had brought down its applied tariff levels in several industries through unilateral liberalisation, it still has the flexibility to raise its applied tariffs in any industry/product to the level at which it has bound multilaterally at the WTO if the need arises. However, in its FTAs with ASEAN, Japan and South Korea, India has committed to reducing or eliminating tariffs in almost all consumer goods, capital goods and intermediate goods.

Equally importantly, under these agreements, India, like several other developing countries, has also made binding policy commitments that are stricter or more liberalising than those under the WTO, which go beyond greater tariff liberalisation to include regulatory aspects that severely impinge on national policymaking sovereignty. Provisions in these FTAs related to trade-related investment measures (TRIMs), intellectual property rights (IPR), agriculture, services, public procurement, investment protection, competition, environment, labour, human rights, etc. have put constraints on the industrial policy space of developing countries to generate domestic value addition sustainably in the context of the growing challenges faced with the spread of GVCs (detailed discussion follows in Chapter 5). These raise potentially multi-layered constraints on developing countries' ability to course a path towards sustainable industrial development.

Thus both GVC dynamics and FTAs have implications for industrial policy, with each policy course involving costs and benefits in terms of the development trajectory that accompanies it. For this reason, debate over the consequences of these policy choices is more important than ever.

The objective of the book

This book is a modest attempt to re-look at the interactions between trade and FDI liberalisation and other industrial policies, and their implications for the attendant restructuring dynamics within industries, for drawing attention to their ramifications for the nature of GVC participation for a developing country like India and its implications for her development trajectory. This includes specifically addressing the challenges presented by FTAs.

We argue that that interactions between trade (including FTAs) and FDI liberalisation and other industrial policies determine firm-level incentives and strategies for production restructuring by both domestic and foreign-invested firms and that these in turn have a critical impact both on how integration into GVCs and upgrading within them can happen for a developing country like India and the extent of benefits obtained by such integration. Our objective is to connect the analyses of the outcomes in GVC-led industrial restructuring and upgrading to industrial policy choices in trade and FDI liberalisation, including through FTAs. It is argued that there has been a critical failure within mainstream approaches to appreciate the implications of the interactions between the different segments of industrial policy and firm-level strategies on industrial restructuring occurring within GVCs. This is brought out through a case study analysis of the Indian electronics industry.

While the role of technological progress in the development process has been well acknowledged by neoliberal and heterodox economists alike, the role of capabilities (built through learning-by-doing *and* knowledge accumulation) in bringing about technological development has been misconceived in the neoclassical framework.[29] The latter has been a crucial reason for the failure of mainstream academia and policy analysts to appreciate the import of different industrial policy measures on firm-level strategies (and therefore on industrial development outcomes).

Different understanding of the nature of technological development leads – as pointed out by Gallagher and Shafaeddin (2009), Reinert and Kattel (2010) – neoclassical or neoliberal approaches to argue that industrialisation comes from 'learning through trading', which as a result, favours free trade and argues for the operation of market forces without government interference. For instance, in open economy growth models pioneered by Grossman and Helpman (1991), trade acts as a transmission channel for international technology spillovers (through import of capital goods). In contrast, neo-developmentalist approaches (owing intellectual debt to evolutionary theorists and going back to early development economists) argue that industrialisation is enabled by promoting 'learning-by-doing' and experience (see also Khan 2010.) Because knowledge is proprietary and firm-specific, it is anything but universally available and free. Because of this, there is a critical need for government intervention for enabling knowledge accumulation as well as for building and upgrading capabilities needed for learning-by-doing. As emphasised by Lall (2005 cited in Gallagher and Shafaeddin 2009), selective and targeted intervention becomes necessary because apart from being firm specific, learning is technology specific and activity specific, given that technologies differ in their tacit features and externalities.

This implies that the absorptive capabilities of the domestic economy agents play a major and fundamental role in bringing out positive spillovers from their interactions with the advanced centres of knowledge through trade or FDI. In fact, according to Reinert and Kattel (2010: 17), up to the rise of Washington Consensus policies and WTO agreements in the 1990s, classical industrial policy used to be about attempting to change micro-level "learned organisational capabilities for innovation and technological change via public policy".

Lack of acknowledgement of the role of learning-by-doing and knowledge accumulation in building up indigenous technological capabilities lies behind the artificial dichotomy that has been constructed between horizontal and vertical industrial policies by neoliberalism. Successful industrialisers are the ones that have seen through the irrationality of this dichotomy and combine the two in ingenious ways to practise industrial policy in its fullness.

The scheme of the book

Industrial policy is one of those ideas that has been repeatedly discovered and abandoned over the last century. In the literature, there have been different, yet inter-related layers of discourse related to industrial policy – some mostly macro, some meso at the sectoral or industrial level and several at the level of firm and/or technology.

The second chapter discusses these different strands while understanding what comes under the ambit of industrial policy and how it is required for sustainable development processes. After a discussion of the industrial policy causalities involved in structural change and sustainable development, it discusses the evolution of the industrial policy debate over the last six decades.

It is observed that, as in the case of mis-interpretation of the East Asian development successes in the 1990s (which remains to date), the mainstream narrative on GVCs has been constructed as if getting integrated into GVCs is a substitute for industrial policy for developing countries. In the third chapter, we therefore pose and examine the counter-question whether industrial policy (as defined in Chapter 2) is an imperative for a country to get integrated into GVCs. This does depend to a significant degree on what benefits the country seeks to obtain from having their firms to be part of GVCs and what the implied costs are. If the benefits are improved technological capabilities, industrial upgrading and sustainable development, rather than transient export growth, the question is what is fundamental to drawing these benefits? It is crucial to understand whether the causality runs from participation in GVCs to achieving technological capabilities and industrial upgrading,[30] or it runs the other way – from technological capabilities to inclusion and upgrading in GVCs. It is one thing to suggest that policies should actively support companies to develop the capabilities to face competition in GVCs and another to suggest that policies should actively promote companies' engagement in GVCs.

For the same reasons, it is very important to move away from a linear understanding of GVCs that (implicitly or explicitly) considers value addition as intrinsic to a sequential process as firms pass from one link in the chain to the next, towards a systemic view. The latter involves considering the increased complexity of GVC networks, which includes, in addition to vertical (efficiency-seeking) FDI by MNCs, horizontal (market-seeking) FDI and non-equity forms of foreign firm engagement. More importantly, a systemic view also incorporates the asymmetric governance structures of value chains, the endogeneity of indigenous technological capabilities in offshoring location decisions as well as how these elements are influenced by institutional and policy contexts.

Against this backdrop, the third chapter examines whether trade and investment liberalisation along with industrial policies of the generic market-promoting kind are sufficient to make use of the opportunities provided by GVCs. Following Gereffi (1995, 2014) and Milberg and Winkler (2013)[31], it is argued that the business model underlying international production networks is built on asymmetric governance relations, where lead firms shape the distribution of risks and profits in their favour. Subsequently, the evidence on developing countries' GVC participation is analysed with a focus on the multiple barriers to GVC entry and upgrading for developing country firms. Evidence from secondary literature of ongoing experiences of developing countries/firms that participate in production networks are brought together to establish that many developing countries and LDCs that do not have some minimum level of technological capabilities have not been able to benefit from even the production segments of GVCs, let alone higher value-added segments. The chapter goes on to discuss how despite the appearance of multinational firms from some emerging economies, mainly China, in select sectors, their ability to 'climb the value chain' remains a challenge. In many cases at present, especially in electronics and automobile GVCs, developing countries are largely involved in 'assembly networks' as assemblers, rather than as the producers of technology-intensive parts and components. It is argued that, if participation in value chains is to deliver *sustainable* growth in terms of output, technology, employment and high wages in addition to export growth (which in turn will need to be reinvested productively for sustainable development), openness in trade and FDI are simply not enough. The spread and dynamics of global value chains have heightened the imperative for industrial policy in developing countries, including India.

Mis-interpreting these causal interactions between liberalisation of trade and FDI, indigenous capability development and GVC participation can lead to wrong inferences, which result in inappropriate policy formulations and unsustainable industrial development trajectories. Despite the fact that the capabilities which India had accumulated on the eve of the 1990s' reforms are a legacy of her domestically-oriented industrial policies in the post-independence decades and that these have played a critical role in her development trajectory, it is common to relate the faster growth rates in Indian exports and the export success of a few sectors solely to the post-1991 import liberalisation and export promotion policies (Francis and Kallummal 2013; Francis 2017). In the absence of the correct diagnosis, the policy prescriptions tend to err on the side of further liberalisation rather than on policy measures that will enable and strengthen Indian firms' ability to link to GVCs strategically. This is critical in strategic sectors like electronics, chemicals, transport equipment, pharmaceuticals, machinery, etc. as well as in labour-intensive industries. This book does not attempt to re-produce the extensive literature or re-tell the debates surrounding India's post-independence industrial policy choices related to import-substitution industrialisation. On the other hand, it attempts to link the policy trajectory from the time of the accelerated policy reforms as it emerged from 1991 to the changes in global development literature and the consequent impact on the manufacturing sector development trajectory. We are, however, concerned about the unavoidable/inevitable path dependence of industrial development. Even as there are exogenous factors that have influenced the policy trajectory and outcomes in specific industries, we argue that more critically, subsequent policy choices become significantly shaped by the outcomes of the previous ones. This is seen through the case study of the electronics industry in the fourth chapter.

The electronics industry has gone through parallel processes of trade and FDI liberalisation, which were carried out with the intention of improving India's export competitiveness and increasing integration into GVCs. However, according to the National Electronics Policy 2012, the value addition in domestically produced electronics products ranged between only 5 to 10 per cent in most cases even two decades after the reforms. Chapter 4 examines Indian electronics industry's experience with GVC participation against the backdrop of the broader industrial policy framework that drove trade and investment liberalisation and other policy changes. It analyses the experience of India's electronics industry with trade liberalisation under the WTO's Information Technology Agreement-1 (ITA-1) and FTAs with ASEAN, South Korea and Japan, with a discussion of the interplay between trade liberalisation with other industrial policies related to the industry since the 1980s. Following a brief discussion on the post-independent evolution of industrial policy in the electronics industry, it analyses the nature of trade liberalisation under the ITA-1 and FTAs and carries out an in-depth analysis of electronics industry trade flows. Subsequently, it enquires into the nature of the observed two-way trade for understanding the development of intra-industry trade (IIT) involving India's major trading partners. This involves the decomposition of India's bilateral electronics industry trade flows into inter-industry trade, horizontal IIT and vertical IIT in order to understand the nature of Indian electronics industry's integration into the industry value chains.

Evidence from both these chapters shows that participation and upgrading in GVCs cannot take place without active industrial policy interventions to build up national technological capabilities, while guiding investments towards increasing returns activities in order to generate domestic value addition in a sustainable manner. However, the deeper and broader liberalisation provisions and regulatory commitments in FTAs signed by developing countries impose significant constraints on their ability to pursue such industrial policies. Therefore, their ability to generate domestic value addition sustainably in the context of the growing challenges faced with the spread of GVCs gets constrained. WTO-plus provisions in FTAs have also heightened the risk of international arbitration of states by foreign private corporations through the inclusion of investor-state dispute settlement (ISDS) provisions. These raise the development costs of policy failures by restricting the state's industrial policy space and also through regulatory chill. These issues are examined in detail in Chapter 5.

India faces significant challenges in formulating vertical industrial policies under the FTAs signed since the mid-2000s. Apart from WTO-plus tariff liberalisation, WTO-plus provisions in FTAs relating to broad definition of investments as well as rules on the operations of investors and protection of investments, indirect expropriation and the ISDS mechanism reduce policy sovereignty and heighten the risk of policy failures by limiting the possibilities to redesign industrial development trajectories towards more sustainable paths. As a result, these comprehensive trade agreements have not only undermined the purported objectives of FTAs, namely, increased investments and greater exports, but may have also undermined India's long-term development prospects. The chapter provides a discussion of WTO-plus provisions in the last four major FTAs signed by India involving investment chapters or separate investment agreement (namely, India-Singapore CECA 2005, India-South Korea CEPA 2010, India-Japan CEPA 2011, and India-Malaysia CECA), which impinge most directly on the policy space for vertical industrial policies; their possible implications that ought to be kept in mind while planning any future trade agreements; and the industrial policy options that can still be exercised within a strategic industrial development framework.

Chapter 6 offers a summary of the main arguments and makes some policy suggestions related to technological capability building and industrial upgrading for developing countries like India in the context of GVCs and FTAs. It is argued that a strategic use of industrial policy tools aimed at improving domestic firms' manufacturing and technological capabilities and addressing the market failures in inter-sectoral coordination to foster forward and backward linkages domestically is called for. It is in figuring out the combination of ingenious policies that create the overall incentive for increased domestic value generation that a developing country like India's greater possibility for gainful and sustainable GVC engagement lies in. This necessarily involves factoring in the industrial policy causalities involved in indigenous technology development, the many structural barriers to GVC entry and upgrading, the impact of trade and FDI liberalisation as well as existing FTAs on firm-level incentives for undertaking domestic production and getting over the industrial policy constraints imposed by FTAs. Going forth, if the large majority of Indians are to benefit from the structural transformations mediated through the windows of opportunity provided by digital revolution, it needs to upgrade its manufacturing and technological capabilities to a significantly higher level through a massive scaling up of its public policy efforts and public investments, so as not to end up with an even higher level of import-dependency (and greater macroeconomic vulnerability) from the emerging digitalised production and consumption patterns.

Notes

1 The maximum recorded value of the share of manufacturing value added in GDP has never exceeded 19 per cent in India. In sharp contrast, that figure peaked at above 34 per cent in Brazil, 40 per cent in China, 31 per cent in Korea and 31 per cent in Malaysia. The comparison in terms of employment in industry relative to total employment was equally worse, with India recording values below 25 per cent, whereas the figure peaked at 36 per cent in Korea, 34 per cent in Malaysia and 30 per cent in China (Chandrasekhar and Ghosh 2017:1). See Nagaraj (2018) for a detailed discussion of the trends in industrial growth in the post-reform period and Chaudhuri (2013 and 2015) for a discussion of the impact of import liberalisation.
2 It has been decidedly settled that the period from 1980–81 marked the break in trend growth rate in India's GDP when compared to the post-independence decades (see Hatekar and Dongre 2005, Nayyar 2006, Mazumdar 2013, among many others). It has also been well

acknowledged that the beginnings of liberalisation had been set in motion since the early 1980s. However, we draw a distinction between the 'pro-business' industrial policy reform measures initiated in the 1980s (such as allowing private sector entry into areas previously reserved for the public sector, removal of hurdles on capacity expansion in activities/industries, enabling import of foreign technology and availability of imported inputs, etc.) from the explicit 'pro-market' and export-led growth strategy and associated liberalisation and reforms from 1991. The former period was considered to be pragmatic 'creeping liberalisation', while the latter is characterised by drastic and comprehensive liberalisation. See Chandrasekhar 1994a; Nagaraj 2003; etc.

3 For detailed analysis of the domestic macroeconomic factors and political/policy decisions that had led up to the acceptance of the IMF loans to tide over the balance of payments crisis, see Nayyar (1994, 2018), Chandrasekhar and Ghosh (2002), etc.

4 For a discussion on the neoliberal prescription for the economic 'framework role' of the state, see Wade (2012: 224–226) and Storm (2015).

5 See Patnaik (2015) for a formulation of open economy macroeconomic model that incorporates some of these implications.

6 As Wade (2012) points out, firms in many middle-income countries find that they cannot compete with firms producing standardised products in lower-wage countries, nor can they compete with firms producing more technology-intensive goods and services in higher-wage countries. In fact, even the second-tier NICs of Southeast Asia – Malaysia, Thailand, Indonesia and the Philippines – which built up production and management skills to match the productivity levels of developed countries in standardised commodities, were not successful in developing their indigenous capacity to design, innovate and commercialise into new and more profitable sectors. Unlike in South Korea and Taiwan, higher-tech manufacturing exports in Southeast Asia remain dependent on MNC subsidiaries (Wade 2012: 233).

7 As Low and Tijaja (2013) observed, different terms have been used by scholars to refer to updated approaches to industrial policy, from Strategic Industrial Policy (SIP) (Gunther and Alcorta 2011), New Industrial Policy (Devlin and Moguillansky 2012) to Global Value Chain-Oriented Industrial Policy (Gereffi and Sturgeon 2013).

8 Exceptions include Menon (2013), Banga (2013), UNCTAD 2014, 2016, ECA (2016), UNIDO (2015 and 2016), etc.

9 This is despite the fact that lack of aggregate demand growth was widely considered to be the principal reason for the relative stagnation (in industrial output) since the mid-1960s. This in turn was attributed to varied factors such as the lack of sufficient growth in the agricultural sector and the adverse income distribution that prevented broad-based and increasing mass consumer demand, a slowdown in public investment and public expenditure, etc. See the papers in Nayyar (1994) and Balakrishnan (2011) as well as Chandrasekhar and Ghosh (2002), Nagaraj (2003), Mazumdar (2013), Patnaik (2015), etc.

10 See also Dastidar (2015) and the literature cited therein for a discussion of the trade and industrial policies under the ISI regime and critiques of the same.

11 Ironically, Williamson (2004) insists that there was no call for zero tariffs or capital account liberalisation in his version of the Washington Consensus. Removing barriers impeding the entry of FDI, though, was very much part of the consensus.

12 Detailed discussion follows in Chapter 2. For an empirically grounded, in-depth theoretical critique of the 'flying geese' theory in the case of Thailand, see Francis (2003).

13 By 1998, FDI was allowed in the small-scale sector too, up to 24 per cent (Mani 2000a: 62). As pointed out by Roy (2013), in the context of liberalised trade from 1991, the rationale for the exclusive protection of small enterprises had become weak. As more products were progressively included in the Open General License (OGL) list (of products that could be freely traded), small enterprises already had to face competition from imported products (Roy 2013: 35). Thus the logic under ISI of protecting small enterprises from large domestic producers and foreign producers had become meaningless under the changed paradigm.

14 The definition adopted for identifying FDI has been merely based on "direct or indirect ownership of 10 per cent or more". Thus India's FDI framework removes the distinction between long-term productive FDI and volatile financial investments, since all capital from abroad meeting this criterion (other than those purchased by foreign institutional investors on the stock market), whether they are financial investors such as private equity funds, hedge funds, etc. or investments by national investors investing in the domestic economy through the foreign route, get counted as FDI. See Rao and Dhar (2011, 2016 and 2018), as well as Francis (2010), for more discussion. Additionally, the associated reinvested earnings and debt instruments are also included under FDI flows and separately reported by the Reserve Bank of India (RBI).

15 A detailed discussion of the changes in FDI policy since 2015 can be found in Rao and Dhar (2018).

16 Several scholars have pointed out that the increased liquidity in the Indian economy resulting from foreign portfolio capital surge has helped sustain a credit-financed, private expenditure-based process of growth during the boom periods of growth in the economy. This has happened along with the significant decline in government expenditure under the conservative fiscal stance promoted by neoliberalism. See, for instance, Ghosh (2013). Meanwhile, recent analysis shows that there has also been increasing dependence on external commercial borrowings by the private corporate sector (see and Bose and Pal 2018).

17 See Rao and Dhar 2016, 2018 for detailed discussions on the methodology and analyses.

18 Due to the different methodology adopted to differentiate financial flows from real FDI and to correct for industrial misclassification in reported flows, these figures differ from the official data reported by the RBI. Rao and Dhar (2018: 29–37) present the FDI trends based on official data.

19 Apart from regulated FDI, the development of the automobile sector in India has benefited critically, in particular, from a local content policy that was in place until 2002.

20 See, for instance, Abrol (2014: 6–9) for details on government support to the pharmaceutical industry. As he has argued, the pharmaceutical sector benefited enormously from the fact that the policymakers delayed – by a decade (when compared to other industries) – the implementation of external liberalisation, the enforcement of strong intellectual property rights (the shift to product patents) and liberalisation of investment and technology (Abrol 2014: 28). Khan (2009) and Jha and Jha (2015) discuss the industrial policy measures related to the automobile industry.

21 In fact, there has been a worrying increase in external commercial borrowings (ECBs) by Indian firms. According to Acharya and Vij (2016), cited in Bose and Pal (2018: 19), most of the firms resorting to ECBs during 2010–2016 belonged to the manufacturing sector (65 per cent) and were largely from the following industries: chemical and chemical products, metal and metal products and transport equipment.

22 For instance, Ranganathan and Murthy's (2013) study of the large private corporate sector represented by the top 500 companies in terms of their assets showed that, even in 2009–2010, except for the pharmaceutical industry, the large Indian companies were neither into high-tech manufacturing nor focusing on R&D. The Planning Commission's 2012 report entitled "Technology and Depth" (cited in Abrol 2014) also found that India was "slipping in the race, for the lack of technological depth in its manufacturing sector".

23 Further evidence in terms of value added in Indian industries is presented in Chapter 3.

24 More than a decade ago, Bhaduri (2007: 1597–1598) made the following observation about the remarkable convergence that has taken place among major political parties in India around the issue of industrialisation: "The role that the governments have assigned to themselves both at the central and at the state level is that of a promoter, an agent of private corporations, not one of a regulator between big business and poor people". In fact, Chibber (2004) had argued that even though the Indian state continued to implement industrial policy and churn out five-year plans, its capacity to implement them had become weaker by the 1970s itself. Das Gupta (2016), which critically analysed how the regulatory reach of all post-independent policy regimes had been limited, attributed it to the expanding power of big capital and the concomitant shrinkage of the relative autonomy of the state.

25 As discussed in Chapter 3, the term GVC (as opposed to global production networks used commonly in the literature previously) covers the much broader evolution of MNC networks beyond production to include pre-production stages like research and innovation and post-production stages such as retail/marketing networks. It also encapsulates the understanding that value added is distributed throughout the chain and not concentrated at the location of production (Milberg and Winkler 2013).

26 The unfortunate inherent bias towards horizontal industrial policies is reflected in statements such as the following in an analysis after twenty years of trade and investment liberalisation in India: "India's growth

and trade patterns are an illustration of adverse impacts generated by inward-looking policies as well as tight controls on foreign and domestic investment" (Anukoonwattaka 2011: 4).

27 Ironically, the level of industrialisation in turn is proxied by revealed comparative advantage in capital-intensive industries and commodity composition of imports. See Suh and Kim (2014: 136–138).

28 For instance, in the words of Kumar (2007b):

> a more important effect of RTAs (compared with 'the market extending effect') is strengthening of overall competitiveness of the region forming it through extensive industrial restructuring or rationalization across the region. This process of efficiency-seeking industrial restructuring is accomplished by intra-regional FDI. It is not a coincidence that the new age RTAs or FTAs generally extend their scope beyond trade to include investment liberalization and facilitation. . . . This restructuring enables fuller exploitation of the locational advantages or synergies between the member countries of the regional trading bloc besides facilitating businesses reaping the economies of scale and specialization.
>
> (Kumar 2007b: 4, 13–14)

29 This difference goes back to a different understanding of the dynamics of technological development within firms, industries and economies (more in Chapter 2; see also the detailed discussion in Reinert and Kattel 2010).

30 For instance, see "Technological capabilities are strengthened by investing in human capital, institutions, improving innovation systems and upgrading in industrial clusters and global value chains" (UNIDO 2016: 23).

31 Milberg and Winkler (2013) in their book *Outsourcing Economics* provides a rigorous analysis of the economics of globalised production, focusing on forces that govern GVCs, in particular, the business strategies of the lead firms in those chains. They also discuss the implications of offshoring for trade and foreign investment theories and economic development, as well as for key policy debates related to deindustrialisation, labour market regulation and export processing zones.

Chapter 2

Industrial policy
Evolution of the discourse

Development literature recognises structural change involving diversification away from primary sectors to industry and further to services as the central process of economic development. It has been known since the 15th century that an increase in productivity – that gives rise to high real wages and demand creation in an economy – which underlies the desirable structural change, is determined by the presence of increasing returns activities.[1] Increasing return activities, in particular, manufacturing activities, have the ability to: (i) create wealth (for reinvestments in more productive capacities and for consumption), (ii) create employment and wage incomes (thus generating adequate demand in the economy and tax revenue for the state) and (iii) solve balance of payment problems (to avoid vulnerability due to external debt build-up) (see Reinert and Reinert 2005). Such activities have the ability for capital accumulation because they enable market control and pricing power through imperfect competition, innovations, etc., all of which enable the generation of profits. Manufacturing production is also generally characterised by a large division of labour leading to benefits originating from specialisation. Moreover, it has great potential for forward and backward production linkages, leading to positive demand-supply externalities (upstream and downstream of various related industries), which in turn generate greater potential for aggregate output and employment growth in the economy. For sustained investments that are needed to maintain these cumulative and synergic causations underlying development, the market power of economic entities in the production space needs to be strengthened and protected in a time-bound fashion by the state through policies aimed at market protection, market expansion and technological upgrading.

It has also been well known that raw material production like agriculture, mining, etc. is typically characterised by diminishing returns and minimal division of labour, because of which it is usually incapable of being a development driver on its own. On the other hand, services typically depend on manufacturing as a source of demand to a far greater extent than *vice versa*. It is only growth in manufacturing that will create the markets for many services such as logistics, transport, trade, finance, etc. as well as other modern business services enabled by information and communication technologies (ICT). Although there have been scale economies and increased productivity in some services, as observed by Ha-Joon Chang, Jostein Løhr Hauge and Muhammad Irfan in ECA (2016: 31), the very increase in productivity will have been achieved by their 'de-basement', which undermines that productivity growth.[2] Of course, with the continuing advance in the ICT 'techno-economic paradigm' (attributed to Carlota Perez), technological progress and productivity increase in the services sector can become a driver of increased manufacturing sector productivity (see Francis 2018a). However, even if there are some ICT services that may share the feature of increasing returns to scale, it becomes difficult to have sustainable development based solely on expansion in such services, if a vibrant ICT manufacturing sector is absent.[3] In fact, no country, except a few states exceptionally rich in oil (e.g., Qatar, Kuwait, Brunei) or very small financial havens (e.g., Monaco, Liechtenstein) has achieved high and sustainable standards of living without developing a significant manufacturing sector (ECA 2016: xii).

It is critical that, simultaneous with the promotion of such increasing returns activities, the state must develop the productive capabilities of its population through investments in education and training, for the accumulation, diffusion and creation of knowledge and bringing in technological change. Technological progress has been recognised as one of the key driving forces of economic development since at least the 17th century. Thus continuous investments in increasing returns activities and generation of human skills and knowledge – both of which lead to productivity gains, sustained demand needed for further investments and technological progress – are integral to the cumulative causations that lead to development (Kattel et al. 2009). Important dynamic feedback effects underlie these virtuous cycles of growth. If state policies are in place to allow the increase in real wages in line with the growth in productivity associated with industrialisation, this will raise the domestic market demand (Storm 2005). At the same time, given that the positive productivity effects of capital accumulation due to increasing returns offset the negative effect of higher real wages on the rate of profit, increasing returns activities enable capital accumulation to continue despite the increase in wage levels.[4] This understanding on achieving development also stresses the crucial inter-sectoral synergies between the primary sector and the increasing returns activities.[5] These synergies mean that there is a crucial need for increasing agricultural productivity simultaneously, for raising real wages and purchasing power domestically and for making the industrialisation process non-inflationary and sustainable.

From around the late 17th century, the history of industrial policy also became integrally linked with trade policy, one of the principal issues surrounding development strategy. Debates related to inward-oriented trade strategies associated with the development of then late industrialisers the United States, Germany, France, etc. in comparison with the trade strategies that enabled Britain to develop and progress through colonial trade had become intense especially since the first Industrial Revolution. These debates continued after the US became the dominant economic and political power in the early 20th century and as a number of former colonies became independent. It was well recognised that the initial conditions as well as the other factors and constraints influencing capital accumulation (and in turn, development) were not the same in the underdeveloped world as in the developed world because of historical processes, including colonialism (see Chang 2002; Patnaik 2006; etc.). The well-known arguments of early development theorists[6] who drew on the work of classical economists are briefly summarised here for their continuing relevance to the debates on industrialisation 'through' global value chains and free trade agreements.

Revisiting the role of industrial policy

Clearly, less developed countries (LDCs) can build up their economic infrastructure and develop by importing capital, raw materials, inputs and technology. However, for financing their imports, countries need to first export in order to acquire the international reserve currency/currencies. In the earliest stages of economic development, for countries rich in natural resources, production and exports largely consist of primary commodities based on natural comparative advantage, while imports comprise mainly

manufactures, both capital- and labour-intensive products. However, while primary products face low income elasticity of demand,
the income elasticity of their demand for imports of manufactured
products is high.[7] As a result, countries rich in natural resources
face declining terms of trade for their exports, which in turn leads
to the worsening of their external payments position. Given that
the latter prevents capital accumulation, the initial conditions of
low productivity, limited capital stock and small market size persist.
Therefore, depending solely on primary exports curtails the ability
of the country to carry out the investments needed towards processing and diversification.

For this reason, even though commodity processing provides
early industrialisation opportunities, the possibilities of maintaining rapid development through deepening and diversification in the
primary sector are limited. Thus historical experience shows that
rich natural resources, even when combined with a well-developed
human resource base, do not automatically lead to processing and
diversification of the economy (Akyuz 2005: 17). This problem is
compounded by the fact that significant levels of protection face
developing country primary exports entering developed country
markets, with more highly processed commodities facing higher
levels of protection (or 'tariff escalation') (Wade 2006: 11. See also
Kallummal (2006)). In general, the financing of growth through
primary product exports would clearly come up against the constraints to development in the form of undiversified production
structure and net financial outflows leading to financial fragility.

The latest manifestation of this is observable in Africa, which –
after the 'African growth tragedy' of three decades of poor growth –
achieved acceleration in economic growth in the late 2000s based
on high prices of primary commodities, that led to a premature
discourse on 'Africa rising' in some circles. But the fall in commodity prices in the second decade of the 2000s has the ECA (2016)
lamenting the failure of most African countries to use the recent
commodity-based growth to start a more sustainable growth based
on the development of the manufacturing sector (including the
processing of primary commodities) or even to achieve upgrading
within the commodity sectors themselves.

Therefore, active policies designed to promote diversification away from activities based on natural or existing (or static)
comparative advantage based on natural resources and existing endowments of labour and capital towards new sectors with

higher productivity potential are required to achieve the capital accumulation required for sustained development. The increasing returns associated with modern industrial production and technological progress has thus been recognised as crucial for achieving development (Jomo and Reinert 2005; Akyuz 2005; Kattel et al. 2009). The reasons were clear from Kaldor's time, who recognised that industrialisation is both the key to structural transformation and growth (Storm 2015). Given the increasing returns and high-income elasticity of demand associated with them, manufactured products allow for more rapid productivity growth and avoid the declining terms of trade that have foiled the growth prospects of many commodity-dependent economies. As it has the strongest backward and forward linkages among all the sectors, export of manufactures can generate productivity growth both within and across industries and sectors. Apart from the scale economies that give rise to increasing returns, this also arises from manufacturing activities' ability to give rise to economies of scope (i.e., capabilities in one set of activities lowering the cost of engaging in other) and to generate knowledge spillovers to other sectors of the economy. By creating capabilities and processes that improve productivity in a continuous and cumulative way, these economies of scale and scope and technological diffusion contribute to raising productivity in a dynamic way (UNCTAD 2016; ECA 2016). Further, higher manufacturing output growth allows an economy-wide deepening of the division of labour, greater specialisation and more rapid learning-by-doing in firms – and all these processes eventually get reflected in higher productivity growth (Storm 2015).

Moving from increasing returns to infant-industry support

It is amply clear that, in order to avoid the balance of payments problems associated with primary goods exports in the initial development stage as well as to improve economy-wide productivity gains required to sustain a dynamic development process, it is necessary to expand other exports along with primary exports (which would be part of a successful development strategy for resource-rich countries), by first developing the domestic manufacturing industry. However, as was recognised by classical development economists, the promotion of manufactured exports in developing countries first requires an increase in production through import substitution/

infant-industry protection for the following reasons (Kattel et al. 2009; Shafaeddin 2005):

- Import protection is required to ensure an increase in demand for domestically produced manufactured goods so that their production may be scaled up to levels that will yield economies of scale required to compete in international markets.
- Protection and promotion of selected manufactured goods (*with increasing returns to scale*) also enables increased productivity growth – through learning-by-doing, training and associated externalities – which can make these products more competitive in the domestic and world markets.
- Initially, there is also a need to restrict imports of goods other than capital goods (mainly consumption goods) for saving the use of limited foreign exchange for importing capital imports.

Typically, at the introductory stage, a new product is introduced in a developing country via imports or foreign direct investment (FDI) from countries at a higher stage of development, and the follower country learns to produce these goods for itself through imitation or borrowed technology. But in each stage of industrialisation, even as existing industries mature and become competitive export industries, a new set of infant industries would need to be nurtured simultaneously to become competitive. This is because rising costs, limits to productivity growth and competition from countries catching-up from behind (due to the erosion of entry barriers with the maturing of technologies) would eventually lead to loss of competitiveness in traditional/existing industries. As all of these reduce the returns to an activity, in each stage, investments have to be guided into activities that would involve greater productivity and thus higher-wage potential than before, such that there is an increase in demand that will keep the growth cycle going. This would involve reducing risks and augmenting profits in activities and industries deemed important for future growth (Wade 1990; Amsden 2001; Francis 2003; UNCTAD 2016).

The post-war consensus was that a viable development strategy should aim at establishing a number of increasing returns activities that would become each other's customers and generate the first virtuous circle of growth. The role of industrial policy was in setting goals and advancing specific sectors. This has to involve targeting and protection focused on increasing returns activities such that the resulting virtuous circles of productivity growth and wage growth act as barriers to entry for competitors in the domestic market, as well as give domestic producers the so-called 'first-mover advantage' in export markets. The first-mover advantage refers to the fact that benefitting from the productivity growth achieved in domestic markets firms can enter first into the export markets for a particular product. This strategic advantage in moving first enables them to further benefit from the economies of scale and scope offered by international markets before others do. As Nurkse argued, these virtuous circles of growth create their own demand and the financing required to make the process sustainable (Kattel et al. 2009). Thus exports of products from increasing returns sectors gives rise to the investment incentives needed for industrialisation. It is impossible, in this context, not to see the connection between this development imperative of LDCs and developed countries' trade policies. As Kregel (2007) emphasised, as in the case of primary products-based exports, developing countries' exports of even simple manufactures like textiles also necessarily depend on the older industrial countries adopting trade policies that support, or at least do not discriminate against, developing country exports of manufactures. This is of course not guaranteed.

Theoretically, foreign capital could also help underdeveloped economies overcome the vicious cycle of low domestic savings (and low capital formation) associated with the low productivity of primary sector dependence in the early stages of development. While all forms of international capital flows (long-term borrowing, official aid, portfolio flows and FDI) allow host countries to invest more than they save, FDI has been traditionally known to be distinct from other forms of capital flows in providing host countries with technology and export market access along with stable forms of capital.[8] In fact, recognising the scope of financial markets to generate erratic movements in exchange rates that are detrimental to industrial development, the post-war international monetary arrangements included restrictions over short-term capital flows to maintain currency stability (see Akyuz 2007; Levitt 2006; Storm and Naastepad 2005).

Furthermore, it is critically important that whether in the form of official aid, borrowing or FDI, foreign capital's role in development is limited, unless it is channelled mostly to savings and investment rather than to an increase in import-dependent consumption. This in turn requires that these strategies must be used together with the targeting of increasing returns activities (Kregel 2007). This is because there is a tendency for foreign aid and foreign-invested firms to finance an increase in imports. The additional imports thus financed could lead to displacement of whatever little domestic industrial production exists in a poor country and prevent further industrial development. Together with the adverse terms of trade in primary exports, this leads to adverse balance of payments situations. This in turn makes a country dependent on further foreign financing to balance the current account. Thus foreign financing becomes unsustainable as the current account becomes dominated by interest payments and profit remittances that exceed capital inflows, causing net capital outflows, depreciation of the domestic currency and further economic problems for the developing country. Foreign capital-assisted industrialisation strategies also, therefore, require targeting and promotion of increasing returns activities.

It was therefore considered as a given in the 1950s and 1960s that developing countries should embark on a path of internally led growth through domestic industrialisation strategies involving import protection.[9] The development history of today's developed countries – such as the US, the UK and Japan – also clearly shows that the policies adopted by these countries had all made important departures from the laissez-faire free-trade rhetoric of the periods in which they were underdeveloped (see Chang 2002).[10]

From state-led industrialisation strategy to the 'flying geese' paradigm

During the 'easy' phase of industrialisation based on import substitution, from the post-war period until the early 1970s (Perez 2002; Storm 2015), industrial growth accelerated throughout much of the developing world at varying rates after World War II. As Perez (2002) asserted, the factors that made possible the varieties of industrialisation paths in post-war Asia, Latin America, Russia, etc. had much to do with the features of the mass production techno-economic paradigm that was in place. These possibilities were exhausted by the early 1970s. Meanwhile, the only countries to manage structural transformation and technological upgrading in a dynamic sense were in East Asia (UNCTAD 2016: 177; Storm and Naastepad 2005; Reinert and Kattel 2010). Many other developing countries, mostly in Latin America and Africa, which had become structurally dependent upon (capital goods) imports and had accumulated unmanageable foreign debts (often denominated in dollars) were pushed into a de facto default and a prolonged debt crisis after the US tripled interest rates in 1982 to fight its domestic inflation (Storm 2015: 667). In Latin America as well as in India, the need for local competitive pressure under the import substitution-industrialisation strategy was severely underestimated (Sridharan 1996). Moreover, as pointed out by Reinert and Kattel (2010), the failure to create dynamic economies of scale led to financial fragility, particularly when foreign capital inflows and lending became prevalent elements in the development strategy.

On the other hand, the rich literature on the history of industrial policy in the technologically advanced early and late industrialisers – the successful 'developmental states' of East Asia, namely, post-war Japan, followed by South Korea, Taiwan and Singapore (see Hughes 1988; Amsden 1989, 2001; Wade 1988, 1990; Lall 1992, 1996; Sridharan 1996; Jomo et al. 1997; Chang 2002; UNCTAD 2003; Storm and Naastepad 2005; UNCTAD 2014; etc.) – has shown how these countries succeeded while following import-substituting industrialisation strategies based on direct state activity as well as regulation of markets. They made use of various forms of industrial policies, which combined a mixture of import substitution and export promotion measures simultaneously and succeeded in setting priorities and in building the domestic linkages required for virtuous development cycles (see also Akyuz 2005; UNCTAD 2016). These have involved 'comparative-advantage defying' measures to engineer a shift towards higher value-added and employment-generating activities with high-income elasticities and more capacities for creating synergies through knowledge creation.

For instance, as Hamilton and Feenstra (2006) cited in Milberg and Winkler (2013: 22) show, Taiwan's specialisation in microwave oven production in the 1970s had little to do with natural endowments and comparative advantage, and all to do with industrial targeting and picking a niche market in the hope of its export potential. Lee (1995) identifies South Korea's movement into the production of higher value-added production between the 1960s and 1980s and attributes it to the emergence of 'non-comparative advantage'-based trade. Amsden (1989) details the strategic policies of the South Korean government to subsidise and target exports in return for export and productivity growth by Korean conglomerates (also see Sridharan 1996 for a comparative analyses of the ISI strategies in the Brazilian, South Korean and Indian electronics industries).

Along with regulated trade policies and the targeting of increasing returns activities by providing incentives that defy market price signals (to promote production, exports, upgrading and employment in increasing returns sectors), the strategies of all these countries also involved public investment in physical and social infrastructure as well as government expenditure to ensure public provision of essential goods and services (see Storm and Naastepad 2005).

Further, these strategies also included policies to enable domestic forward and backward linkages as well as performance requirements on FDI to support sustainable industrial development and structural change towards higher value-added activities. The risk of failure associated with selective state promotion has been managed with mechanisms for monitoring performance, observing underperformance and either rectifying or removing state assistance (Lall 1996; Amsden 2001; Storm and Naastepad 2005; UNCTAD 2016).

But as well known, the minimum entry barriers and skill requirements become higher while moving from low-technology products to medium- and high-technology industries. This meant that the risks involved in entry of firms of developing countries into new activities increased, and government intervention required to improve firm-level competitive advantage became more important once the easy phase of industrialisation was over. The successful East Asian countries were the ones that were able to meet the technocratic/governance challenges that arose and overcame the information and coordination market failures. Such industrial policies were combined with macroeconomic policies that allowed stable exchange rates and financial stability. These strategies have had important implications for the subsequent industrial development trajectories in these countries.

However, over the 1980s, evidence of the superior economic and industrial performance of the seemingly market-led export-led first-tier East Asian countries over the relatively poor record of other developing countries which adhered more closely to the state-led and regulated inward-looking policies, including India, led to the emergence of a 'new orthodoxy' in economic policy advocacy. The Latin American and East Asian industrial growth experiences were interpreted as proof that, while developing country governments that intervened strongly in markets suffered from gross inefficiencies (like in Latin America and India), those relying on competitive markets operating broadly on neoclassical principles could foster high levels of economic efficiency and rapid self-sustained growth (as in East Asia; see Ghosh 2009; Reinert and Kattel 2010).

Although gradually this interpretation came under increasing attack, especially in terms of the crucial role of government intervention in the market-oriented economies in East Asia, one element that mainstream economists have continued to highlight is the apparent openness of these countries to FDI, which facilitated their rapid economic restructuring. Consequently, the sustained growth and industrialisation experienced by the late industrialisers of East Asia until the mid-1990s saw the 'flying geese' paradigm being adopted to explain the pattern of industrial restructuring and development of the countries in this region (see Trade and Development Report 1996; World Investment Report 1995, 1999; Kwan 1994; Yamashita 1991; Suthy 1991; etc.).

'The flying geese syndrome'

The growth sequence of imports, domestic production and exports – typical of late-industrialising developing countries – was first highlighted by the Japanese economist Kaname Akamatsu (1961, 1962) in the case of Japan. This is similar to the product-cycle theory, which fits the strategic behaviour of a developed country innovating firm and the life cycle of a product and industry developed in an advanced economy through innovation. However, the 'flying geese' model is essentially a 'catching-up product cycle' (CPC) model constructed from a late-industrialising developing country's point of view, where the cycle begins when the product is introduced through imports, rather than innovation (Francis 2003).

Originally, Akamatsu had used the 'flying geese' pattern to illustrate how Japan followed and tried to catch up with the US and Western Europe beginning in the late 19th century, with the production first of simple consumer goods introduced from abroad, then consumer durables and eventually capital goods (Francis 2003). The industrialisation of the country was perceived as proceeding in the manner of imports and import substitution followed by export expansion of successively advanced products and industries, in a sequential pattern of industrial upgrading.

Akamatsu's and the later Japanese studies which substantiated the CPC theory clearly recorded "*the continuity of Japanese import-substitution policies while pursuing export expansion*" (own emphasis) and, equally significantly, "*a very low level of dependence of Japan on external capital (especially FDI")* during its period of CPC development (see Yamazawa 1990: 35).[11] However, in subsequent adaptations, the 'flying geese' paradigm was used to argue that, rather than attempting to domestically generate and accumulate the technology and managerial resources required for catching-up industrialisation through trial and error and/or relying on imported machines and new technology under licensing agreements (that is, non-equity forms of technology transfer), CPC development can be hastened for a late-industrialising country through inward FDI, which brings in capital, technology, external market access and managerial and marketing techniques in a packaged form.

According to these later variations of the CPC model (see Yamazawa 1990; Kwan 1994; UNCTAD/WIR 1995; Dobson and Yue 1997; Ramstetter 1991; etc.), FDI (rather than imports) by firms from mature industries in a more advanced economy accelerates import substitution and export expansion of new products and industries in the less developed host economy and enables its rapid catching-up and industrial restructuring (Francis 2003). Japan was the original lead goose offshoring production in its mature industries (such as textiles, electronics, etc.) to successively cheaper locations in neighbouring countries at different stages of development (the first-tier newly industrialised countries or NICs), in a manner mutually beneficial to home and host countries. The shift observed in the East Asian countries (commencing with Japan in the 1870s), from light industry such as textiles to a range of heavy industries one after another, beginning with basic material producing industries such as chemicals and metal industries and then further to processing-assembly machinery sectors like automobile and electronics industries, was pointed out to be a standard example of such industrial upgrading and diversification.

However, ironically, CPC development through FDI was not the way the first-tier NICs – particularly the countries that developed the most diverse, deep, complex and technologically dynamic industrial sectors, namely, South Korea and Taiwan – industrialised. The share of FDI inflows in gross domestic capital formation (GCF) in the NICs shows that South Korea and Taiwan had the least reliance on inward FDI during their industrial catching-up phases (Lall 1996: 202) in the 1950s, 1960s and 1970s. The ratio of FDI inflows to gross capital formation remained less than 2 per cent for Korea and Taiwan until the mid-1980s (see also Jomo et al. 1997).

Taiwan's ratio increased slightly thereafter, but remained between 2–3 per cent until 1997.[12]

Equally problematically, the flying geese paradigm assumes that there is a natural or automatic inclination for the linear progression from FDI-led domestic production growth to import substitution and then to exporting by the host country (Francis 2003).[13] This is untenable as we show below. Further, as Yokokawa (2013) points out, there are also possibilities for non-linear development, that is, leapfrogging, available to late industrialisers, because they can introduce the most advanced technology available (Yokokawa 2013: 38, citing Gerschenkron 1962).

What is critical to note is that, contrary to what a once-for-all technology transfer process implies, technology development is cumulative and dynamic in nature, involving acquisitive, operative, adaptive and innovative capabilities. If FDI is to lead to technology upgrading and diffusion enabling industrial upgrading in the host economy, the production of foreign-affiliated firms in the country must be linked to indigenous firms in the supporting and related industries in that country (Francis 2003). The beneficial impact of FDI on the development of local capabilities through spillover channels of demonstration effects, training effects and linkages is influenced, *inter alia*, by learning, experience, skill development and the accumulation of knowledge by the labour force of the host country (Gallagher and Shafaeddin 2009: 5). This clearly means that indigenous technology development and other forms of technology transfer such as technology licensing, subcontracting, etc. must therefore take place along with FDI, for the purpose of breaking the cycle of foreign technology dependence and even for FDI to have developmental impacts for the host economy. This is the role played by industrial policy.

The critical importance of indigenous technological development becomes clearer when we look at the requirements for sustained competitiveness at the industry and firm level.

Industry-level imperatives for productivity growth

As first elaborated in Francis (2003), there are two necessary conditions that should be met for an expansion in an industry's output in a developing country, even when there are foreign-affiliated firms producing locally. Firstly, an increase in the price competitiveness of domestic producers vis-à-vis imports is necessary if the domestic product is to replace imports (whether imports of the product are restricted or not). Secondly, there should be entry of indigenous firms into the industry. The entry of indigenous firms into the industry following/envisaging a growth in demand can come about through (i) the emergence of private indigenous firms due to the presence of strong entrepreneurial capabilities in the economy or (ii) the emergence of indigenous firms through government participation and promotion. While the latter condition is not necessary for expanding the industry's output or for import substitution, it becomes critical for the sustainable growth of the industry over time.

Price competitiveness of domestic producers (both indigenous and foreign-affiliated firms) may improve in either of the following ways:

1   subsidies to domestic producers in a variety of ways (including tax concessions and subsidised credit) to offset the higher productivity/lower prices of imports;
2   presence of a managed exchange rate advantage;
3   imposing quantitative restrictions on imports and/or providing tariff protection to domestic firms; and
4   increase in productivity, which may come about due to:

   (i)   increased availability of competitive factor inputs through (a) successful linking up with firms in supporting industries domestically, or (b) through access to more competitive imported inputs;
   (ii) faster increase in labour productivity in comparison to wage rise;
   (iii) successful technological development or technology transfer; etc.

However, productivity increase becomes a necessary condition for the sustainability of the industry's growth in the medium to long term. Import substitution in an industry may be achieved by indigenous firms through price competitiveness obtained under prolonged use of tariff protection, import bans, subsidies, etc. However, they may continue to produce for the protected domestic market with significantly lower productivity.[14] Meanwhile, locally established foreign producers may achieve higher productivity and export successfully due to the international production network/GVC strategy of the parent firm. Such a situation may lead to a dichotomised industrial structure. This in turn leads to intra-industry trade with large trade deficits, which occur because of exports of low value-added goods and imports of higher value-added goods belonging to the same industry. If this occurs across several industries, the country would eventually run unsustainable trade deficits, which may jeopardise further industrial development. Further, while this co-existence is possible under protection, the domestic market-oriented segment will find it extremely difficult to survive if and when protection is withdrawn suddenly, unless they improve their productivity consistently.

Similar considerations apply when we consider a country's entry into export markets in a sector. This may come about from a combination of the following possibilities:

1 direct entry into export markets by indigenous firms;
2 an export strategy of foreign-owned/affiliated firms (as part of GVC network); or
3 indirect entry of indigenous firms through subcontracting or other non-equity forms of foreign alliance.

In any of the above scenarios, an increase in the price competitiveness of domestic products vis-à-vis export competitors[15] becomes a necessary prerequisite for entry into export markets and expansion in exports.[16] Relative price competitiveness of a country's products may improve in either of the following ways:

1 subsidisation of domestic production to offset the lower productivity of domestic producers vis-à-vis imported products in a variety of ways (such as tax concessions and subsidised credit);
2 presence of exchange rate advantage for exports through devaluation; and
3 increase in productivity; which could come about through:

    (i) increased availability of competitive factor inputs (a) due to the presence of a diversified domestic industrial structure which enable successful linking up with firms in supporting industries domestically, or (b) through access to more competitive and high-technology imported inputs;
    (ii) faster increase in labour productivity in comparison to wage rise; or alternatively,
    (iii) through improved technology.

The first two options could offer price advantages in the short term. But such advantage would be transient given that many other countries are also providing similar tax or credit incentives or because the currencies of economies which are competing in similar export segments may be depreciating simultaneously. Furthermore, devaluation is not often a policy option in an open economy dependent on volatile foreign capital inflows to finance its current account deficit. It is also not a viable option in an economy with a growing external debt-to-GDP ratio. Equally importantly, devaluation may not lead to an increase in net export earnings when exports are already significantly import-dependent.

In the third case, the option of increasing productivity through liberalised access to competitive imported inputs and intermediate products – a significant incentive for carrying out extensive tariff liberalisation by many developing countries[17] – will also not be long-lasting, given that the importing country can end up in an unsustainable trade deficit situation in the absence of domestic industrial upgrading (Francis and Kallummal 2013; Francis 2015a). Only upgrading indigenous industrial and technological capabilities that make several competitive factor inputs – upstream and downstream – available domestically[18] and enabling the introduction of higher value-added and more advanced products successively leads to structural transformation along a sustainable path (Francis 2015a).

The fact that building and upgrading capabilities require learning and knowledge accumulation has been emphasised in the post-war and modern theoretical and empirical literature since the pioneering article on learning-by-doing by Arrow in 1962 (Gallagher and Shafaeddin 2009). As suggested in Amsden (2001), knowledge needed to compete in world markets – as distinct from factual information – comprises unique skills, sui generis capabilities, novel product concepts and idiosyncratic production systems. Because knowledge is proprietary and firm-specific, it is anything but universally available and free. This is why there is a critical need for government intervention in learning-by-doing as articulated in the 'capability building theory'[19] (see also Khan 2010). The latter is related to the evolutionary theory's understanding that innovations and economic growth in general take place because of knowledge and skill agglomeration and continuous upgrading and technological change (Karo and Kattel 2011), which are engendered by highly embedded policymaking of increasing coordination, dialogue and cooperation managed by a highly capable state and administration.[20]

On the other hand, the neoclassical tradition argues that the main drivers behind innovations and growth are trade and competition: the former using the comparative advantage of nations to bring more, better and cheaper goods to consumers (higher efficiency); and the latter creating pressures for companies to incessantly innovate and outcompete the competitors and to push prices down in the process (higher efficiency, again). This difference goes back to a different understanding of the nature of technological development and its impact on firms and economies (see Gallagher and Shafaeddin 2009; Reinert and Kattel 2010; Karo and Kattel 2011).

As explained by Reinert and Kattel (2010: 16, 17):

> The evolutionary school argues that technological development is almost always path-dependent; neo-classical arguments assume that technology is essentially freely available to all, competitors and countries alike, . . . and that technological development is more or less linear. . . . To evolutionary economists, technological development is anything but linear and technology is anything but freely available. Path dependencies, linkages, spillovers, externalities, winner-takes-all markets and highly imperfect and dynamic competition make technology an unpredictable, high-risk and possibly high-return endeavour. These characteristics engender long-term structural changes in the economies in form of technology trajectories, techno-economic paradigms and geographical agglomerations. . . . Thus, while neoclassical economists set out to rectify market failures that prevent the dissemination of technologies and skills, in the eyes of evolutionary economists, entrepreneurs seek technological innovation in order to create market failure. . . . In trying to hedge their balance sheets through innovations companies rely on skills and routines they have developed, or as Alfred Chandler called this, companies rely on 'learned organizational capabilities' that include technical know-how, management and marketing skill, established networks, etc.[21] These capabilities, however, develop and evolve in a wider context which can be called a national system of innovation that can have a huge variety of features from the legal system to particularities of education and R&D.

Thus it is well acknowledged that the outcomes of firms' technological learning and upgrading efforts are affected by the environment in which learning is taking place, i.e., the innovation systems (Low and Tijaja 2013: 8). Firms located within an efficient innovation system can cope better with the complexity of global value chain transactions and undertake technological learning at relatively lower costs (Low and Tijaja 2013). Innovation systems can be strengthened through effective science and technology policy and targeted activities and initiatives such as industry-specific dialogues, science competitions, internships or work placements, collaboration with universities/research institutes, R&D support, joint R&D, science parks, business incubators and personnel mobility. Many of these policies may seem horizontal in the first instance, but the peculiar nature of technology means that after a certain (low) threshold, effective intervention will necessarily become sector-specific (Lall 1992).

Further, as discussed earlier, because of rising entry barriers, the importance of government intervention becomes more critical in indigenous technology development as a country attempts to move from low to medium and high-technology activities – within industries and across industries.

The shift to passive/horizontal industrial policies

However, with the advent of stabilisation and structural adjustment programmes from the mid-1980s onwards, industrial policy as understood in early development literature – with the goal of advancing specific sectors that bring economy-wide productivity gains required to sustain a dynamic development process – had already begun to be discredited and shunned in international policy discussions. The different interpretations of post-war industrial policy regimes in Latin America, Africa and East Asia led to the next phase of the state-versus-market debate in development literature globally.

The World Bank praised the few successful late industrialisers in East Asia as developmental miracles driven by market-led and efficient outward-oriented policies (World Bank 1993). East Asia's story was told in a way as if feedback linkages and positive externalities emerging in these economies through state-led industrialisation played only an exogenous role in these countries' development, because technological progress and innovation were simply left out (Reinert and Kattel 2010: 24). Focus on export-led growth and, in particular, FDI-led export growth became paramount in the subsequent development debates. In the Asian region, throughout the 1990s (and into the early 2000s), neoliberal writings continued to point to the 'flying geese model' of FDI-led industrial upgrading for supporting the case for trade and investment liberalisation in successful export-led industrialisation by late-industrialising developing countries.

Ex post, it is evident that industrial policy was always a part of the Washington Consensus, albeit in a different form. The approach to development under the latter shifted the focus away from capital accumulation for productive investments to a reliance on improved efficiency in factor allocation led by market forces achieved by 'getting prices right'. Trade liberalisation, removal of price controls and subsidies and financial sector and public sector reforms came under the supply-side policies of structural adjustment. Trade liberalisation included import liberalisation in the form of moving from import quotas to tariffs and reducing tariffs (often eliminating them) and reduction or removal of export controls and subsidies. The neoliberal policies following the Washington Consensus ensured that the developing world could no longer go against, but rather had to follow its static comparative advantage – determined by the relative abundance of unskilled labour and/or natural resources and the relative scarcity of capital (Storm 2015: 667). Thus financial liberalisation was seen as the primary source of the investments needed for the export-led growth model. Liberalisation of FDI inflows followed, which included reducing or eliminating restrictions on which sectors FDI can enter, relaxing rules about extent and modes of foreign ownership, technology transfer, repatriation of profits, etc.

Industrial policy of the selective kind became equated with state intervention, corruption and rent-seeking, inefficiency and misguided economic incentives.[22] Accordingly, the policy prescriptions by international financial institutions like the International Monetary Fund (IMF) and the World Bank shifted to 'passive' or horizontal industrial policies (Francis 2017), supposedly of the non-price-distortive kind of state intervention.

As described in UNCTAD (2016: XIV, 185–188), a horizontal industrial policy framework (also called functional industrial policy; see Lall 1996: 126) essentially accepts existing factor endowment-based static comparative advantages and mainly aims to reduce the costs of doing business, while carrying out hands-off trade and financial liberalisation to allow greater play of market forces. The reduction in the costs of doing business (ease of doing business) is achieved through broad policy measures for improving infrastructure, energy supply, business entry and exit regulations, taxation and customs administration, investment promotion and facilitation, etc. Fundamentally, these broad-based policies aimed at increasing competitiveness by creating 'an enabling environment' are applicable economy-wide, as opposed to any particular sector, industry or firm. Sticking to the neoclassical framework, they are not intended to affect prevailing relative prices in any product markets (Low and Tijaja 2013: 4; Lall 1992, 1996). Trade liberalisation included import liberalisation in the form of moving from import quotas to tariffs and reducing tariffs (often eliminating them),[23] and reduction or removal of export controls and subsidies. Liberalisation of FDI policies included reducing or eliminating restrictions like limits on which sectors FDI can enter, relaxing rules about extent of ownership, technology transfer, local content, foreign exchange balancing, repatriation of profits, etc. Export processing zones (EPZs), infrastructure investments and FDI promotion became the policy buzz words.

Evidently, lagging infrastructure development (including energy supply) is an important supply-side factor impacting firm-level competitiveness, as it does the overall development of a country. Cumbersome administration of tax and customs is also efficiency reducing. However, other horizontal policies that are advocated like labour market 'flexibility' (meant to address the so-called 'rigidities' in the labour market) and reduction in tax rates have critical development implications in terms of inadequate demand and government revenues, and the generation of significant inequalities, all of which lead to unsustainable growth trajectories.[24] These are linked to what is known as the 'low road' to industrial restructuring.

'Passive' industrial policies are quite in contrast to 'active' or vertical industrial policies that were practiced and continue to be practised by some of the other late industrialisers such as China and Brazil (UNCTAD 2016: XIV, Also see Lall 1996; Gallagher and Shafaeddin 2009; Yu et al. 2015; Kasahara and Botelho 2016; etc.). Vertical industrial policies seek to influence the pattern of national industrial development by policy interventions that guide and promote investment domestically towards new activities and sectors with higher productivity, better paid jobs and greater technological potential (i.e., increasing returns activities) (UNCTAD 2016). As noted earlier, income benefits associated with higher productivity activities are necessary to generate the domestic market size required to break the path of import dependent production. Moreover, as Lall (2005 cited in Gallagher and Shafaeddin 2009) emphasises, selective and targeted intervention becomes necessary because learning is technology specific, firm specific and activity specific, and technologies differ in their tacit features and externalities. Performance requirements imposed on foreign investors aimed at promoting backward and forward linkages between foreign-invested enterprises and domestic supplier firms in particular sectors also belong to the category of vertical industrial policies.

Be that as it is, since the 1990s, along with the spread of an export-led economic growth paradigm, there has been a much wider shift towards passive industrial policies across the developing world. This was driven primarily by their Uruguay Round (UR) commitments on tariff liberalisation, as well as the restrictions on domestic policies deemed as trade-related investment measures (TRIMs) and trade-related intellectual property rights (TRIPs) under the WTO from 1995 onwards. These along with the General Agreement on Trade in Services (GATS) brought several domestic policy regulations related to foreign investments, intellectual property rights (IPR), services, etc. under the WTO's multilateral disciplines by deeming them 'trade-related' (more discussion follows in Chapter 5).

In the case of trade policy measures, although the WTO had mandated the conversion of various non-tariff measures to tariffs, it did not require countries to eliminate all tariffs or even substantially reduce them. The assessment made by the WTO Secretariat showed that the share of non-agricultural tariff lines that were bound[25] at the multilateral level by developing countries in 1995 increased from 21 to 73 per cent (Dhar and Das 2015: 257). But many developing countries had bound their tariffs at levels higher than their actual applied levels at the time, leaving some room for adjusting tariffs to meet particular domestic policy objectives (Shadlen 2005: 756–757) if they wanted. Despite this, there was an overall abdication of tariffs as an industrial policy tool, which was due to both external pressures as well as internal political economy dynamics of different developing countries. This is reflected in the fact that many countries, including India, undertook unilateral tariff liberalisation that went much beyond their multilateral commitments at the WTO, bringing down tariffs significantly lower than their bound levels. Simultaneously, they also liberalised their FDI regimes in ambitious drives towards attracting FDI for achieving East Asian-like growth, which was perceived (as discussed) as FDI-driven export-led growth under passive industrial policies (or in other words, due to the 'flying geese syndrome').

Such shift to horizontal industrial policies was cemented by the other WTO agreements such as TRIMs and TRIPs mentioned above. As Shadlen (2005: 754) observed, often, there was a difference between formal degrees of flexibility granted by the WTO and effective flexibility enjoyed by many developing countries given the pressures they faced to exceed their WTO obligations. Apart from the conditionalities of the World Bank and the IMF, such pressures bore upon developing countries indirectly through the competition among them for foreign capital inflows under perceived benefits of greater trade and investment liberalisation. To the extent that the technocracy and the elite in some developing countries also believed in the merits of such an approach (along with the political economy of the interests of foreign-invested domestic companies and liberalised financial sectors), the shift to horizontal industrial policies was also 'autonomous' in those countries.

The 'outliers'?

But there are countries that clearly understood that "as the easy stages of industrialisation are crossed, greater effort is needed to diversify production and find new and dynamic markets, both at home and abroad" (UNCTAD 2016: 177). Passive industrial policies – neither under Washington Consensus' 'getting prices right', nor under 'getting institutions right' as the post-Washington Consensus had come to advocate by the late 1990s – allow for such interventions. However, some developing countries (especially China and Brazil) continued with the more strategic industrial policy approach to widen and deepen their industrial development.

Notably, China did not join the WTO until 2001. Reinert and Kattel (2010) have argued that China and India, and increasingly Brazil, have become powerful countries within the WTO, such that they are able to push through their own clear agenda. They point to the fact that all three countries have made significant changes to their intellectual property laws, which while being WTO-compliant (that is TRIPs-compliant), give important advantages to domestic producers. While this is indeed true, it is only China that has made noticeable exceptions in not allowing total freedom for foreign investors and capital movement (see also UNCTAD 2014: 98–99).[26] The closed financial system has served a critical role in insuring against speculative attacks on China's currency.

Felipe et al. (2010a) highlights that China's high growth rates since the early 1960s (while being the result of massive investment and successful integration into the world economy through trade) only make sense in a context of high assimilation and absorption capabilities, increasing capacity to employ new methods of production and new inputs, and significant upgrading. This was done by protecting certain capital and technology industries, giving them monopoly positions and subsidising them through various price distortions, including suppressed interest rates. These price distortions often created shortages and the government had to resort to using administrative measures to allocate resources directly to non-viable firms in priority industries. China had also adopted the Technology Transfer in Exchange for Domestic Market (TTEDM) access strategy in the late 1980s. Under this, the government encouraged advanced technology transfers from MNCs by offering them access to the Chinese domestic market in exchange (Zhongxiu Zhao et al. 2007).

China also encouraged technological innovation through government funding, while establishing technical standards. Both for regulating technology transfer from MNCs and in ensuring returns from public investment in technology funding, the government could leverage the large size of the domestic market through the regulation of market access/import growth. As reported in the Trade and Development Report (2014), efficiency-seeking type of FDI into China has benefited from the kinds of incentives generally associated with activities located in special economic zones, such as selective value-added tax rebates, corporate tax holidays and the provision of infrastructure that facilitates international trade (Zeng 2011, cited in UNCTAD 2014: 98). By contrast, the market-seeking type of FDI has been subject to varying foreign ownership limits, such as minority equity stakes in the steel and banking sectors or 50–50 joint ventures in the automobile industry. Encouraging several joint ventures in the automobile sector has been used as an instrument to maintain that sector's competitiveness, making it more attractive for foreign investors to transfer and upgrade their technologies used in production in China. This has been further supported by massive increases in the government's R&D expenditures. Moreover, government procurement and state investment in infrastructure, such as the building of a highway system, have been used to boost the demand for cars (Lo and Wu 2014, cited in UNCTAD 2014: 98–99). Storm and Naastepad (2005), Lee and Mathews (2013), and Yu et al. (2015) also discuss the policies adopted by China for industrial targeting, export orientation and sequential upgrading with an emphasis on learning and capability building, towards the 'creative restructuring' of domestic firms (Yu et al. 2015).[27]

Based on a review of studies on the revival of industrial policy in Brazil, Kasahara and Botelho (2016) show that, after almost two decades of neglecting industrial policy, the first term of President Lula Inácio da Silva (2003–2006) represented a turning point. While the BNDES (the National Bank for Economic and Social Development) and Brazil's innovation agency (FINEP) played a key role in preserving the legacy of traditional industrial policy, the launch of the Industrial, Technology and Foreign Policy (PITCE) document in 2004, followed by the creation of the National Council of Industrial Development (CNDI) and the Brazilian Agency for Industrial Development (ABDI), have been hailed as landmarks of the rebirth of industrial policy. The Brazilian development bank BNDES succeeded in supporting the consolidation of new activities such as the pharmaceutical and wind turbine industries. In both sectors, the 'nurturing' strategy of combining a stable public demand (i.e., drugs and wind energy) with market-based incentives for private sector (domestic and foreign) producers facilitated the establishment of a variety of new companies (Kasahara and Botelho 2016: 102).

Kasahara and Botelho (2016) counters the frequent criticism in the literature that Brazilian industrial policy subsidised consolidated companies that are solid enough to borrow funds in regular financial markets rather than supporting new and innovative sectors.

> BNDES's participation as a minority shareholder seemed to improve companies' performance and capital expenditure, especially for stand-alone firms. Informatics, for instance, is one sector that is still alive and kicking in Brazil's industrial policy. The sector has been a pioneer in the use of local content requirements and public procurement to stimulate R&D, despite criticism about the results. The resilience of this sector

inspired the creation of a new state-owned company (CEITEC) in 2008, with a mission to build microchips.

(Kasahara and Botelho 2016: 105)

UNCTAD (2014) analysis also shows that, in Brazil, the main objectives of tax reduction measures adopted in 2012 in a 5-year programme known as Inovar Auto had been to slowdown import growth and encourage the development local suppliers in the automobile sector. The policy implied a 30-percentage point increase in the excise tax on industrial products (IPI) levied on cars imported from outside MERCOSUR and specified the eligibility requirements for firms to join the programme and be granted IPI tax credits. Some of these requirements were linked to domestic content and investment in innovation. These measures complement other support policies for the domestic automobile industry such as relatively high tariffs on automotive parts imported from outside MERCOSUR. This proactive approach towards the development of domestic automobile industry has allowed Brazil to attract additional FDI by new vehicle assemblers and a progressive delegation of innovation activities to Brazilian affiliates and their local suppliers (UNCTAD 2014: 100).

As discussed in the first chapter, many developed countries, such as the US, Japan, Ireland and Israel and those of the EU (less significantly), have also continued practising industrial policy, even if their goals were often hidden and not couched in conventional industrial policy terminology (see UNCTAD 2014). As has been known widely, the US has pursued the formulation of national visions and national programmes by centralised coordination agencies to develop specific industries. For instance, a number of its institutions such as the Defense Advanced Research Projects Agency, National Institutes of Health, National Institute of Standards and Technology and the Central Intelligence Agency, have sought to build a knowledge economy linking innovative firms, public resources and new sources of finance (UNCTAD 2016: 178). But several scholars have established that the US has increasingly used a more de-centralised approach wherein a variety of federal and state-led initiatives and programmes have lent support to strategic industries, both traditional and emerging (UNCTAD 2014; Wade 2012; Mazzucato 2013; Brandt and Whitford 2017; etc.). For example, the several programmes initiated by the Obama administration to support American manufacturing industries include: the 'National Network for Manufacturing Innovation' (NNMI), which consists of seven institutes hoping to bring together 'talents and capabilities from the public and private sector into a proving ground for cutting-edge technology'; the 'Investing in Manufacturing Communities Partnership' (ICMP), which presumes to help designated communities to develop more coordinated economic development strategies by 'synchronizing grant programmes across multiple departments and agencies'; and other such programmes (Brandt and Whitford 2017: 332). The US is thus viewed both as an "entrepreneurial State" and a "coordinating State" (UNCTAD 2014: 93).

While the EU industrial policy remains less comprehensive than that of the US, the Horizon 2020 Programme introduced in 2014 includes complementary and more targeted measures to foster investment in innovation, such as €80 billion earmarked for research and innovation to support key enabling technologies. The Programme also finances prototypes and demonstration projects in order to facilitate commercialisation of innovations (UNCTAD 2014: 95–96; Dhar 2014; Pianta et al. 2016).

On the other side, despite the decline in global interest in Japanese industrial policy after the late 1980s, and contrary to the popular story of internationally competitive Japanese firms operating in a 'normal' economy, industrial policy failed to die in Japan (Noble 2003: 284). It continues to play an active role in attempts to smooth the adjustment of traditional industries coping with structural decline such as coal and textiles that were declining economically but were politically influential. Equally importantly, industrial policy has continued to play a major role in the promotion of 'new' areas such as nanotechnology. It has also played a significant role in internationally competitive but temporarily weakened industries, including steel, semiconductors and even cars, where MITI played a prominent role in the restructuring of Nissan and other troubled firms (*ibid.*).

Despite such industrial policy measures in various shapes to reverse the decline in the manufacturing sector comparative advantages even in the developed economies, neoliberal economists continue to be reluctant in accepting the role of industrial policy in developing/maintaining dynamic competitiveness. Relatedly, what Palley (1994) pointed out in the early 1990s about the remarkable tendency among orthodox economists to continue to promote free-trade policy despite doubts about its benefits even within their own theoretical paradigm, remains true even now. At another level, the neoliberal stream of research continue focusing on the welfare question, which remains unsettled, even while agreeing that there are instances where infant-industry protection led to higher growth.

In their OECD review study, Harrison and Rodriguez-Clare (2009) argue that the infant-industry framework typically assumes that the mere expansion of a sector will generate all sorts of positive effects that will increase industry-wide productivity. But this may not happen, and the economy may simply end up with a larger version of the inefficient sector it began with. This is despite their acknowledgement that investments that will increase productivity may not occur without public intervention because of coordination failures.

Harrison and Rodriguez-Clare (2009) also reviewed research that suggests that FDI has been particularly important in cases where governments were actively engaged in strategies of technological upgrading in certain sectors and brought in foreign companies *as part* of those strategies. Typically, these efforts were part of a set of complementary policies that included increasing the supply of skilled workers in a targeted industry, improving regulation and infrastructure, promoting new activities and innovation and increasing exports. In many of those cases, the government probably encouraged joint ventures. By contrast, as Chandra and Kolavalli (2006: 19) have concluded in their overview of 10 cases of successful technology upgrading, "without host country policies to develop local capabilities, MNC-led exports are likely to remain technologically stagnant, leaving developing countries unable to progress beyond the assembly of imported components". Chandra and Kolavalli (2006) concluded that "in every case, getting it right depended upon the degree of synchronization between institutions and government policies to motivate learning among exporters. The hallmark of these policies was industry specificity" (cited in Harrison and Rodriguez-Clare 2009: 75). However, after their review of research, the conclusion drawn by the OECD paper is that the direction of causality between industrial policy and success with FDI involvement is not so clear.

Back to the basics in development economics

Even so, by the mid- to late-2000s, there was recognition even among some quarters of neoliberal economics that the Washington Consensus policies had not led to the desired effect in developing countries (Rodrik 2008). Research had already begun to emerge discussing industrial stagnation, deindustrialisation and middle-income traps in developing countries (Wade 2006; Felipe et al. 2012; the papers cited in UNCTAD 2016). According to the World Bank, out of the 101 economies classified as middle income in 1960, only 13 had graduated to high income in the five decades that followed: Equatorial Guinea, Greece, Hong Kong (China), Ireland, Israel, Japan, Mauritius, Portugal, Puerto Rico, the Republic of Korea, Singapore, Spain and Taiwan. Most countries in Latin America, as well as in the Middle East and North Africa, reached middle-income status during the 1960s and 1970s and have remained there. Even in East Asia, the second tier of new industrialisers, such as Malaysia and Thailand, has experienced growth slowdowns in recent years that could be conceived as an MIT (World Bank 2013, cited in UNCTAD 2016: 40). Storm (2015) showed that there was not just deindustrialisation, but also a drastic intra-industry restructuring in line with static comparative advantage. Thus while Mexico and some small Central American economics went for assembly manufacturing by catering to US markets, Southern Cone countries went for natural resource processing. As in Latin America, African countries deindustrialised prematurely, at levels of per capita income which were significantly lower than the levels at which the advanced countries had deindustrialised.

Around the same time, there emerged papers by mainstream economists discussing growth and development in the tone of classical development economists. For instance, Hausmann et al. (2007), Hidalgo et al. (2007), Hidalgo (2009), and Hidalgo and Hausmann (2009) have argued that growth and development are the result of structural transformation, and, more crucially, established that not all products carry the same consequences for a country's development. This came out of the reality that developing countries face serious problems when they try to become competitive in a new product or when they try to enter a new market, and especially when they try to shift production and exports toward more sophisticated products. Hausmann et al. (2007) showed that the specific set of products that a country exports has important consequences for the pattern of development. Hausmann et al. (2007) also argued that the varied economic performance of different countries is partly explained by the goods that they produce. Their explanation is that goods that provide more opportunities for learning-by-doing and for technological and institutional upgrading ultimately benefits the whole economy. On these grounds, Hidalgo et al. (2007) argued that development has to be understood as the process of accumulating more complex sets of capabilities and of finding paths that create incentives for those capabilities to be accumulated and used. The implication is that a growth miracle sustained for several decades must involve the continual introduction of new goods, not merely continual learning on a fixed set of goods.[28] In effect, these studies imply that countries should promote new areas of comparative advantage, which offer greater potential for economy-wide learning and externalities through increasing returns. To analyse development and structural transformation from this perspective, Hidalgo et al. (2007) developed an analytical tool called the product space. This has been incorporated into subsequent research from the Harvard University's Growth Lab.

Meanwhile, renewed interest in industry's role as a dynamic instrument of growth in the developed economies after the global financial crisis has coincided with a renewed concern for industrialisation and structural change in the mainstream of development economics as well (Storm 2015). Storm (2015) points to the World Bank's Commission on Growth and Development (2008), UNIDO's Industrial Development Report (2013), McMillan and Rodrik (2011), Rodrik (2007, 2008, 2013), Justin Yifu Lin (2009, 2012) etc. as manifesting this renaissance in thinking about structural change and industrial policy (see the literature cited in Storm 2015).

In the US, the bastion of neoliberalism, as Wade (2012) observed, the financial crisis of 2007–2009 and the ensuing long slump tarnished the neoliberal consensus around 'the self-regulating market'. As observed in UNCTAD (2014), while the share of industrial activity in developed economies' GDP has been declining for some decades as part of their evolution towards a post-industrial society, the pace and extent of this shift, which accelerated in the early 2000s, has begun to worry policymakers in several developed economies. Such worries, and attendant concerns about the hollowing out of the middle class in these economies, intensified after the 2008 global crisis, reinforcing the argument that policymakers should now use industrial policies as part of a rebalancing of the economy away from the lopsided domination of the financial sector. As we saw in Chapter 1, the Obama government's response to the post-2007 slump included an unprecedented programme of targeted industry assistance. Subsequently, the President's Council on Science and Technology have explicitly called for state co-investment

with industrial partners, without calling it industrial policy. It is
pertinent to quote Brandt and Whitford (2017):

> Prominent and powerful groups such as the American 'Presi-
> dent's Council on Science and Technology' must publicly
> eschew 'industrial policy, in which the government invests in
> particular companies or sectors', since such policies are so asso-
> ciated with visions of hamhanded and corruptible bureaucrats
> trying to 'pick winners'. Somehow, though, they are nonetheless
> 'unabashed' in their call for a new 'innovation policy' wherein
> the American state (or states) would help 'firms and industries
> compete globally' by identifying 'industrial partners willing to
> co-invest with the government [in] for example, . . . technology
> infrastructure and the creation of clusters' and the like.
>
> (PCAST 2011 cited in Brandt and Whitford
> (2017: 332), emphasis in original)

Ironically, in the developing world, from around the mid-2000s,
the policy discourse on industrial development saw a broad shift
towards participation in global production networks and global
value chains (GVCs) as the 'new' panacea for underdevelopment.
As we saw in the previous chapter, this shift has been observable in
Indian policy discussions too.

The emergence of the GVC paradigm and the partnership with FTAs

GVCs have been traditionally used to refer to the geographical fragmentation of production processes by large firms (mainly based in
industrialised countries), which rely on networks of suppliers across
countries connected by service links. It is important to note that
GVCs are hardly a new phenomenon that emerged suddenly on the
global scene in the 2000s. Production networks in East Asia go back
to the 1960s, particularly in textiles and electronics (semiconductors). In the literature, they have been alternatively designated as
global production networks (Gereffi 1995), global supply chains,
international production fragmentation (Jones and Kierzkowski
1990), production relocation, global production sharing (Yeats
1997), vertical specialisation (Hummels, Ishii and Yi 2001), international outsourcing, 'slicing up the value chain', offshoring, etc.
The rapid spread of GVCs needs to be seen in the context of
long-term changes in technology and the associated organisation

of production – especially the shift since the 1970s from the fourth technological revolution based on oil and mass production to the microelectronics-based information and communication technologies (ICT). This shift in what neo-Schumpeterian economists refer to as the 'techno-economic paradigm' has involved the transformation of business organisation models from the rigid hierarchical and integrated pyramids of the Fordist mass production age into flexible, de-centralised network-based organisation of production and innovation (see Perez 2001; Francis 2018a). The significant decline in transport and communication as well as computing costs leading to major leaps in supply chain management – all facilitated by the ICT revolution, has been an important underlying driver of the wider spread of value chains. The development of international standards for product descriptions and business protocols has further facilitated the spread of GVCs (De Backer and Yamano 2010). Simultaneously, the autonomous and exogenously imposed policy changes that occurred across the developed and developing world (examined earlier) which have continuously liberalised trade and capital flows (FDI and non-FDI investments) along with the shift from import substitution to an export-led growth strategy have been important handmaidens in the spread of GVCs.

For Milberg and Winkler (2013: 12), offshoring – a key component of the globalisation of production within/through/involving GVCs – is part of the larger corporate strategic shift over the past 25 years which attempted to realign the interests of shareholders and managers. This changed corporate strategy involves a search for lower costs and greater flexibility to implement a process of 'mass customisation', along with a desire to focus on 'core' activities and allocate greater resources to financial activity and short-run shareholder value while reducing commitments to long-term employment and job security. For the economy of the lead TNC's home country, the impact of the offshoring of routine tasks is thus considered to help sustain manufacturing competitiveness. On the other side of the bargain are the developing country host economies, for which, the trade in intermediate goods and services within GVCs is considered to provide cheaper, better or a broader variety of intermediate inputs and thereby reduce costs and improve productivity in downstream industries (see, for instance, Nordas 2009). It is assumed that the rise in profitability leads to further investments and growth in the economy concerned. Thus participation in GVCs is proposed as a win-win situation.

Consequently, production has become more trade-intensive, lead-ing to significant increase in intra-industry trade. Given that sup-plier firms have to often import parts, components, machinery and services in order to export, vertical specialisation has increased sig-nificantly. While the fact that vertical fragmentation associated with GVCs has been an important driving force for deepening interna-tional specialisation since the 1970s has been well acknowledged by scholars of East and Southeast Asian countries, as discussed in Chap-ter 1, Indian academia discovered it around the mid-2000s – soon after India's Look East Policy began assuming increased significance.

As Milberg and Winkler (2013) point out, the fact that the enor-mous expansion in the scope of value chains has offered substantial opportunities for some developing countries to expand exports and move into the production of higher value-added goods and services, has led to 'upgrading' in such value chains becoming synonymous with economic development (see also Banga 2013; Low and Tijaja 2013; UNCTAD 2014, 2016 countering such claims). 'Linking into GVCs' per se is increasingly being considered as the new devel-opment challenge by policymakers in many developing counties (Banga 2013). Apart from continuing the wrongly told experiences of the first-tier NICs of South Korea and Taiwan, China's manu-facturing export success and India's IT services exports are also considered as examples of upgrading that have occurred through integration into value chains.

Just as the 'flying geese' paradigm was propagated from the late 1980s into the 1990s, GVCs began to be propagated as the 'ideal' platform for developing countries to launch themselves and further their globalisation projects/efforts. GVCs in fact became the new-found basis for wider and deeper trade and financial/investment liberalisation in developing countries. Industrial policies are being reshaped in order to adjust to this new dimension of trade, and for-eign direct investments are being encouraged with the hope of rais-ing the possibility of linking into the value chains (Banga 2013: 4). Even trade facilitation was sold on the basis of the gains to be had from increased participation in GVCs by undertaking these reforms.

The rationale behind the need for trade and investment liberalisa-tion for getting included in GVCs has been made in many variants, one of which is provided in Nordas (2009: 9):

> While technical separability and comparative advantage
> for different stages in the production process make vertical

fragmentation feasible, the gains from it depend on a trade-off between the prices of the outsourced parts, components and tasks and the additional transaction costs arising from dealing with a supplier at a distance and across an international border. Since parts and components cross international borders several times in an international production network, firms located in countries with high tariffs and time-consuming border procedures are at a disadvantage when it comes to participating in international supply networks.

Thus trade liberalisation becomes an imperative for countries to be able to participate in GVCs.

Because of their focus on relative factor-cost advantages without incorporating technological factors, the ongoing mainstream discussion in developing (and developed) countries, typically, focuses on how developing countries can rely on their comparative advantage based on existing factor endowments and undertake trade and FDI liberalisation along with passive industrial policies to facilitate new foreign investments and exports. Liberalisation of FDI norms will attract FDI and enable developing countries to participate in GVCs, while trade liberalisation will provide greater flexibility to these MNCs to source components from or undertake tasks in partner countries at different stages of development and increase intra-firm trade within the GVCs. Both together will help increase exports from the host developing countries and lead to dynamic gains from trade that accompany industrial upgrading (see Anukoonwattaka 2011). In Asia, trade liberalisation through free trade agreements (FTAs), in particular, has been argued to enable rapid and 'efficient industrial restructuring' by allowing countries to participate in GVCs (see Kumar 2007a; and other literature cited in Francis and Kallummal 2013; Anukoonwattaka 2011; Suh and Kim 2014; etc.).

Conclusion

At the level of ideas, industrial policy has been repeatedly discovered and abandoned over the last century. Industrial policy as understood in early development literature – with the goal of advancing specific sectors that bring economy-wide productivity gains required to sustain a dynamic development process – had been discredited and shunned in international policy discussions since the 1980s. Developing countries like China and Brazil are outliers as they have continued with the more strategic industrial policy approach to widen and deepen their industrial development.

But there was recognition by the mid- to late-2000s that the shift to horizontal/passive industrial policies along with liberalisation of trade and FDI under neoliberal consensus had led to industrial stagnation, deindustrialisation and middle-income traps in many developing countries. Developed economies have themselves been increasingly relying upon various explicit and implicit industrial policy measures to reverse the decline in their manufacturing sectors. Renewed interest in industry's role as a dynamic instrument of growth in the developed economies after the global financial crisis has coincided with a renewed concern for industrialisation and structural change in the mainstream of development economics and the varied role to be played by industrial policy.

By contrast, the typical focus in the ongoing discussion in developing countries is on how they can rely on their comparative advantage based on existing factor endowments and undertake trade and FDI liberalisation along with passive or functional industrial policies to facilitate new foreign investments. The latter will enable their firms to participate in GVCs and increase their exports and obtain dynamic gains from trade that accompany industrial upgrading. Furthermore, free trade agreements (FTAs) have been argued to enable rapid and 'efficient industrial restructuring' by allowing countries to participate in GVCs by attracting efficiency-seeking FDI. The mainstream discourse on GVCs have thus been constructed as providing yet another rationale for trade and FDI liberalisation in the continuing saga of economic growth tied to export performance. The next chapter will examine whether participation in GVCs is a panacea for development or a development challenge and whether horizontal industrial policies are sufficient to make use of the opportunities provided by GVCs and reap the benefits from participating in them.

Notes

1 See Reinert and Reinert (2005) which traces the origins of "production-focused mercantilist policies" and their "interdependency with nation building" to the development experiences of 15th-century Europe, starting with England in 1485. Notably, this contradicts the neoclassical interpretation of mercantilism, which draws its origins to Adam Smith and projects it as being solely centred on trade-led development strategies.

2 This is true of services such as retail trade and finance. For instance, the 2008 global financial crisis clearly revealed that much of the recent productivity growth in finance had been achieved through the de-basement of the products – that is, the creation of overly complex, riskier and even fraudulent products (ECA 2016: 31).

3 This aspect is discussed further in Chapter 4 while analysing the electronics industry.

4 Increased market size also allows for more economies of scale, which can support lower prices and greater product variety.

5 Such synergies are that (i) a growing agricultural sector provides sufficient wage goods at affordable prices to the growing industrial workforce; (ii) expanding farm incomes provide a growing domestic market for the infant industrial sector; and (iii) the expanding manufacturing sector supplies ever more productivity-enhancing intermediates and capital goods to both the agricultural and service sectors (e.g., fertilisers and other chemicals, agricultural machinery, etc. to agriculture and transport equipment and other machinery including ICT equipment to services). See also Storm (2015).

6 See the detailed discussions of the contributions of early development economists in Kregel (2007) and Kattel et al. (2009). For discussions on Kalecki's contributions, see Ghosh (2005), Storm (2015), etc.

7 This follows from Prebisch (1959) and Singer (1950), which related the size of the elasticity parameters of exports and imports to the manufacturing and technological content of the products exported and imported. The income elasticity of demand for exports increases as we move up the value-added chain from commodities to semi-processed goods and labour- and resource-intensive goods, then to manufactures with low, medium and high skill and technology content (see Ali and Perez 2006).

8 Problematically, these distinctions have become blurred with the advance of financial liberalisation and problems in the way in which FDI is defined in many countries. See Francis (2010) for a detailed discussion.

9 However, contrary to the criticism by neoclassical economists later on, early development economists did not advocate dirigiste and autarkic policies. Dutt (2005) counters the indictment of early development economists as providing the intellectual underpinning of inward-looking development policies under state-led import substitution industrialisation (ISI) strategies in the 1950s and 1960s (which led to economic stagnation in many LDCs by the 1970s). He shows how their work has been mis-represented.

10 As Chang (2002) points out, while the "official history of capitalism" credits the industrial success of 18th century laissez-faire Britain and 19th century America to the superiority of free-market and free trade policies, they were the pioneers and frequently the most ardent users of interventionist trade and industrial policy measures in their earlier stages of development. See also Reinert (2008) and Reinert and Kattel (2010). See Johnson (1982) for a discussion on how Japan coordinated its industrial policy through the Ministry of International Trade and Industry (MITI) during its post-war catch up industrialisation phase.

11 According to TDR 1996, the ratio of FDI flows to gross fixed capital formation in Japan was historically a minuscule 0.1 per cent and continued to be the same even during 1981–1990 and 1991–93 (Francis 2003).

12 Francis (2003), based on Table 2.1 in Jomo et al. (1997: 14). As pointed out by several analysts, only the much smaller economies of Singapore and Hong Kong possessed open economic environments, mainly due to their roles as trading and (later) financial hubs (see McNally 2008: 113).

13 See Yokokawa (2013) for another critique of the 'flying geese' theory. He argued out that the industrialisation processes of the second-tier NICs (Indonesia, Malaysia, the Philippines and Thailand) did not follow the original 'flying geese' pattern as they skipped the first two processes – imports and import-substitution production.

14 Similarly, domestic market-oriented production undertaken by foreign-affiliated joint ventures under long periods of assured protection may also operate with low productivity and be relegated to rent-seeking investment.

15 Here, a firm that is competitive in export markets is assumed to be competitive against import competition in the domestic market also. However, this may not always be the case, such as when a developing country firm's export success occurs in LDCs, while it is unable to compete with developed country firms in its domestic market.

16 Clearly, external demand is a critical determinant factor too, whether for entry into export markets or for expansion in exports of any product; whether of low value added or of high value added products. However, external demand is an exogenous variable over which national policymakers have very little control. See the discussion in Francis (2015a).

17 The argument has been that trade in intermediate goods and services provides cheaper, better or a broader variety of intermediate inputs and thereby reduces costs and improves productivity in downstream industries. See, for instance, Nordas (2009).

18 Interestingly, recent economic geography literature refers to the access/availability of domestic downstream customers and upstream suppliers as 'thickness of markets'.

19 As observed by Gallagher and Shafaeddin (2009), the theory of capability building is built on the infant-industry argument of Frederick List who regarded 'mental capital', or the accumulation of knowledge and experience as the main element of 'productive power' (development) and industrialisation.

20 For a discussion of the underlying theoretical arguments in evolutionary economics, see Francis (2018a).

21 In fact, according to Reinert and Kattel (2010: 17), up to the rise of Washington Consensus policies and WTO agreements in the 1990s, classical industrial policy used to be about attempting to change micro-level "learned organizational capabilities" for innovation and technological change via public policy.

22 It is useful to see the extensive review carried out by Harrison and Rodriguez-Clare (2009), which argues that the conditions needed for infant-industry protection to produce higher growth in developing countries are not often satisfied. It is argued that the theoretical

justification for intervention requires at a minimum either industry-level rents or a latent comparative advantage (i.e., sectors that are intensive in knowledge and human capital), as well as large Marshallian externalities from production. The criticism against industrial policy then is that policymakers cannot easily identify these necessary conditions ex ante. It is also argued by them that there is no evidence suggesting that developing countries have generally protected sectors with latent comparative advantage and Marshallian externalities. Rather, protection has been used as a tool to protect sunset industries instead of sunrise industries. Therefore, state intervention has an inherent bias against promoting sectors with a latent comparative advantage (and is thus presented as failing).

23 Ironically, Williamson (2004) insists that there was no call for zero tariffs or capital account liberalisation in his version of the Washington Consensus. Removing barriers impeding the entry of FDI, though, was very much part of the consensus. However, as Kanbur (2009: 36) pointed out, "the Washington Consensus became what it did, not what it said" (as in Williamson's originally meant list).

24 This can be related to the work by theorists such as Lance Taylor and Luigi Pasinetti, who emphasize that secular growth and structural change are propelled by aggregate demand and by the distribution of incomes. See the detailed discussion in Storm (2015: 680). For a critical examination of the theory underlying the labour market flexibility argument, see Roychowdhury (2018).

25 The MFN bound rate is the tariff rate above which a country cannot raise its tariffs on a particular product for imports from any WTO member, without giving compensation to an injured member country.

26 Similarly, Russia also consciously delayed its entrance into the WTO agreements until 2012 as it was set to experiment with various industrial policy means such as priority industrial sectors, local content requirements, public procurement for innovation, import tariffs, etc. In fact, Reinert and Kattel (2010: 20–21) considers the period starting with Vladimir Putin's first presidency in 2004 as emerging state capitalism or, particularly after 2008, as neo-developmentalist.

27 While arguing that conceptions of the Chinese state must differ from those of the Asian developmental state (due to China's state socialist legacy, large size, timing of entry into the world capitalist system and other factors), McNally (2008: 116) has pointed out that China's capitalism remains heavily shaped by the hand of the state. He however, also discussed the important role played by the 'network capitalism' of overseas Chinese businesses. Fuller (2016) too has argued that foreign venture capital embedded in ethnic Chinese networks have driven technological development in China's high-technology industry. Ernst and Naughton (2008: 56, 40) have argued that, while Chinese capitalism involves a hybrid mixture of ownership and corporate governance patterns, Chinese government policies are pervasive, and specific interventions, common.

28 See https://growthlab.cid.harvard.edu/publications/policy-area/product-space.

Chapter 3

Global value chains

Heightening the industrial policy imperative

Global value chains refer to the vertical disintegration and coordination of upstream and downstream segments of the value chain of a product[1] by multinational corporations (MNCs) across national borders, which are centrally organised by them through multiple networks across firms linked through equity and non-equity relationships. Changes in business organisational strategies facilitated by rapid advances in information and communication technologies (ICT) and the decline in transportation costs has been a fundamental driver of global value chains (GVCs). This is related to the accelerated shift since the 1980s from the fourth technological revolution to the present fifth one based on ICT, which has seen continuing transformation of business organisation from the old rigid, internal hierarchical pyramids of the mass production age into flexible organisation and adaptable networks (Perez 2001). On the other side, liberalisation of trade and financial flows (FDI and non-FDI), along with the shift to export-oriented industrialisation strategies by developing countries, has been the most important handmaiden in the spread of GVCs (Francis 2017). The spread of GVCs, in turn, has been used as a catalyst to promote further trade and financial liberalisation in developing countries.

The term 'global value chain' (as opposed to 'global production networks' used commonly in the literature previously) covers the much broader evolution of MNC networks beyond production to include pre-production stages like research and innovation and post-production stages such as retail/marketing networks. As emphasised by Milberg and Winkler (2013), the term 'global value chain' also underlines the widespread recognition that the location of production at any stage does not reflect the total value added until then. The deepening international division of vertical specialisation and 'segmentation of key technological markets'[2] driven by MNC-led value chain fragmentation clearly means that parts and components as well as tasks are produced/carried out in a number of countries before assembly in a particular country.

The spread of GVCs

The vast literature on international production networks and value chains since the late 1980s has pointed to the various kinds of contractual networks (with or without FDI) and cooperative arrangements that have emerged in different industries, beginning with textiles and electronics across East Asia in the 1960s. GVCs have been typically categorised into producer-driven networks and buyer-driven networks, thus differentiated based on the nature of the firm that controls a value chain (UNESCAP 1991; Lall 1996; Ernst 1997; Gereffi 1995; Dicken 1998; UNCTAD 2016). While manufacturing sector MNCs control producer-driven value chains and are therefore the lead firms in them, the lead firms in buyer-driven value chains are typically commercial capital. Consequently, producer networks involve backward linkages of manufacturing firms with suppliers at various tiers through subcontracting and a variety of other arrangements such as original equipment manufacturing (OEM), contract manufacturing, etc. By contrast, buyer-driven chains involve forward linkages of manufacturing companies with distributors, marketing channels, value-added resellers and end users.

Buyer-driven value chains usually occur in labour-intensive consumer goods industries such as apparel, footwear, toys and food and beverages (Gereffi 1995; Milberg and Winkler 2013). Among buyer-driven chains, at one level are the GVCs driven by large retailers such as Walmart, Nike, Fisher-Price, Starbucks, etc. They source directly from subcontracted manufacturers and import goods fully assembled – containing the lead firm label or package, while they themselves focus on design, the setting of product standards and marketing as well as finance. They often engage in obtaining and sharing information on consumer tastes and behaviours with their subcontractors.[3] Milberg and Winkler (2013: 18) point out that major retailers in all industrialised countries now actively control their global supply chains. Another kind of buyer-driven chains is controlled by 'brand-name firms' (Luthje et al. 2013) that were previously involved in manufacturing, but now purchase finished goods for sale as their own brand while focusing on their core competences (again design, marketing and finance). Such 'fabless' manufacturers (manufacturers without factories) are in sectors ranging from clothing (The Gap); to toys (Mattel); and electronics and computers (IBM, Apple, Dell, Toshiba) to even servers (Cisco Systems) and semiconductors (Xilinx) (Perrow, as cited in Milberg and Winkler 2013: 34; Luthje et al. 2013).[4]

On the other side, outsourcing or producer-driven value chains are more common in medium-to-high capital- and technology-intensive industries – that are also characterised by significant scale economies – such as automobiles, electronics and aircrafts (Milberg and Winkler 2013; UNCTAD 2016). For instance, it was found that European firms in the electrical and optical equipment industry (25 per cent) and automotive and transport equipment manufacturers (24 per cent) are particularly active in outsourcing, followed by machinery and equipment manufacturers (18 per cent) and the chemical industry (14 per cent) (Kinkel 2014).[5] The lead MNC manufacturing firms of these chains have traditionally expanded through FDI and also subcontract many or most aspects of production (often providing technical and communications support to smoothen operations), but they usually keep R&D with themselves.

Modifying the framework discussed in Chapter 2 in the context of FDI-driven export-led industrialisation strategy, we can observe that a developing country's entry into export markets as part of GVCs may come about from any or a combination of the following possibilities:

1   export strategy of foreign-owned/affiliated firms located in the developing country (as part of MNCs' GVC strategy),
2   indirect entry of indigenous firms through subcontracting or other non-equity forms of foreign alliance (as part of MNCs' GVC strategy) or
3   direct entry into export markets by indigenous firms.

Some large subcontracting supplier firms – in both buyer-driven and producer-driven chains – have also captured economies of scale and developed modular production systems. This enables such supplier firms to produce a range of related products, allowing them to supply intermediate inputs and finished goods to many companies within a sector and sometimes even across sectors on a contractual basis. This has been observed especially in automobiles, apparel, footwear and electronics, as well as in business services (Milberg and Winkler 2013; Ernst 2014 for Taiwanese and Chinese case studies).

In addition to FDI and subcontracting arrangements, there have also been cooperative arrangements for co-production that involve some sort of knowledge sharing and regular extra-contractual relations between buyer and supplier firms (UNCTAD 2016), as well as technology cooperation networks (for technology exchange and joint technology development) and standards coalitions. Standards networks are initiated by potential global standard setters with the explicit purpose of locking-in as many firms as possible into their proprietary product, architectural or interface standards, especially relevant for electronics industry, but increasingly true in many others such as food processing, pharmaceuticals, automobiles, etc. (UNCTAD 2016; Ernst 2016). This is also increasingly the trend in digital technologies (Francis 2018a), which has critical cross-sectoral implications for many emerging new manufacturing technologies.

Traditional understanding on GVCs has pointed out that more knowledge-intensive parts of the production process, innovation, etc. are retained by the lead firms in developed countries, while more routine tasks (or those involving less complex knowledge or more readily available skills) have greater propensity to be outsourced to suppliers in developing countries (Nathan, Tewari and Sarkar 2016). However, recent research has shown that increasingly 'ubiquitous globalization' is moving beyond markets for goods and finance into markets for business services, technology, intellectual property rights and knowledge workers (Ernst 2016; Nathan et al. 2016; Nielsen 2017). Progressive modularisation of all stages of the value chain and their geographical dispersion by corporations have been driven by increasing digitisation of services in finance, accounting, medicine, software, design, payroll management and marketing (Milberg and Winkler 2013). As a result, as Gereffi (1995) and Baldwin (2006) argued, the international division of labour and vertical specialisation are now occurring at a much finer level of disaggregation, with specific tasks – that were previously considered non-tradable – being offshored. Increased codification of substantial parts of knowledge involved in the different segments/tasks involved has led to the offshoring of knowledge-intensive tasks too. For instance, Nathan et al. (2016: 16) point out that, in garment manufacturing, some developing country intermediary suppliers such as Li & Fung have moved from full package supply to the joint development of products, including design. Similarly, activities such as R&D of some high-tech products are being located in centres in economies like China and India. Continued codification of parts of knowledge along with the modularisation of tasks has made it possible to finely slice what were integrated tasks into parts that could be outsourced (Damodaran 2016: 395). In fact, as Low (2013) pointed out, the role of services in production and trade within GVCs has been understated.

Given that firms have begun to offshore aspects of the production, application and exploitation of knowledge, discussion on 'global innovation networks' has appeared in the literature recently (Montalvo 2014). As observed by Ernst (2016: 58), a defining characteristic of the new geography of knowledge is that "learning and innovation are also fragmented or 'modularized' and geographically dispersed through multi-layered global corporate networks that integrate software development, engineering, product design, and research and development across firms and countries". However, given that the GVC concept envelops upstream processes including research, design and development, we consider the term 'global innovation networks' a misnomer. What is significant is that, here again, a variety of network structures are possible. These networks range from loose linkages that are formed to implement a particular project and are dissolved after the project is finished – so-called 'virtual enterprises' – to highly formalised networks and 'extended enterprises', with clearly defined rules, common business processes and shared information infrastructures (Ernst 2016: 57–58). These formalised networks may or may not involve control of equity stakes.

As a result of all these developments in organisational structures involving functional and geographic fragmentation, GVCs have grown in scale of operations and network complexity, involving multiple supplier-buyer relationships (sometimes including home-based production) with various degrees of lead firm's investment, technical support, subcontracting and control in network firms.[6] Increasingly dense networks have emerged,[7] which involve arms-length market transactions, internalised transactions and those in between, geared to an increase in vertical and horizontal integration along value chains, with trade and investments organised within them.

'Accounting' for GVCs: networked FDI and network trade

This obviously has implications for the FDI literature, which is often not considered as part of the GVC literature. Traditional mainstream FDI theory defined two types of FDI: (i) horizontal FDI or 'market-seeking' FDI wherein production becomes multi-national to avoid trade costs (attributed to Markusen 1989); and (ii) vertical or 'efficiency-seeking' FDI originating from production stages being distributed geographically to exploit cost differences (attributed to Helpman 1984). Consequently, in the market-seeking case, FDI and trade in goods are substitutes, as was the case in tariff-jumping FDI under traditional import-substituting industri-alisation. On the other side, in the efficiency-seeking case, trade and FDI are complements. Subsequently, Dunning expanded this in his ownership, location and internalisation (OLI) advantages framework as four main types of FDI: resource-seeking, market-seeking, efficiency-seeking and strategic asset-seeking (Dunning 1980, 1988).

A review of theoretical and empirical FDI studies by Baldwin and Okubo (2012) revealed that FDI literature began catching-up with the spread of GVCs in the 2000s. Hanson, Mataloni and Slaughter (2001, 2005, cited in Baldwin and Okubo 2012) documented addi-tional types of FDI where affiliates (i) produce for export to third markets (export platform FDI), (ii) add value to inputs sourced from their parents or (iii) act as wholesale distributors. Yeaple (2003) found that many firms engage in horizontal and vertical FDI simultaneously and placed them in a catch-all category called 'com-plex FDI'. Clearly, this is increasingly the case with the expansion in tariff-free trade that reduces the incentives and need for horizontal FDI. Accordingly, an MNC's investments in various host nations participating in a GVC can be complements or substitutes of each other, while trade and FDI may be complements and/or substitutes for a particular host country.

In an empirical investigation of Yeaple's 'complex FDI', Bald-win and Okubo (2012) focused on the trade behaviour of affili-ates (rather than on parent-affiliate characteristics or affiliates' sales alone). They defined an affiliate's vertical-ness as its non-local sourcing share: if most sourcing of associates is non-local, then efficiency-seeking was probably the important motive. That is, ver-tical FDI is associated with low 'domestic' backward linkages.[8] By contrast, an affiliate's 'horizontal-ness' is defined as its local sales share; if most output is sold locally then market-seeking was probably the dominant motive. Given that there are foreign affiliates engaging in local and export sales as well as local and import sourcing of intermediate inputs, Baldwin and Okubo (2012) considered all affiliates with intermediate levels of local sales and local sourcing as 'networked FDI'. Such facilities are viewed as part of international supply chains. Clearly, efficiency-seeking and market-seeking differentiation of FDI gets blurred here, and therefore the networked FDI concept comes the closest to understanding the role of foreign affiliates within GVCs. However, this concept of networked FDI is still inadequate to capture the prevalent GVC complexity, as it leaves out non-equity forms of engagement utilised by MNCs to engage and control various nodes of their value chains across different countries/industries.

Meanwhile, Baldwin and Okubo (2012) put forth their 'sales-sourcing box' for illustrating typical development strategies involving FDI. According to them, the traditional import-substitution strategy, for example, involves starting with local assembly and pushing multinationals to produce more intermediates locally. The eventual goal is to achieve export competitiveness with a high degree of local sourcing. The 21st century version of this – pursued by China and other East Asian nations, according to them – starts from 'outward processing' and seeks to induce multinationals to source more intermediates locally (see Baldwin and Okubo 2012: 7, Figure 2).

While useful in elaborating the typology, this is a misleading interpretation of development strategies using FDI for participation in GVCs for a number of reasons. Firstly, once again, non-FDI forms of foreign firm engagement in GVCs are left out in this conceptualisation. Secondly, in the usual mainstream tradition of considering increased productivity as arising from reduced costs of intermediates, Baldwin and Okubo (2013: 24) suggested that affiliates with high degrees of 'vertical-ness' (that is, high imports) might be thought of as having a larger impact on local productivity than affiliates with a high degree of 'horizontal-ness' (or domestic market orientation). We have already shown in Chapter 2 that depending solely on competitive imports to increase productivity will not lead to a sustainable development strategy. So if a country begins by using vertical FDI with a high degree of dependence on imports as the development strategy for taking part in GVCs, it may not lead to the productivity increase required for sustainable catching-up using the 'moving up the value chain industrialisation' strategy.

Thirdly, while as mentioned earlier, Baldwin and Okubo (2012) point out that "the eventual goal is to achieve export competitiveness with a high degree of local sourcing" by inducing "multinationals to source more intermediates locally", there is no consideration of the industrial policy strategies adopted by the East Asian countries and the indigenous technological capabilities they built up, which played a fundamental role in enabling them to achieve this "moving up the value chain industrialisation" possible. As elaborated in Chapter 2, and as highlighted in Ernst (2009), the relatively strong catching-up region of East Asia has managed to create sustainable links to global production and innovation networks through highly targeted and selective government policies that have created capabilities and steered the actions of actors participating in these global networks to increase local value addition and positive externalities. Thus the underlying framework of those advocating an FDI-led industrial upgrading strategy through GVCs also falls prey to the 'flying geese syndrome' in that it draws an automatic causation as flowing from openness to FDI (in this case, especially of the vertical type) to participation in GVCs and to sustainable industrial development in a simplistic manner, without linking the underlying industrial policy framework as necessary conditions for entry and upgrading. Moreover, the manner in which localisation is induced – for the substitution of local production for imports to increase local value added – determines the long-term impact of FDI-led GVC participation and benefits to the national economy for technology upgrading.[9]

On the trade side, even as GVCs have given rise to complex cross-border flows of goods, investment, services and people, it has been traditionally viewed in terms of trade in goods that has come to be concentrated in parts, components and sub-assemblies. Yeats (1997) was the first to use trade in parts and components to measure the phenomenon he called 'production sharing'. Subsequently, it has become a stylised fact that production sharing between countries involved in GVCs typically involves the import of inputs for assembly or additional processing, as well as the export of intermediate goods for assembly or additional processing by third countries. Several studies have shown that production sharing typically leads to a significant expansion in two-way trade (simultaneous increase in exports and imports) between the countries involved, in particular, intra-industry trade in intermediate goods (Athukorala 2003; Fukao et al. 2003; Haddad 2007; IMF 2013; Nielsen 2017; etc.). Hummels et al. (2001) described vertical specialisation as based on trade between different countries with each specialising in a particular production stage. Accordingly, trade in intermediate goods has been considered as an upper boundary of measures of vertical specialisation. A lower boundary measure is provided by Hummels and others (2001) who defined vertical specialisation as the use of imported intermediate goods in products that are subsequently exported. They found that the share of vertical specialisation in exports had increased from about 15 per cent in 1970 to about 20 per cent in 1990, using data for 13 OECD countries plus Taiwan – a sample that covered 60 per cent of world trade.

Subsequently, there has been growing recognition that trade data – designed to capture trade flows in final products – is incapable of capturing the extent of countries' participation in vertical specialisation brought about by GVCs, because of the following characteristics of growing network trade (see De Backer and Yamano 2010; Banga 2013; Milberg and Winkler 2013; etc.):

• Trade in intermediate products is growing faster than trade in final products, while trade data is expressed in only output terms.
• Several intermediates are being used commonly across different industries.
• There is an increasing services component as value chains have extended beyond products to include services too.

Given that trade data includes the value of intermediates imported at each border crossing, it tends to overstate the implicit value (or factor content) exchanged between countries. In fact, with growing use of imports for export production, this has been a major problem with using export data for identifying countries' competitiveness, technological intensity of exports, etc. High levels of vertical specialisation – high import content of exports – clearly implies that increased export value generates proportionally less domestic value added. Further, trade data often excludes the value-added contribution of services.

Accordingly, input-output (I/O) analyses has been considered to provide a useful alternative to trade data, given that they classify goods according to their use (as intermediate or as final good) and also include information on inputs of and in services sectors.

Following this approach, Stehrer et al. (2012) provides a comprehensive picture of the increase in fragmentation within GVCs of Japan, the EU and the US during the 1990s and 2000s. It used data from the World Input-Output Database (WIOD) project,[10] which allowed for analysing the structures of sourcing and vertical specialisation in detail. They used aggregation of direct and indirect (through suppliers) imports incorporated into the exports of a given country as a combined measure for production fragmentation and country's specialisation. According to this analysis, in 1995 the foreign content of exports from the EU-15 and Japan ranged from 6 to 8 per cent.[11] The figure for the US in 1995 was higher at about 11 per cent. By 2007, in all the three, the foreign content of exports had increased to levels of about 14–16 per cent. The share of domestic content (which is relatively high at around 85 per cent) has been on a downward trend in all the cases, mirroring the upward trend in foreign content (Stehrer et al. 2012; Baldwin and Lopez-Gonzalez 2013; Kinkel 2014; Casini and Kay 2014).

Milberg and Winkler (2013) provide evidence on increased average materials and services offshoring intensities across all 35 manufacturing and services sectors for the US, defined as imported inputs as percentage of total non-energy inputs, based on US input-output tables. Average materials offshoring intensity in manufacturing alone increased from 4.1 per cent in 1974 to 6.2 per cent in 1984 to 12.5 per cent in 1998 and 16.4 per cent in 2010. Average services offshoring intensity in manufacturing alone increased strongly between 1998 and 2010 with an intensity of 0.43 per cent in 1998, 0.48 per cent in 2006 and 0.78 per cent in 2010. Sectoral materials offshoring intensities grew in all 21 manufacturing sectors and in 10 out of 14 service sectors and reached more than 25 per cent in some sectors, including apparel and motor vehicles. Services offshoring intensities also showed positive growth rates in 20 manufacturing and 13 service sectors (Milberg and Winkler 2013: 47).

Baldwin and Okubo (2012) provide similar support for increased spread of GVCs using extensive firm-level data on Japan's foreign affiliates called "The Survey on Overseas Business Activities" prepared by the Research and Statistics Department of the Japanese Ministry of Economy, Trade and Industry (METI). The yearly survey conducted by METI covers all Japanese affiliates in all sectors and in all nations. The biggest FDI/offshoring sectors for Japanese parent firms based on assets and employment were electrical and mechanical machinery, clothing and certain types of services that require local presence such as finance and insurance. But in terms of assets alone, other sectors like auto parts and chemicals were also important, apart from wholesale trade. The study showed a clear picture that most sectors saw a decrease in the local sourcing of intermediates between 1996 and 2005 and the emergence of 'networked FDI' – i.e., FDI where the affiliates import substantial shares of their intermediates and export substantial shares of their output (Baldwin and Okubo 2012: 8–10). Japanese affiliates in most sectors and most nations became more vertical between 1996 and 2005. The 'production unbundling' phenomenon has most prominently occurred in the machinery sectors – especially in the mechanical machinery and electronics sectors. In 1996, many machinery sectors had host economy local sales and sourcing shares over 80 per cent. By 2005, however, no machinery sectors had more than 80 per cent local sales and sourcing share, reflecting the internationalisation of supply chains in the machinery sector.

Overall, the review of the available indicators on GVCs in De Backer and Yamano (2010) also shows that the indicators on imported intermediates, offshoring and vertical specialisation all illustrate the growing fragmentation of production across more economies. Recent studies also clearly show that network trade arising from vertical specialisation increasingly stretches out to the services sector: offshoring increased significantly over the period 1995–2005 especially in the services sector in almost all countries (see Banga 2013 and Casini and Kay 2014).

We now consider empirical evidence for developing country participation in GVCs based on both trade data and input-output data.

Evidence on developing countries' GVC participation

Sturgeon and Memedovic (2011) show that the share of intermediates trade in manufacturing and services from developing countries as a share of global trade in manufactured intermediates has increased significantly from 26 per cent in 1992 to 35 per cent in 2006, while the developed countries' share fell from 72 to 63 per cent. While China accounted for 8.5 per cent of the world total in 2006, other significant developing country contributors were Taiwan (3.9 per cent), Hong Kong (2.6 per cent), Mexico (2.4 per cent) and Malaysia (1.7 per cent). India stood among the others with a 1.2 per cent share, along with Thailand (1.3 per cent), Brazil (1.0 per cent) and Turkey (0.9 per cent).

Casini and Kay (2014: 46) point out that, typically, small and open countries source more intermediate goods from abroad, and therefore, the vertical specialisation component is generally high for such countries. By contrast, large and more resource-rich countries can afford to be less involved in GVCs and their participation is predominantly in the forward part of GVCs as exporters of commodities or primary inputs. An example cited as obvious is Russia's energy exports. Similar is the case with Brazil, South Africa and Indonesia according to Banga (2013: 16). Even so, evidence from De Backer and Yamano (2010: 111) shows that the offshoring of intermediates has increased in large emerging countries such as Brazil, India (typically considered as important beneficiary of services offshoring), Argentina and China too, although their level of offshoring remains lower than the OECD average.

The fact that developing countries' share in global exports of manufactures greatly increased is often cited as an evidence for the beneficial impact of globalisation led by the spread of GVCs: this share increased from less than 20 per cent in 1995 to about 30 per cent in 2014 (UNCTAD 2016: 106; see also Alcorta 2014: 81). It must be noted that this increase however happened in the context of a decline in the share of manufactures in global merchandise exports, which fell from about 76 per cent to about 67 per cent over this period (UNCTAD 2016: 103, Chart 4.1). Further, there has been a weakening of developed country markets as a destination for developing country exports and *relative increase* in the prominence of South-South trade. However, what is notable is that the rise of both North-South and South-South trade in manufactures is attributable mainly to Asia. West Asia and North Africa, sub-Saharan Africa, and Latin America and the Caribbean exhibited a growing trade deficit in manufactures between 1980 and 2013. These patterns have been interpreted to mean that most international production networks are not only regional in nature, but are also highly concentrated within the Asian region (UNCTAD 2014, 2016: 106–109). Other studies have pointed to a regional trend in offshoring by the EU-15 firms and among the three NAFTA members (Canada, Mexico and the US). This would seem to point to some role being played by regional market integration schemes.

This tendency for regional agglomeration of production networks could also be related to the technological asymmetry within production networks highlighted by Baldwin et al. (2013)'s distinction between 'headquarter economies' and 'factory economies'. Typically, technologically advanced headquarter economies (mostly the US, Japan and Germany) buy and sell intermediates (especially importing-to-export) to and from a wide range of partners, while factory economies are heavily dependent on one partner, which is always the nearest technologically advanced manufacturing giant (US, Japan and Germany). Importantly, firms in the headquarter economies arrange the production networks, while factory economies provide the labour. China does not fit neatly into this two-way categorisation; in general, China is exporting low-tech industrial intermediates (supplying a broad range of partners on the sales side), while importing high-tech intermediates (sourcing mainly from the three technologically advanced headquarter economies and Korea). The most intensive supply-chain trade relationships are in North America. In Europe, there is a hub-and-spoke arrangement around Germany and the system includes the factory economies as well as the other headquarters economies (Britain, France and Italy with large manufacturing sectors) (Lejour et al. 2012, cited in Baldwin and Lopez-Gonzalez 2013), Consequently, Baldwin and Lopez-Gonzalez (2013) also argue that global production networks are marked by regional blocks they call Factory Asia, Factory North America and Factory Europe, with the US, Germany and China being the hubs for their respective regions. The off-block exceptions all involve one of the four giants (US, Germany, Japan and China) as seller or buyer.

However, while the regional agglomeration effect cannot be denied, it must be noted that the reference here is to production networks, not value chains. The inclusion of services intermediates is likely to increase the global nature of backward (and forward) integration for developing countries in GVCs (as seen earlier). In fact, Baldwin and Lopez-Gonzalez (2013: 21) themselves established that supply chain trade in services is far less regionalised that it is for goods. Even in the case of production networks, it may not be possible to generalise their regional character across all industries. Baldwin and Okubo (2012) found that, while the auto industry in the US has a regionally networked production structure (because of NAFTA and Mexico), those in Asia and Europe involve much more internationally networked production structures. In the case of electronics, however, it was found that production networks in Asia are more regional in nature, not global.

As discussed in Chapter 1, what is observable is that there has been a tendency for production networks to agglomerate around countries in East and Southeast Asia that were already integrated into production networks from the 1970s and 1980s (Francis 2003, 2010; Menon 2013, and the literature cited therein; see also Borrus et al. 2000). Such regionalisation is fundamentally related to the gains made by these countries under their post-independence developmental state policies, in particular, to the build-up of manufacturing capabilities (including clusters),[12] which are essential for entry and upgrading in value chains. By the same logic, India's relatively less successful induction into the IT offshoring activities could also happen because of the capabilities built up in the software sector in the post-independence decades.[13] In addition, as Yeung (2006) has argued, while the developmental role of the national state is a necessary condition for regional development to take place, the complex strategic coupling of large business firms operating in specific regions in Asia with their lead firm counterparts orchestrating production networks on a global basis has played a significant role in shaping regional development trajectories. Arguably, such coupling leads to the emergence of domestic interest groups that come to play an important role in furthering regionalism subsequently through further trade and financial liberalisation. As argued in Francis (2015b), the emergence of domestic exporters and increased number of outward investors in particular sectors from the Asian developing countries have also contributed to the emergence of such interests, for whom greater regionalism advances their prospects for increased market access for exports or foreign investments or both. As mentioned in Chapter 1, the mainstream analyses of GVCs are also increasingly highlighting the role of agglomeration economies in East Asian production networks, although they derive different policy implications.

Whether regional or global in nature, the trade patterns seem to be point to increasing domination by China. For instance, in his examination of the foreign value added in the exports of the EU, Japan and the US (based on I-O tables), Kinkell (2014) found that China accounted for about 10 per cent of import content in the EU-12, 15 per cent in the EU-15 and about 20 per cent or more for Japan and the US. For the EU-15, China as a source surpassed even the EU-12 in the latter years.[14] In 2007, the BRII group (Brazil, Russia, India and Indonesia) accounted for only about 10 per cent or less of the import content of most countries (with a larger share for the EU-15). As Kinkell (2014) noted, the BRII group – though it includes India, which is comparable in size to China – does not account for higher shares of vertical integration (particularly not with the US). Further, during the global economic crisis, between 2007 and 2009, when the overall share of the foreign content of exports in all these countries/regions went down, China still had a growing share, whereas the share of all other partner countries and regions declined.

When considered in terms of foreign content of exports, China's share increased from a negligible figure in 1995 in the EU-12 to more than 15 per cent in 2009, mostly at the expense of the EU-15 and the BRII countries. In the EU-15, its share increased from slightly above 5 per cent to about 20 per cent (at the expense of Japan and the US). An even more pronounced increase is to be seen in Japan, where China's import share rose from about 5 to 30 per cent (in this case with a shrinking share of the EU-15 and the US). For the US, there was a similar change in China's share (from about 5 to 20 per cent) at the expense of the EU-15 and particularly Japan, whose share dropped from almost 20 per cent to less than 10 per cent (Kinkel 2014: 17–18). Similar empirical results supporting China's increased role were established by Baldwin and Lopez-Gonzalez (2013).

GVC governance structure and its implications

As we mentioned, explanations of GVCs/production networks based on traditional mainstream trade theory focus on how international fragmentation takes place if costs can be reduced due to differences in labour productivity (Ricardian model) and/or differences in factor supplies and prices (Heckscher-Ohlin model) between locations (De Backer and Yamano 2010; Milberg and Winkler 2013). Within this framework, MNCs determine the division of labour or vertical specialisation between countries on the basis of factor intensity of production stages and differences in factor prices between countries. When factor-cost savings are large relative to the costs of fragmenting business activities across countries (that is, offshoring costs), a multinational firm will decide whether or not to fragment the production into stages as well as where to locate those fragmented units (Anukoonwattaka 2011: 11–12). For Baldwin and Venables (2010) also, fragmentation of stages of the production process by a firm is determined by the trade-off it faces from international cost differences creating the incentive to 'unbundle' and the centripetal forces of agglomeration benefits (of co-location of related stages). This line of thinking is complemented by explanations based on transaction costs and other technical factors such as advances in ICT that have reduced the cost of coordinating operations internationally. For instance, according to Lall et al. (2004), cited in Nordas (2009), four major factors affect vertical specialisation through the production offshoring decisions of MNCs: (i) technical divisibility of the production process; (ii) differential relative factor intensities across different stages of production; (iii) technological complexity[15] and (iv) high value-to-weight ratio of the products being outsourced.[16] WTO (2011) also considers that decisions on production offshoring involve a trade-off between gains derived from lower manufacturing costs at distant geographical locations, and costs incurred in transportation, managing risks and coordination across different locations. Thus the mainstream literature addresses GVC-related issues within the framework of the 'cost minimisation problem' that confronts MNCs in their production fragmentation decision.

Because of their focus on relative factor-cost advantages without incorporating technological factors, the ongoing mainstream discussion in developing (and developed) countries, typically, focuses on how developing countries can rely on their comparative advantage based on existing factor endowments and undertake trade and FDI liberalisation along with passive industrial policies to facilitate new foreign investments and exports. Liberalisation of FDI norms will attract FDI and enable developing countries to participate in GVCs, while trade liberalisation will provide greater flexibility to these MNCs to source components from or undertake tasks in partner countries at different stages of development and increase intra-firm trade within the GVCs. Both together will help increase exports from the host developing countries and lead to dynamic gains from trade that accompany industrial upgrading (see Anukoonwattaka 2011). In Asia, trade liberalisation through free trade agreements (FTAs), in particular, has been argued to enable rapid and 'efficient industrial restructuring' by allowing countries to participate in GVCs (see Kumar 2007b; and other literature cited in Francis and Kallummal 2013; Anukoonwattaka 2011; Suh and Kim 2014; etc.).

One underlying argument has been that, through the multiplier effect of tariff reductions on production fragmentation trade, reduction or elimination of tariffs within the free trade area may make it more profitable[17] for goods that were previously produced entirely in one country to become vertically specialised, exploiting differences in cost competitiveness across members of the FTA. It follows from this argument that the proliferation of FTAs has supported the spread of production networks (as reflected in an increase in intra-regional trade), and therefore the continued growth in production networks will be enhanced by expanding or increasing the number of FTAs (see Yi 2003; Athukorala 2012 cited in Menon 2013: 9; Suh and Kim 2014). The associated second rationale for FTAs' role has been linked to their ability to attract vertical FDI, which will enable 'efficient industrial restructuring' across the countries participating in GVCs (see Kumar 2007b).

This understanding of the implications of developing country firms' participation in GVCs fails to factor in the consideration that technological capabilities are endogenous to the determination of cost competitiveness of different locations for a particular production/process segment as argued in Francis and Kallummal (2013). The mainstream analyses also eschew the broader framework in Milberg and Winkler (2013), Gereffi (2014), Nathan and Sarkar (2011), etc., which considers how the business model underlying GVCs is built on asymmetric governance relations.

The main focus of the GVC framework developed in Milberg and Winkler (2013: 16–17) is the governance of the supply chain and includes:

• the nature of contracting with suppliers;
• the degree of sharing of technology;
• the extent of entry barriers along the supply chain; and
• the ability of firms to 'upgrade' within the supply chain by moving into aspects of production generating higher value added per worker.

For Milberg and Winkler (2013: 12), who have integrated the financial sector and financialisation into the analysis of GVCs, offshoring is in fact part of the larger corporate strategic shift over the past 25 years which attempted to realign the interests of shareholders and managers. This changed corporate strategy has involved a search for lower costs and greater flexibility to implement a process of 'mass customisation', along with a desire to focus on 'core' activities and allocate greater resources to financial activity and short-run shareholder value while reducing commitments to long-term employment and job security. Consequently, "GVCs are not governed for the purpose of generating economic development, but to expand lead firm shareholder value" (Milberg and Winkler 2013: 23).

The relationship between lead firms and their suppliers may take several forms as we discussed earlier. Whichever is the form of relationship between lead firms and their suppliers, what is of critical relevance is that the business model underlying GVCs is built on asymmetric governance relations, as Gereffi (2014) has argued. Asymmetric market structures are created within GVCs with oligopolistic lead firms (and in some cases supplier firms) at the top – with a high degree of mark-up pricing power and industry concentration (through product differentiation and branding strategies) and highly competitive markets among suppliers at the lower tiers (Milberg and Winkler 2013. See also Nathan and Sarkar 2011; Sturgeon and Memedovic 2011; Luthje et al. 2013; Casini and Kay 2014; etc.). According to Milberg and Winkler (2013), the ability of lead firms to generate and maintain this asymmetry – which is at the core of their cost-cutting and rent maximisation strategy – is endogenous to the formation and governance of GVCs. This is because lead oligopoly firms' mark-up pricing power is accomplished by the shift to core competences and shareholder value, while keeping input prices low through mass customisation and cost-cutting, which are both managed through offshore sourcing in GVCs (Milberg and Winkler 2013: 124, 143).

Lead firms seek to reduce the cost of organising the chain, coordinate with dispersed and varied suppliers, decide what is to be produced and by whom and monitor performance (Das and Hussain 2017). Because the lead firms select and place orders on suppliers (Sturgeon and Memedovic 2011), supplier firms are often subject to intense pressure from them on supply price, delivery time, quality and payment schedule (Milberg and Winkler 2013). Further, some lead firms with control over both upstream and downstream processes cause double marginalisation effects for suppliers and influence the benefits of GVC participation significantly (Casini and Kay 2014: 48).

Consequently, lead firms shape the distribution of risks and profits in their favour by imposing disadvantageous contract conditions on developing country participants. Suppliers whose products are easier to produce or who are replaceable by lead buyers (buyer-driven value chains such as in garments), and producers who are dependent on suppliers of advanced inputs and technology that cannot be easily sourced elsewhere (producer-driven value chains such as in electronics) are usually at the receiving end of imposed contract conditions (UNIDO 2015). Lead firms can set relatively short-term contracts, allowing them the ability to respond to changes in final good demand conditions or supply side changes more rapidly, on issues ranging from changes in product design to changes in wage, exchange rate or policies in the supplier countries or potential supplier countries (Milberg and Winkler 2013; Luthje et al. 2013). It must be noted that restrictive contractual arrangements together with fierce competition in each market segment create significant business risks associated with hold-ups or uncertainty for developing country suppliers, in particular, for SMEs that take part in them (see Casini and Kay 2014).

Thus as Gereffi and Korzeniewicz (1994) had stated way back, the principal profits are not realised in manufacturing itself, but in the corporate coordination and control of the entire 'global assembly line'. Based on a review of case study literature on GVCs, Milberg and Winkler (2013: 127–130) established that lead firms ensure their profits by the generation and maintenance of 'endogenous asymmetry' within the GVC through mainly four different strategies:

1   inducing competition among suppliers (which Nathan and Sarkar 2011 call horizontal competition), thus reducing costs and raising flexibility;
2   offloading risks to suppliers;
3   erecting entry barriers through branding even in industries with standardised production technologies (such as apparel, footwear, airlines, computers, consumer electronics and to some extent, automobiles); and
4   minimising technology sharing.

But as pointed out by Nathan and Sarkar (2011: 54–55), not all intermediate product suppliers are of the above type. Microsoft and Intel, for instance, are component suppliers who are also standard setters. Given that their products are industry standards and that intellectual property rights protect their products, they earn considerable rents from this position.

Clearly, the balance of power within GVCs is always tilted in favour of, and therefore, maximum rents accrue to, firms which maintain technological leadership. The much discussed 'smiley curve' posits that activities which essentially involve services like applied R&D, design, marketing and branding create higher returns than the manufacturing function (Banga 2013: 20). That is, value-added share rises at both extremes of the upstream and downstream activities along the value chain. Lead players maintain a higher share in value addition due to their ownership of well-established brand names, proprietary technology such as patents and trademarks or access to exclusive information on different input and product markets (Banga 2013; UNIDO 2015: 21).

Even in the few cases where large subcontractors from developing countries such as Brazil, China, India and Turkey have emerged in autos, apparel, footwear and electronics, as well as business services, there is little evidence that such firms have successfully transformed size into pricing power. Scale does not necessarily translate into an ability to increase value added per worker (see Nolan 2012 cited in UCNTAD 2014: 121).[18] This is because even when they coordinate complex resources and exert considerable purchasing power within the value chain, they lack the technological competence and the financial and political leverage of established brand-name firms (Luthje et al. 2013: 25), except in rare cases. That is, the governance structure of global value chains and the power of lead firms constrain the ability of even such lead suppliers to achieve the sorts of price increases that could boost wages and improve labour standards (Milberg and Winkler 2013; UNCTAD 2016: 121). It is the skewed bargaining strength of the lead firms over the suppliers, rather than market forces, which determine the distribution of incomes among different segments of the value chains (Das and Hussain 2017: 16).

Clearly, all these have implications for the nature of developing country participation in and their gains from GVCs and, therefore, for the distribution of value-added gains across countries involved in a value chain. These in turn have implications for wage growth, domestic demand and sustained productive investment (and therefore, the scope for industrial upgrading) in the GVC participating developing country. This approach fits the analytical framework of industrial development discussed in Chapter 2, as also our focus on examining whether and how GVCs facilitate industrial upgrading in developing economies. Our examination of the empirical evidence from trade and value-added analysis in the following sections is carried out within this broader framework.

Barriers to GVC entry and upgrading for developing country firms

It is now increasingly acknowledged that consequent upon the governance strategies of GVC lead firms, pervasive global division of labour through GVCs has caused the commoditisation of many industrial goods and components and resulted in acute price competition. Increased participation of developing countries in global exports of lower- and medium-tech manufactures has in itself generated greater competition between developing countries. The resulting sector-wide excess capacity (referred to as 'the fallacy of composition') has led to falling manufacturing prices globally. Estimates show that long-term average manufacturing prices declined by 13 per cent between 1970 and a further 33 per cent between 1990 and 2010. Altogether prices have nearly halved for similar products during the last 40 years (Alcorta 2014: 81).

UNCTAD (2016) points out that the simultaneous pursuit of export-led strategy in similar low value-added products by several developing country exporters has compressed price (and ultimately wage) growth even for the most successful manufacturing exporters in Asia. As a result, the terms of trade (measured as the ratio of export prices to import prices) for developing country exporters of manufactures declined at an average annual rate of 1.1 per cent between 1980 and 2014. In the case of Asian exporters of manufactures, this drop was higher, at 1.5 per cent (UNCTAD 2016: x).

Both greater competition among developing countries and declining trends in their manufactured export prices have strengthened the bargaining and pricing power of lead MNCs based predominantly in developed economies (to exert oligopsony power in input markets). This has led to a consolidation of power (Nolan 2012; Milberg and Winkler 2013; Ernst & Young and FICCI 2015; UNCTAD 2014) and increasing appropriation of profits in GVCs by lead firms. Rouvinen (2014) suggests that each interface between two modules in a value chain may define a new market in GVCs, and the locus of competition has expanded to virtually all intermediate, as well as final products and services. Not only does the competition take place at a finer resolution, it is also more real-time, insofar as uncompetitive providers may be dropped instantly. Therefore a refined global value chain is a collection of the most competitive providers and their best practices globally (Alcorta 2014: 81). A recent examination of the national profit shares of the top 2000 corporations by sector shows the continuing dominance of firms from the advanced countries, particularly the United States (UNCTAD 2014: 104–105). Thus the market structure within GVCs is asymmetric, with oligopolistic lead firms at the top and competitive markets among the lower tier suppliers (Milberg and Winkler 2013: 123; Nathan and Sarkar 2011).

The combination of investment strength and the ownership of proprietary assets (such as patents, copyrights, etc.) and intangible assets[19] of lead firms have thus increased the competitive challenges for firms from developing countries trying to enter production networks (UNCTAD 2014, 2016). Moving up the value chain into more capital-intensive or higher value-added production is particularly challenging in such an environment, because in the first place, it necessitates relationships with lead firms at the top (UNCTAD 2016: 120–121) in one form or another (including non-equity modes). The evidence from Southeast Asian economies, where tariffs are quite low, is telling.

Wignaraja et al. (2013) explored role of technological capabilities in GVC participation possibilities for a sample of Malaysian and Thai firms using a technology index (consisting of eight technical functions) based on the taxonomy of technological capabilities developed by Lall (1992). These results showed that participation in production networks and supply chains was positively correlated with technology upgrading at the firm level. Foreign buyers and subcontractors view internal quality standards as increasingly compulsory for enterprises to qualify as potential suppliers. Going beyond learning-by-doing, this requires firms to undertake conscious investments in skills and information to operate imported technologies. Capability building involves a range of technological activities, including actively acquiring new technologies through foreign licences, implementing international quality standards and developing new products supported by patent protection.

In another study, Wignaraja (2014) undertook a comparative, firm-level econometric investigation of factors influencing participation in supply chains in Southeast Asian economies using a large cross-sectional enterprise dataset from the World Bank collected in the late-2000s. It covered 5,900 firms in five economically important outward-oriented Southeast Asian economies – Indonesia, Malaysia, the Philippines, Thailand and Vietnam. This investigation drew on recent literature emphasising the notion of heterogeneity of firms and highlights key enterprise characteristics (e.g., firm size, technological capabilities, skills and access to finance) underlying success.

In the analysis of firm-level data (which include both direct and indirect exporters), Wignaraja (2014) found that only a minority (37 per cent) of the sample firms in Southeast Asian economies are involved in supply chains through exports, input supply and subcontracting. More developed economies such as Thailand and Malaysia have a higher share (60 per cent) of their firms in supply chains than other Southeast Asian economies. This is true of SME participation as well.[20] Moreover, there was a clear dominance of large firms[21] in supply chain participation (with 72 per cent of large firms participating) and a minor role for SMEs (22 per cent) (Wignaraja 2014: 13). Clearly, large firms have more capital resources to meet the fixed costs of entry into supply chains (e.g., information, marketing and technology expenses). In fact, the study found that apart from firm size, efficiency, particularly investment in technological capabilities and skills and access to commercial bank credit affect the probability of supply chain participation. Here technological capabilities were represented by three variables which captured whether a firm had (i) a technology licence; (ii) internationally agreed quality certification (e.g., ISO 9000 or 9002); and (iii) a patent.

At the same time, Wignaraja (2014) found that the foreign ownership variable had a positive and significant effect on the probability of joining supply chains for both manufacturing firms as a whole and for SMEs. This reflects the stylised fact that access to the superior marketing connections and know-how of parent companies enables direct and indirect exporting by firms. Read in conjunction with the result that investment in technological capabilities and skills were an important determinant of supply chain participation, this implies that once foreign investment took place in firms with certain technological capabilities, their probability of GVC participation increases.

In fact, Borrus et al. (2000) and the papers therein based on case studies covering the Asian production networks of electronics firms from the US, Japan, Taiwan and South Korea established that, in the electronics sector, production networks were not simply constructed to access cheap factor inputs (that is, vertical FDI) or to gain access to expanding markets (horizontal FDI). Even where those factors might have motivated initial investment, they found that IPNs had been increasingly designed to both foster and exploit the region's highly heterogeneous technological capabilities. IPNs have been organised and coordinated across countries to access locational advantages at each network node associated with the increasingly specialised technology, skills and know-how that are resident there.

A recent study by Dash and Chanda (2017) on determinants of Indian automotive firms' participation in GVCs also found that large firms or firms with partial or full foreign ownership had higher probability of being in GVCs when compared to small or medium firms and firms without foreign ownership. It appears that foreign-invested firms' access to parent companies' accumulated learning experience of export production as well as access to sophisticated technologies and management experience will improve technical efficiency of such firms further. These results also reaffirm the role of technological capabilities in GVC participation (and upgrading) possibilities. That is, while the earlier empirical literature (cited already)[22] had established the role of (vertical) industrial policy measures in building up indigenous capabilities in the successful cases of FDI-assisted industrial and technological upgrading of domestic supplier bases in particular industries in Southeast Asia, it is clear that the same is a necessary condition for participation in MNC-driven GVCs.

All these clearly establish as Low and Tijaja (2013: 8) pointed out that,

> what allow participating domestic firms to seize the learning opportunities from GVC participation for eventual upgrading are technological capabilities possessed by them. Among the roles of industrial policy is the promotion of successful technological learning by providing a conducive environment and supporting the development of firm-level technological capabilities.

Thus evidence from analyses of ongoing experiences of developing country firms that participate in production networks shows that successful GPNs tend to contract and rely on local suppliers who have both the capabilities to absorb the knowledge disseminated by the networks and meet the standards of production required by them. Many developing countries and LDCs that do not have some minimum level of technological capabilities have therefore not been able to benefit from even the production/manufacturing segments of GVCs (UNCTAD 2012: 41. See the literature cited therein and the case studies in Borrus et al. 2000).

Therefore, if participation in GVCs – whether directly by developing country suppliers or by the setting up of production by MNCs in a developing country through FDI or subcontracting – is to happen, domestic producers have to be at a minimum level of technological capability. As pointed out by Casini and Kay (2014), a greater degree of know-how is required to compete in a GVC, also because firms must understand and interact in markets that go beyond national and regional borders, embrace separate legal systems, different languages and distinct business cultures. This environment poses many challenges particularly for SMEs, which may find it hard to develop the necessary skills in-house in order to compete globally.

Consequently, with some exceptions in Southeast Asia, most developing country producers tend to be part of labour-intensive, buyer-driven chains (UNIDO 2015: 21). African economies' participation in value chains remains primarily in upstream production of low-value commodities. Only with entry, there is potential for gaining market shares (at whichever level of entry). However, pressure from lead firms and competition from other suppliers to keep labour costs low raises the risk of developing countries becoming locked into low value-added activities. As discussed in Chapter 2, such patterns of global integration by developing countries would tend to reinforce ongoing specialisation patterns owing to the features associated with low-productivity activities.

This is why a considerable proportion of the production, exporting and innovation within GVCs has been occurring only in a few developing countries in East Asia as well as China, Brazil, India, etc. (UNCTAD 2012: 39–41). Importantly, evidence presented in the Technology and Innovation Report (2012) shows that emerging capabilities in these economies have been clearly supported by growing R&D investments *domestically* (own emphasis). These countries had a greater share of patents and earnings from royalty and licensing fees generated domestically.

That is, the entry of a developing country firm into the GVC of a particular industry/industry segment is crucially dependent on whether the existing industrial and technological capabilities in the country offer higher productivity levels than other competing countries for the specific segment of the production process involved (Francis and Kallummal 2013: 114).

However, even with entry into a particular value chain, neither upgrading by firms within the entered segments nor entering segments of higher value addition is automatic or assured, as we will see in the next section.

Contribution of GVCs to industrial upgrading efforts

Overall, there is evidence of an increase in the technological intensity of exported manufactures over the period 1980–2013 (UNCTAD 2016: 110). However, for many developing and transition economies, even when the commodities exported are classified as being of medium or high technological intensity, there is not much of this type of manufacturing activity overall. While at one level this reveals the limited scale of success in exports of manufactures, the increased trade in intermediate goods that results from the spread of GVCs also needs to be factored in (UNCTAD 2016).

Indeed, as De Backer and Yamano (2010) point out, GVCs directly challenge measures of competitiveness based on export market shares and indicators of revealed comparative advantage. Clearly, as countries' exports are increasingly made up of imports of intermediates inputs, analysis of indicators based solely on favourable export data of final goods does not necessarily indicate a competitive edge in the production of a specific good. It might hide the fact that a country is merely specialised in the final assembly of that good by importing intermediate inputs while adding/creating less or no value to the good itself. Given the significant proportion of two-way trade in intermediate products associated with the rise of GVCs, the technological sophistication embodied in the goods exported by developing countries may not coincide with the exporting country's contribution to them. Therefore, we consider evidence of contribution of GVC participation to the industrialisation efforts of developing and less developed countries in terms of net gains in value addition.

Distribution of value-added gains in GVCs

Studies have recently been able to examine gains from GVC engagement after the OECD and WTO jointly released Trade-In-Value-Added (TIVA) dataset in May 2013 (see De Backer and Yamano 2010; Banga 2013; WTO and IDE JETRO 2011; IMF 2013; etc.).

UNCTAD extended this to include developing as well as least developed countries. As pointed out in IMF (2013: 7), there is no internationally agreed methodological framework for measuring trade on a value-added basis. Measures of trade on a value-added basis have therefore focused on the use of international input-output tables, which have been constructed by combining the national input-output tables available from national statistical agencies. Given that trade in value-added aims to capture only the domestic content/value that countries add to goods and services[23] (and not the gross value of goods and services traded), it is expected to give a relatively better picture of the benefits of GVC participation.

Using OECD-WTO TIVA dataset (May 2013), Banga (2013) estimated GVC participation for each of the 58 countries covered by the dataset (34 OECD countries; 5 BRICS – Brazil, Russian Federation, India, China and South Africa; 8 NICs; and the category 'rest of the world' which comprises all developing and underdeveloped countries excluding BRICS and NICs). Participation in GVCs for a particular country is measured as a sum of 'foreign value added in its gross exports' (backward linkages or imports of foreign value-added) and its 'domestic value added that goes into other countries' gross exports (forward linkages or exports of domestic value-added).[24] A more recent study Banga (2016) uses the newer TiVA (August 2015) database. The latter defines forward linkage as the domestic value added in gross exports of intermediate products that can be exported or consumed by a partner country as a share of gross exports. The earlier version included only that part of value-added exports of a country which entered the exports of the partner country. As a result, for a given year, the absolute value of forward linkage of many countries has significantly risen in the newer version of TiVA as compared to the earlier one.

In both the studies, trends in the share of domestic value addition in gross exports, which are indicative of the value-added gains for a country from exports, for the period 1995–2010 (Banga 2013), and for 1995–2011 (Banga 2016) showed that domestic value added in gross exports had declined substantially for many developing countries. Decline in the share of domestic value added in gross exports was very high for countries like China (21 percentage points), South Korea (17 percentage points) and India (12 percentage points). According to the new definition for forward linkage used in Banga (2016), domestic value added in gross exports declined by 15 percentage points for India between 1995 and 2011. Similar results can be seen for Thailand, Vietnam, Chinese Taipei and Malaysia. On the other side, estimation of the foreign value added in gross exports (i.e., backward linkages) shows that the foreign value-added (FVA) content of gross exports has substantially increased in many countries, including India. In Brazil, Russia, India, China and South Africa (BRICS), only China reports a fall of FVA share in gross exports (1.2 per cent) (Banga 2016: 642–643). FVA share in gross exports has increased by 3 per cent in Brazil, 0.46 per cent in Russia, 14.7 per cent in India and 6.3 per cent in South Africa. Other countries with tangible increases in FVA share include Cambodia (24 per cent), Korea (19.4 per cent), Vietnam (14.9 per cent) and Malaysia (10 per cent) (Banga 2016: 642–643).

By contrast, the US has much stronger forward linkages as compared to its backward linkages (ratio of 2.53), because its domestic value-added which enters other countries' exports are much higher than the foreign value added that enters exports of the US. The ratio of forward linkages to backward linkages was only 0.5 for China, which indicates that China's domestic value-added that enters other countries' exports is much lower than what it imports from other countries. Thus even as China appears to be integrated in GVCs at a much higher level compared to other developing countries in terms of backward linkage, its forward linkages in gross exports are not equally strong in terms of creating domestic value-added. This is despite the fact that China has increased its export market share gains in all the major developed country markets at the expense of Latin American, African and even Asian exports of manufactures (see Wood and Mayer 2011, cited in Milberg and Winkler 2013: 14).

Share of a country in the total value-added created by forward and backward linkages in GVCs (i.e., summing over all countries) is used by Banga (2013) to provide a measure of the extent of a country's participation and its relative gains in GVCs. It was found that the US, Germany and China have high total participation in GVCs. Using TiVA 2013, Banga (2013) finds that this ratio is 0.93 for India in 2009, indicating that India's net gains from linking have not been positive. Using TiVA (Oct 2015)'s new definition, it is found that, while the ratio for India is greater than one for the time periods considered (see Table 3 in Banga 2013), it has significantly declined over time, which reflects falling net gains (and increasing import dependence). In the case of India, Gupta (2016: 20) also found that post-2000s, the forward linkages/backward linkages ratios had declined in all the sub-sectors of machinery and textiles industries.

The low/falling domestic value addition in developing countries that are integrated into GVCs explains the weak evidence for a positive causal connection between GVC participation and industrialisation (UNCTAD 2014, 2016; Banga 2013). UNCTAD (2016) mapped the association between changes in the import content of export-oriented manufactures and changes in manufacturing value added as a share of GDP between 1995 and 2011 for all developing countries for which data were available. While much of the Asian region shows a clear and strong positive association between GVC participation and industrialisation, developing countries in other regions show the opposite relationship.[25] That is, the positive contribution of GVCs to structural change in Asia does not apply to other regions (UNCTAD 2016: 119–120). This has weakened the overall causal relation between GVC participation and industrialisation.

Further, as Chandrasekhar (2013: 66) pointed out, given that most high-tech industries can be broken down into a range of processes and components involving very different levels of science and technology (S&T) intensity, gains in terms of higher value-added shares in only some sub-processes or sub-sectors would be actual high-tech gains, whereas gains in other areas may just be a reflection of the relocation of less technology-intensive segments to cheaper locations (see also Kattel et al. 2009; Karo and Kattel 2011). In fact, Banga (2013: 27) has shown that even in industries where developing countries like China have the highest share in global exports – e.g., electrical and optical equipment, a large part of value-added is sourced from developed countries from where most of the TNCs emerge. On the other hand, in low-tech industries like textiles and leather – although the comparative advantage of developing countries is higher by standard definition as they involve large-scale low-wage employment – backward linkages with developed countries in terms of foreign value-added used in exports was high.

Baldwin and Lopez-Gonzalez (2013) also showed that, while China moved up the value chain in terms of gross production between 1995 and 2009 in terms of markedly high gross output growth in high-tech sectors like electrical and optical equipment, transport equipment and chemicals,[26] its value-added growth in these high-tech sectors was below its gross output growth in these sectors. As they observed, the gap between high-tech output and high-tech value added is clearly symptomatic of China's position in

regional supply chains; China was increasing its imports of intermediates in high-tech sectors faster than it was increasing value-added
contribution to these sectors. They established that China's dependence on imported intermediates did not abate in the higher-tech
sectors such as electrical and optical equipment, transport equipment or chemicals. Large switches away from foreign sourcing – by
replacing imported intermediates with locally produced ones – happened only in light manufactures (textiles and clothing, leather and
footwear and wood and related products).

Similarly, the implications of linking into GVCs can change dras-
tically for developing countries if we use other alternative ways of
measuring participation in GVCs involving firm-level data, rather
than gross exports and imports data. The widely quoted 2007 study
by Linden et al. which is a detailed analysis of the fragmentation
of the Apple iPod value chain and associated value-added shares,
clearly demonstrated the discrepancy between trade performance
and value creation across countries (Linden et al. 2007). The analysis showed that China was merely specialised in the assembly of
the imported intermediates into the final product, which generated
relatively very little value. That is, even in a producer-driven chain
expected to deliver more in terms of dynamic gains, the largest part
of the value creation throughout the production process was done
and captured by the producers of high value components (located
in the US and Japan) and the seller, who undertakes the design and
branding of the iPod (Apple in the US) (see De Backer and Yamano
2010; Milberg and Winkler 2013: 33–35, 41). The iPod example
clearly showed that the concept of competitiveness may sometimes
needs to be assessed at a detailed level, in order to fully understand
what drives the international performance of countries (De Backer
and Yamano 2010) in seemingly high-tech industries. Again, this is
true even in the case of China whose share in global exports and
global value added in high-tech manufacturing industries, including
in the computer and office machinery industry, increased dramatically after 2001 (see Chandrasekhar 2013).

As UNCTAD (2016) point out, the extent of forward participation in GVCs might be expected to be higher at both low and high
levels of industrialisation than at the middle. At the lower stages of
development, forward participation in GVCs occurs through the
supply of relatively unprocessed goods to foreign markets, while at
the higher development stages, it occurs because of shifting out of
processing into the types of headquarter activities that accompany

greater technological development (OECD 2015 cited in UNCTAD 2016: 119). Evidence put together in the Trade and Development Report (UNCTAD 2016: 118–119) reveals that Asian countries show a strong negative correlation between changes in forward participation and manufacturing value added. The former result could reflect the fact that, except for Singapore and Hong Kong, which might offer higher value-added services that fit the category of headquarter activities, the forward participation of many other Asian countries considered in the analysis might be through the exports of relatively low value-added products. This translates into a negative relationship between forward engagement in GVCs and manufacturing value added also.

At another level, it is true that making use of the technology upgrading opportunities that exist within GPNs, especially those that allow them to progress from manufacturing to designing and onwards to becoming original brand creators, a number of firms in developing countries have become originator firms of global production networks in some sectors. However, despite the appearance of firms from some emerging economies, mainly China, in select sectors, their ability to climb the value chain remains a challenge. According to Starrs (2014), cited in UNCTAD 2016, despite being the largest exporter in the electronics sector, China accounts for just 3 per cent of the share of profits derived from this sector. Once again, this reflects the low contribution of GVC participation to domestic value generation. Koopman et al. (2008) showed that the share of foreign value added in Chinese manufactured exports was about 50 per cent. In the case of processing exports, which benefit from duty exemptions on imported raw material and other inputs 'as long as they are used solely for export purposes', this foreign share rose up to 82 per cent (see De Backer and Yamano 2010).

Electronics industry case studies by Luthje et al. (2013: 25) also showed that

> contract manufacturing within GVCs engenders significant potential for industrial upgrading **within respective facilities** [own emphasis] and their manufacturing capabilities. But such developments are often limited by the centralised global decision making on product allocation by contract manufacturers and their brand name customers as well as by the dominant pattern of neo-Taylorist organisation[27] of work and the related

deskilling of the industrial workforce. Industrial upgrading remains highly precarious under these conditions.

It must be noted that, in some cases, developing countries' export success has been aided in part by expansion of export processing zones (EPZs) where MNCs and their management of process trade played a significant role (Milberg and Winkler 2013: 40). However, several studies point out that such zones have been successful only in those cases where significant agglomeration effects – or the positive externalities arising from knowledge spillovers and backward and forward linkages among upstream and downstream producers of and/or services clustering in a specific location – were generated. But in the first place, certain conditions or ecosystem must be in place to facilitate the common location of enterprises in an area (Nawrot 2014: 77) for the development of cluster formation. Further, agglomeration benefits from cluster formation do not occur automatically. If such zones have to become channels for indigenous innovation and cause the gradual development of backward and forward linkages, state has to play an active role, which go beyond providing the hard infrastructure.

After studying Taiwan's success with the well-known Hsinchu Science Park, Mathews (2010) showed that the steady hand of government as collective entrepreneur was needed to make the breakthroughs necessary in Taiwan's progress, from labour-intensive manufacturing activities based on low-cost labour inserted into GVCs, to skills and technology upgrading combined with openness to flows of capital, technology and people (particularly exchanges between Hsinchu and Silicon Valley). The steady hand of the government was also necessary to provide the 'new shoots' of industrial development to maintain the pressure in the long process of change from imitation to innovation, and from contract manufacturing to full-branded enterprise. The state laid the ground for a dynamic process of circular and cumulative causation at work, generating the sustained increasing returns enjoyed by firms in the Hsinchu park.

Examining the high level capabilities developed and obtained by the domestic IT industries in Ireland, Israel and Taiwan, Breznitz (2006) also showed that, in successful cases of rapid innovation-based industrial development, the state's initial role has been that of a key factor in the creation of a network/cluster. The state agencies first create a set of firms and industrial actors (organisations that are involved in the industry but are not private firms) and then seek to develop a deeply meshed network among firms and between firms and the state. The state also helps to embed firms into international financial and production markets and networks. The state at first creates a hierarchical network and then in the course of a co-evolution process (that is, a process in which two or more parties influence the development of each other) the network becomes denser as well as more egalitarian and international, with the state moving from a position of power and control into a position of centrality. It was only consequently, that the state becomes more of a facilitator organiser and less of an overall commander.

Overall, it has been observed that it is only when backward participation in GVCs (reflected in increased foreign value added of exports) occurs in a larger context of greater production and exports of manufactures (as in Cambodia and Vietnam, for instance), that GVC participation can complement industrialisation and structural change (whether through EPZs or otherwise). However, this might not happen if increasing backward participation in GVCs reflects a reduction of domestic sourcing in a context of weak export performance for manufactures (UNCTAD 2016: 119). Most of the evidence discussed above in terms of increased import dependence as well as weak forward linkages in GVCs establishes that this has largely been the experience of developing countries.

The role of FTAs[28]

In the absence of domestic industrial and technological upgrading, the net impact of production restructuring effected under GVCs could lead to a decline in domestic sourcing/production also in the case of a country that carries out simultaneous tariff liberalisation under overlapping free trade agreements (FTAs). While strict rules of origin in a bilateral or regional PTA can force localisation of certain parts of production within the older PTA members, broader region-wide trade liberalisation removes the need for MNCs to maintain horizontal national operations (Francis 2015b). This clearly impacts the production and trade structures resulting from such FTAs.

As elaborated in Francis (2015b), broader PTAs with cumulative rules of origin enhance the possibility of sourcing inputs from the larger region at preferential rates or zero duty, which allows MNCs to locate different segments of the production process for a particular product in different countries (with competition now spread across a wider set of countries), and export to or import from those countries. A combination of broader and overlapping FTAs can also lead to the scenario that an MNC can locate the entire production process for a particular product in a single country that it considers the most suitable and import tariff-free into all other markets in the region (Kumar 2007a; Francis 2015b).[29] Note that this would clearly be the case when any of the FTA partner countries have a well-diversified and developed supplier base. Ironically, this gives the exact opposite outcome of the proposition that FTAs help increase vertical specialisation or fragmentation trade. As noted in Chapter 1, this was one of the arguments put forward by researchers like Yi (2003), Athukorala (2012), etc. while suggesting that FTAs will help increase the spread of GVCs.

Therefore, as argued in Francis and Kallummal (2013: 114), in the case of liberalised trade, investment and cumulative rules of origin under overlapping FTAs, the net impact of the division of labour under regional or global value chains on a participating country's productivity, output growth and job creation will depend on:

- whether that country is chosen for the production of particular product lines that offer scope for sustained productivity gains and externalities;
- the extent of foreign facility closures in that country in conjunction with new investments in other host countries;
- the extent of closures by domestic companies due to the increased foreign competition in the domestic market[30]; and/or
- the nature and pattern of outward FDI from this country.

In the above list, the first decision is shaped by the specific position of the developing country firm within the sector-wide global value chain, which in turn is dependent on its manufacturing and technological capabilities. To the extent that such region-wide industrial restructuring due to the FTAs means closing factories in India in favour of production in a partner country, there would clearly be output and employment losses in India (Francis 2015b). Even as there might be a rapid increase in intra-industry trade involving Indian firms, the country could experience decline in local value addition if Indian firms lag behind in dynamic competitiveness embedded in indigenous capabilities. The associated production restructuring experienced in particular sectors may also lead to a reconfiguration of two-way trade from intra-industry to inter-industry in those sectors, apart from a change in the geographic composition of trade flows (Francis 2015b). This clearly means that the outcome of 'extensive industrial restructuring or rationalisation' enabled by region-wide FTAs (Kumar 2007a, see Chapter 1) can be counterproductive for countries that have lagged behind in utilising industrial policy measures to build up indigenous capabilities and backward linkages in its foreign-invested enterprises.[31]

Menon (2013: 11, 20) makes the argument that FTAs have little additional trade impetus to offer in the case of most industries involved in GVCs and fragmentation trade because most, if not all, product fragmentation trade already travels at duty-free or at very low tariffs across the region, either because of the ITA that covers trade in electronics parts and components; various duty-drawback schemes or the fact that most multinationals operate out of export processing zones, where they are duty-exempt. However, as we will see in the next chapter, in the case of electronics trade, India's FTAs have indeed been ITA-1 plus. Moreover, the impact of FTAs on industrial restructuring occurring within GVCs need to be analysed as discussed above, going beyond their implications for fragmentation trade. Clearly, the exact nature of restructuring dynamics under GVCs and the scope for industrial upgrading for a specific country (under the impact of FTAs too) can be verified only at the industry level.

The scope of services

It has been observed that backward linkages within GVCs are not strong for developing countries in the case of services also. As Banga (2013: 21–22) points out, services play a much more dominant role in value-added contribution to exports of developed countries as compared to manufactured products. Overall, in OECD countries, contribution of domestic value-added to total exports from services is greater than contribution of domestic value-added to exports by manufactured products. The higher share of services is seen in the case of the US, France and the UK. Domestic value-added in exports by manufactured products play a dominant role in developing countries. In China, most of the value-added by exports was created in the manufacturing sector, while services contributed 29 per cent of total value-added exports in 2009, with 40 per cent imported from other countries. In India, by contrast, most of the value-added exports are from the services sector, which contributed 53 per cent to value-added exports. However, foreign value added for manufactured products and services was almost equal in the case of India.

As discussed, given that most of the rents in GVCs come from the services component of manufactured exports dominated by developed countries, developing countries may stand little chance in maximising gains through such integration in the services part of the value chains. The driver for export-led growth in India is the business services sector, which includes both software and IT-enabled services. But the share of business services in total value-added revenues in market-oriented services (that is, excluding education and health services) fell from close to 50 per cent in 1985 to 38 per cent in 2007 (Chandrasekhar 2013: 74). Indeed, the GVC participation of services sector estimated by Banga (2016) using TiVA 2015 showed that for services sectors, growth in backward linkages was generally significantly higher than growth in forward linkages for the study period 1995–2011. Within business services sectors, the highest growth in backward linkages (1995–2011) was observed to be in post and telecommunications, R&D and other business activities, and transport and storage. These were followed by hotels and restaurants, the renting of machinery and equipment and computer and related activities. For R&D and other business services, forward linkages had actually declined over time (Banga 2016: 749–750). However, in the case of R&D processes being out-sourced to India, it is possible that, as in the case of pharmaceutical companies, knowledge-intensive projects are more likely to be assigned to internal teams, while data-intensive projects are more likely to be outsourced (Damodaran 2016: 395, citing Contractor et al. 2011).

Further, it need not be true that a country displaying success in knowledge-based services (or industries) actually controls the knowledge needed for such production (Chandrasekhar 2013: 76). Despite the fact that emerging economies like China, India and Brazil have increased their R&D expenditures compared to the 1990s, the US, and in particular, US MNCs, still monopolise the control over knowledge. Licensing the use of this knowledge ensures

significant revenues to firms from the US (through intra-firm transactions with their foreign affiliates), far exceeding that received
by other countries (Chandrasekhar 2013: 77–78). In fact, the US
dominated foreign ownership of patents in India too. In the case of
Brazil, Kasahara and Botelho (2016: 104) point out that, although
the overall number of patent filings in Brazil increased from about
21,000 (for 2001–2004) to 27,000 (for 2007–2011), the patents
filed by Brazilian companies have remained stagnant since 2004.
This clearly indicates that foreign companies have increased their
role in innovation in the country. This has been attributed by Kasahara and Botelho (2016) to the fact that Brazil had not still put
innovation at the heart of its industrial policy strategy. Data until
2013 showed that total national expenditure on R&D and most of
the financial instruments created to promote innovation was on a
clear decline when compared with BNDES loans – the main industrial policy instrument (Kasahara and Botelho 2016: 104).

Re-examining import-driven productivity growth

Thus in many cases at present, especially in electronics and automobile GVCs, developing countries are involved in 'assembly
networks' as assemblers, rather than the producers of technology-
intensive parts and components (UNECA 2016: 216). In the electronics industry, for instance, Reinert and Kattel (2010: 23–24)
pointed out that "Asian labs remain focused primarily on repeti-
tive detailed engineering and product development tasks". In the
absence of industrial policies to promote linkages between local
firms and MNCs, or to improve national technological capabilities, the experiences of Mexico and Central American countries as
assembly manufacturers and the performance of the electronics and
automotive industries in Eastern and Central Europe also show that
these involve only limited success. While there has been significant
'internal upgrading' within MNC affiliates, it has involved very few
spill-overs to the domestic economy in the form of productivity
improvements and imitation by domestic firms, partly due to limited linkages of MNCs with local firms and labour markets (see the
country case studies and other literature cited in UNCTAD 2016:
118–119; Kattel et al. 2009; Puyana 2007, 2011; Gallagher and
Zarsky 2007; Palma 2010). Similarly, despite Mexico's and several East European countries' close geographical proximity to and
preferential trading arrangements with large developed markets,

Mexico experienced broad-based decline in real wages, while the East European countries saw their presence across supply chains reduced to the lower end (Milberg and Winkler 2013: 242).

It is more than evident that, even as catching-up developing countries might seem to both industrialise (measured by an increasing share of industry in GDP) and catch up technologically (measured by a raising share of 'high tech' exports), none of these indicators necessarily imply an increased capacity to develop and to pay higher real wages (Reinert and Kattel 2010: 23–24, see also Milberg an Winkler 2013). This is because domestic linkages may remain weak, while intense global competition and 'commodification' keeps wages and profits low as already pointed out. This is why, calculations based on the OECD-WTO database on Trade in Value added (May 2013) show that, while 67 per cent of total global value created in GVCs accrued to OECD countries, the share of NICs and BRICs countries was 25 per cent. Only 8 per cent of the total value added was attributed to all other developing countries and LDCs (UNIDO 2015: 21).

That is, under extensive trade and investment liberalisation and passive industrial policies, export-oriented manufacturing takes place in an enclave manner, where manufacturing inputs get increasingly outsourced from lower-cost producers abroad that are part of GVCs.

It is true, as discussed in Chapter 2, that, despite very low domestic value addition, the effect of importing cheaper, better or a broader variety of intermediate inputs can be positive for productivity at the firm (and industry) level as it reduces costs and improves productivity in downstream industries. There have not been many empirical studies that measure the impact of trade in intermediate inputs on productivity in downstream industries directly. Amiti and Konings (2007) used an indirect approach by analysing the impact on productivity among downstream firms of tariff cuts on intermediate goods in Indonesia. They found that a 10-percentage point fall in input tariffs improved the productivity of importing firms by 12 per cent. In the case of India, some recent econometric studies have found evidence of increase in productivity linked to trade liberalisation. Topalova and Khandelwal (2011) found significant efficiency improvement in 4,000 large formal firms, which they attributed to increased competitive pressure from lower output tariffs and increased volume of imported inputs. A recent study on India by Rijesh (2017) using panel data estimation for 1980–2013 found that, while increased import penetration had a significant impact on productivity with a 1-year lag, this improvement in both labour and total factor productivity exhausted in the second period as the coefficient became negative after 2 years. However, these studies did not examine the impact of intermediate goods separately. In an earlier study, Veeramani (2014) had found that imports of capital goods had exerted a stronger positive impact on growth than intermediate goods imports and attributed this result to the fact that capital goods embody higher levels of knowledge than intermediates.

In the analytical framework in Chapter 2, we showed that productivity improvement and export growth arising from increased access to imported inputs is not sustainable. Furthermore, growth in overall production in the economy may slowdown relative to total employment as a result of both low domestic value addition (which reduces the capital available for re-investment) as well as due to a slowdown in demand from falling employment,[32] both of which makes the process unsustainable (Francis 2015a; UNCTAD 2016: 113).

Reinert and Kattel (2010: 23–24) pointed out that productivity-reducing type of structural transformation due to low domestic value addition and demand slowdown from falling employment and wages has been occurring especially in Africa and Latin America, as well as Eastern and Central Europe (as discussed above), but also in Asia barring a few exceptions. This is the case even when there seems to be evidence of emerging catching-up country innovation hubs (technology parks, production agglomerations, R&D centres by MNCs, etc.) in highly innovative fields such as ICT in economies like Estonia, Mexico, India, etc.

It is clear that, while GVCs constitute opportunities for developing countries to become part of the global economy, to absorb knowledge and technology, add value to their products and expand exports (UNCTAD 2014), the very entry of developing country firms into GVCs is conditional upon their existing level of technological capabilities (Francis 2017). This was also observed by Low and Tijaja (2013: 9): "It will be difficult for any country to participate effectively in GVCs, let alone to upgrade its participation, if the economy does not have enough innovation capabilities and/or its domestic GVC participants do not possess sufficient technological capabilities". Thus if participation in value chains is to deliver sustainable growth in terms of technology, employment and high wages along with export growth, which in turn will need to be reinvested productively for sustainable development, openness in trade and FDI are simply not enough. Clearly, industrial policy has to come into the picture to play its role in building up capabilities.

Growing challenges in industrial development

The need for industrial policy measures in the development process is further enhanced by the urgency for developing countries to respond to the increasing challenges arising from climate change, rapidly evolving digital technologies as well as emerging 'backshoring'[33] and 're-localisation' trends in manufacturing industries (that may or may not be associated with the first two).

As Zarsky (2010) has conceptualised, climate-resilient development is a socio-economic trajectory that generates and sustains human livelihoods in ways that both mitigate and adapt to global climate change. Central to mitigation is the transition to non-carbon energy sources. For developing countries, mitigation will primarily consist of ensuring that new investments are in low-carbon and/ or renewable energy technologies (Zarsky 2010: 8). But many of the emerging green technologies are also dominated by developed country MNCs as of now. In the light of the above discussion, it is clear that there is an urgent need for vertical industrial policies to support the development of such new technologies in developing countries and ensure sustainable development.[34]

Meanwhile, the processes of globalisation and the accompanying division of labour across the world are evolving continuously. Several concurrent trends have been noted. Nordas (2009) had already pointed out that vertical fragmentation appeared to be levelling off and consolidating at its mid-2000s' level. This was first observed among the major OECD countries, but since 2000, vertical specialisation appears to have been reaching a plateau also in Asia. Evidence from Casini and Kay (2014) also shows that, while the international sourcing of intermediates has on average been more important in manufacturing, it increased relatively little over the period 1995–2005 in most countries except for Eastern European countries. Nevertheless, the offshoring of services still appears to be on the rise, albeit from a low base compared with total trade or total demand for business services (Casini and Kay 2014).

In fact, Montalvo (2014), Alcorta (2014), Kinkel (2014), Ernst (2016) discuss several factors that are leading to changes in firm-level competitive strategies based on a re-evaluation of the advantages and disadvantages in globalised organisation of production. Some of these are:

- erosion of profit margins among MNCs as the offshoring model has been mastered by many;
- relative increases and levelling over time of wages of competing hosting regions as a result of their economic catching-up processes, rendering comparative cost advantages more and more marginal;
- productivity increases in offshoring countries' firms;
- new major concerns regarding the efficiency of offshoring operations[35] as well as vulnerability to damages in one of the links in the supply chain;
- trends of individualised consumption and demand modes, making it necessary to develop and produce customised solutions close to local clients, as opposed to the development and production of standard, mostly less complex products in large batches;
- continuing technological developments in ICT and manufacturing technologies supporting individualisation and automation, e.g., additive manufacturing technologies using 3D printers with their disruptive potential to deliver 'individualisation for free';
- massive market shifts towards emerging markets,[36] etc.

Some of these factors are supporting 're-localised manufacturing' trends (such as in large markets in emerging economies); others appear to lead to a 'backshoring' tendency. In the case of the EU, a study by Dachs and Kinkel (2013) showed that, while the new EU member states (EU-12) and China were the main target countries for production offshoring by European firms, these countries (EU-12, less so for China) were also the main source countries for backshoring. Reflecting some of the factors listed earlier, there is also evidence of considerable backshoring activities from EU-15 locations, in particular Germany, and from the US (Dachs and Kinkel 2013). When distinguishing between backshoring from high-income locations (the EU-15 countries, the EFTA countries and the US) and from low-income locations with a GDP per capita of less than 3,000 USD (the EU-12, other Central and Eastern European countries, Russia, China, India and other Asian countries except Japan), the results revealed that, while backshoring from high-income countries is often related to a lack of flexibility, transportation costs and labour costs, by contrast, production activities of European firms in low-income countries suffer above average from a lack of quality and a lower availability of skilled personnel. Quality was reported to be the major concern particularly in China and India (where more than three fourths of all backshoring was related to quality problems) (see Dachs and Kinkel 2013).

Overall, firm-level data on European companies' production relocation activities show a decrease across most countries, sectors and firm sizes in the initial phase of the 2008 crisis. Evidence from longer ranging time series analysis of German data suggests that this decrease in offshoring might be part of a larger trend, which started as early as 2003 and continued after the crisis in the years up to 2012. Despite a general decrease in offshoring, offshoring to Asia, and China, in particular, has stayed stable. This may be explained by the fact that the offshoring decision in these cases is not dominated solely by potential labour cost savings, but also by customer and market access motives (Stehrer et al. 2012) and the advancements in ICT simultaneously.

According to Montalvo (2014: 128), new ICTs and manufacturing technologies are enabling the reorganisation of two core aspects of industrial organisation. First, the remote monitoring and control of key aspects of manufacturing activities (materials, inventories and flows, quality monitoring and maintenance of machinery). Second, the digitisation and creation of design platforms for customer intimacy directly linked to the production of goods and services now promises the conduction of relative low cost manufacturing beyond modular to individualised design and production, leading to fully individualised mass customisation. There is increasing compulsion of subcontracting firms in GVCs to move their design, production and delivery systems towards fulfilling customised wishes of the individual customer with greater intimacy. New digitisation technologies enable that the wishes of a single customer organise a unique and entire value chain and production network (see Dietel 2013; EFFRA 2013; Sauer 2013, cited in Montalvo 2014).

Another trend provoking fundamental changes in business organisations as technology-based competition has been intensifying is the globalisation of R&D (Ernst 2016). The globalisation of R&D appears to be driven both by the development of GVCs and by the dynamics of global innovation processes themselves (see detailed discussions of motives driving the offshoring of R&D by MNCs in Sachwald 2013; Montalvo 2014; Kinkel et al. 2014). There are potential benefits associated with the increasing trend to locate new R&D units in emerging countries, on innovation in host countries. If there is, for example, a higher likeliness to introduce worldwide innovations in the host country, it could also benefit the host economy indirectly through supplier linkages and knowledge spillovers. However, once again, it has been pointed out that the extent of such beneficial effects, if any, will also depend on 'the embedded-ness of the foreign affiliates' (that is, their linkages with the host economy) and the absorptive capacity of the local firms and the host country (see Wolfmayr et al. 2013; Kinkel 2014).

Conclusion

GVCs are characterised by hierarchical governance structures, with highly centralised control in the contractual relationships between oligopolistic lead firms and highly competitive supplier firms, which lead to asymmetric distribution of the value-added gains and rents across firms and countries involved in a value chain. Maximum rents accrue to firms which have and maintain technological leadership. Moreover, lead firms shape the distribution of risks and profits in their favour by the continuous "generation and maintenance of endogenous asymmetry" within GVCs (Milberg and Winkler 2013: 127–130) by inducing competition among suppliers, offloading risks to suppliers, erecting entry barriers, minimising technology sharing, etc. The mainstream understanding of the implications of developing country firms' participation in GVCs fails to factor in these asymmetric governance relations within GVCs.

It also fails to acknowledge that technological capabilities are endogenous to the determination of cost competitiveness of different locations for a particular production process/segment/task within GVCs. While GVCs constitute opportunities for developing countries to become part of the global economy and contribute to a diversification of exports, the very entry of developing country firms into GVCs – whether through FDI or otherwise – is conditional upon their existing level of technological capabilities. For FDI to lead to technology upgrading and diffusion enabling industrial upgrading in a country, the production of foreign-affiliated firms in the country should be linked to indigenous firms in the supporting and other related industries.

However, under extensive trade and investment liberalisation and passive industrial policies, export-oriented manufacturing within

GVCs takes place in an enclave manner, where manufacturing inputs get increasingly outsourced from producers abroad that are part of GVCs leading to an erosion in domestic production capacities. This is because technological capabilities and agglomeration benefits are endogenous to these MNC outsourcing decisions (rather than pure relative cost competitiveness) and the former are built up by state's active role. For the same reason, a country that carries out simultaneous tariff liberalisation under overlapping free trade agreements (FTAs) will find that the net impact of production restructuring effected under GVCs would only result in a decline in domestic sourcing/production – in the absence of domestic industrial and technological capabilities and their upgrading, and/or policy-driven incentives for localised production.

The discussion in the previous sections clearly established that the participation of developing countries in GVCs at low value-added positions within the chain with limited productivity externalities and domestic linkages does not lead to the kind of structural transformation that leads to sustained industrial development. Productivity-enhancing structural change can be obtained only in the case of specialisation patterns that are more conducive to technological upgrading than others, even when they are combined with the right forms of public investment and policy support (UNCTAD 2016). This is again related to the main argument discussed in the Chapter 2 – only increasing returns activities have the ability to lead to productivity growth and externalities required for generating virtuous cycles of growth. This necessitates a role for active industrial policy interventions that guide investment towards increasing returns activities.

Moreover, even with entry into a particular value chain, neither upgrading by firms within the entered segments nor entering segments of higher value addition is automatic or assured for the same reasons. Despite the appearance of large supplier firms from some emerging economies, mainly China, in select sectors (which is itself linked to a legacy of domestic capability building through industrial policy measures), their ability to climb the value chain remains a challenge. The governance structure of international production networks and the power of lead firms constrain the ability of even such lead suppliers to achieve the sorts of price increases that could boost wages and improve labour standards. The latter comes dominantly through the rents accruable through technology ownership.

It is evident that, if participation and production restructuring in GVCs is to deliver sustainable growth in terms of value added, technology, employment and high wages (going beyond a growth in exports), which in turn will need to be reinvested productively for sustainable development, openness in trade and FDI are simply not enough. All these point to the heightened need for vertical industrial policies to support developing countries' participation in GVCs and to draw development benefits from their engagement.

Mis-interpreting these causal interactions between liberalisation of trade and FDI (including through FTAs), indigenous capability development and GVC participation can lead to wrong inferences, which result in inappropriate policy formulations and unsustainable industrial development trajectories. It is therefore important to examine these interactions and the attendant restructuring dynamics in particular industries in a systematic manner. This is critical in strategic and technology-intensive sectors like electronics, chemicals, transport equipment, pharmaceuticals, machinery, etc. as well as in labour-intensive industries such as textiles and garments, leather, etc.

In the case of India, the electronics industry is one which has gone through parallel processes of trade and FDI liberalisation, which were carried out with the intention of improving India's export competitiveness. Some of the FTAs were also rationalised based on the argument that they would increase India's integration into the electronics industry value chains centred around East and Southeast Asia and lead to an expansion in India's exports. However, according to the National Electronics Policy 2012, the value addition in domestically produced electronics products ranged between only 5 to 10 per cent in most cases, even as electronics exports continued to show dismal performance (see Francis 2015a). The following chapter will therefore examine Indian electronics industry's experience with GVC participation against the backdrop of the industrial policy framework that drove trade and investment liberalisation and other policy changes in that industry.

Notes

1 These are the pre-production stages involving research, design and development; production process stages involving procurement, manufacturing and assembly; and the post-production stages of marketing, trade, servicing and disposal. Transportation, logistics, etc. are overarching service sector components in a value chain. Broader

understandings of value chains adopt a cyclical system view as the flow of products from primary production to consumption, with a focus on resource use, waste management and recycling. See, for instance, UNIDO (2015).

2 Luthje et al. (2013: 24).

3 Subcontracting involves an intensive kind of cooperation under which the parent firm assures off-lift of all of the ancillary production or a substantial portion of it over an extended period of time at a fair, mutually acceptable price. Further, the parent firm extends support in the form of technical know-how, provision of drawings and training. See UNESCAP 1991: 241.

4 Among computer and other electronic companies, this had happened as part of the shift to the Wintelism paradigm, when many old computer companies in the US and Europe, most notably IBM, moved away from the Fordist-style vertical integration to network-centric models of organisation (Luthje et al. 2013: 35–36). The new model that emerged at the end of the 1980s came to be known as electronics manufacturing services (EMS).

5 It is pertinent to note that chemical industry has been traditionally quite reserved about production relocation strategies due to high capital intensity and high degree of process integration (Kinker 2014). Baldwin and Lopez-Gonzalez (2013: 13) also showed that the big supply chain trade flows are in sectors like transport equipment, electrical and optical equipment and chemicals.

6 Montalvo (2014) points out that some GVCs sometimes involve as many as 30 or more different players and locations.

7 Baldwin and Venables (2010) have argued that most production disintegration (what they term 'unbundling') processes are complex mixtures of two types of configurations: (i) the spiders, whereby multiple limbs (parts) from different sources come together in one place to form a body (assembly), which may be a component or the final product itself, and (ii) the snakes, wherein the good moves in a linear manner from upstream to downstream with value added at each stage. They point out that, in practise, the two are combined: spiders might be attached to any part of a snake, and multiple snakes might join into a spider.

8 It is explained that, when affiliates import intermediates for further processing, it is likely that further processing is cheaper in that host nation but the intermediates are cheaper abroad – a clear indication that the affiliate's location is at least in part motivated by efficiency-seeking. See Baldwin and Okubo (2012).

9 Francis (2003) has shown that localisation achieved when indigenous firms are able to enter into subcontracting with MNCs for the supply of parts and components, offers the highest degree of transfer and diffusion of technology and management know-how (and therefore wider externalities in the economy). While the procurement of inputs by MNCs from indigenous firms in the open domestic market offer the next best scenario, the 'internalisation of production' by MNCs or foreign-invested/foreign-affiliated domestic firms through backward

integration (that is, by setting up downstream units locally) offers the least diffusion and externalities (see the detailed arguments developed in the theoretical framework in Francis 2003). This in turn has clear implications for how policies related to FDI should be formulated.

10 WIOD is a joint effort by a consortium of 11 research institutions led by the University of Groningen and funded by the European Commission (Timmer et al. 2015). This database shows where each sector in each nation obtains its inputs and sells its output, distinguishing between purchases of the goods for intermediate usage and final usage (www.WIOD.org).

11 By contrast, it has been suggested that the EU-12 countries had a much higher vertical specialisation (at 21 per cent in 1995) than the other countries partly due to the strong forward linkages these countries already had as providers of intermediates for (mainly) the EU-15, but also because the country group consists of relatively small countries. Its integration intensified even further over time to about 34 per cent in 2007.

12 Examining the experiences in leapfrogging and catching-up through regional clustering in East Asian countries, Nawrot (2014: 81) clearly showed that accumulation of knowledge and capabilities was essential to building clusters as internationally competitive industrial destinations. The state and its institutions were essential facilitators and catalysers of those processes. Additional incentives resulted from deepening the cooperative efforts through regional initiatives, including AFTA (ASEAN Free Trade Area), ACFTA (ASEAN-China Free Trade Area) or AICO (ASEAN Industrial Cooperation).

13 More discussion follows in the next chapter. In fact, the Indian software industry is one of the standout examples of prolonged and effective state intervention in India (Saraswati 2013). See also Kumar and Joseph (2004), Saith and Vijayabaskar (2005), Mathur (2007), Kallummal and Francis (2012), Das and Sagara 2017, etc.

14 This is despite the fact that the EU's single market for goods has enabled a high degree of intra-EU trade integration involving east European countries (EU-12).

15 This refers to the range of activities from routine tasks and standard low technology, labour-intensive processes to skills-intensive, high-technology tasks contained in the production of the good in question (Nordas 2009).

16 The higher this ratio, the smaller the transport costs relative to total revenue, and the more easily the component can be sourced from a distance (Nordas 2009). In this reasoning, the sectors that most easily lend themselves to fragmentation are electronics and clothing.

17 The logic behind this assertion rests on the fact that, unlike trade in final goods, product fragmentation trade generally involves multiple border crossings. Since a tariff can be levied each time a good-in-process crosses a border, the reduction or elimination of tariffs within the free trade area can lead to a multiplier effect on trade stimulation, whereby the cost savings is a multiple determined by the number of border crossings within the FTA (see Yi 2003; Menon 2013). On the

other side, Anukoonwattaka (2011: 17) argued that, in practice, the actual benefits of PTAs with regard to increasing the trade of participants in IPNs depends much on the nature of the rules of origin built into PTAs. Trade-distorting effects of rules of origin can be more detrimental to trade in IPNs than the conventional style of trade in which firms only trade in final goods because trade costs arising from the bureaucratic process of utilising tariff preferences will be accumulated over multiple cross-border trading in parts and components at different stages of production. Moreover, maintaining trade barriers against non-members may distort the natural expansion of fragmentation trade across countries.

18 The scale of production has not been associated with a proportional increase in mark-up pricing power in China also. (See Appelbaum 2008, cited in Milberg and Winkler 2013: 123.)

19 Ownership of intangible assets (R&D, design, marketing and branding) are based on unique resources and capabilities that other firms find difficult to acquire and they are therefore sources of superior returns (Kaplinsky 2005 cited in Milberg and Winkler 2013).

20 This was reflected in national-level data – SMEs made relatively little contribution to the country's exports relative to the sector's employment or GDP contribution. Even more industrially developed Southeast Asian economies (e.g., Thailand and Malaysia) lagged behind the SME export shares of advanced East Asian economies such as Japan, South Korea and the PRC. See Wignaraja (2014).

21 Following OECD classification, large firms were defined in this study as enterprises with more than 100 employees and SMEs as those with fewer than 100 employees.

22 Another instance is given in Nawrot (2014: 76) which discussed the cases of the automotive cluster in Thailand, the electronics clusters in Malaysia and Singapore and the chemical and biomedical industry in Singapore. For example, the local content requirement policy implemented by Thai government resulted in more investments of automotive assembly companies in Thailand and more support for local supplying firms in order reach the quality standards required by parent firms who established local production bases to meet the local content requirements. See also Francis (2003) and the literature cited therein.

23 According to Baldwin and Gonzalez (2013: 8), a nation's imported intermediates from a given partner usually contain intermediates from third nations and even from the nation itself. When the recursion is fully worked out – so that the origin of all primary factor inputs in exports is identified – we have 'value-added trade', which was earlier called 'factor-content trade'.

24 It must be noted that foreign value added (FVA) in gross exports of a country reflects the total value-added created in other countries which enters the exports of a country, as it includes all direct imports as well as indirect imports from countries where there is no direct trade. That is, in multi-country value chains, it contains not just the foreign value-added content in bilateral trade, but also the foreign value added included in the exports of the country's bilateral trading partner (which

has gone into the intermediate product exported to the first country). See Banga (2013).
25 See Chart 4.7 in UNCTAD 2016: 120.
26 In terms of gross output, below average gross output growth was experienced in sectors like agriculture and related products, non-metallic minerals, leather and footwear, textiles, etc. (Baldwin and Lopez-Gonzalez 2013: 44).
27 This concept refers to the combination of segmented assembly line work in highly automated factories with extreme flexibility of working and employment conditions and specific strategies for motivating workers in companies with no brand-name products and cultures of their own. The term has been used in industrial sociology and political economy to characterise corporate strategies to reform the Taylorist model of work without sacrificing its basic elements of work segmentation and control (Luthje et al. 2013: 24).
28 This section includes portions from the essays previously published as Smitha Francis and Murali Kallummal (2013), 'India's Comprehensive Trade Agreements: Implications for Development Trajectory', *Economic & Political Weekly*, Vol. XLVIII (31), August, pp. 109–122, and Smitha Francis (2015b), 'Preferential Trade Agreements: An Exploration into Emerging Issues in India's Changing Trade Policy Landscape', in Jayati Ghosh (ed.), *India and the World Economy*, ICSSR Research Surveys and Explorations (New Delhi: Oxford University Press). The extracts have been reproduced with the permission of *Economic & Political Weekly* and Oxford University Press India © Oxford University Press 2015.
29 See Sukegawa (2009), cited in Francis (2011a), for an illustration of how the export strategies of the Sony Electronics company across Asian production platforms were re-aligned based on different countries' productivity and skill levels after the Indo-Thai Early Harvest Program and later when the India-ASEAN FTA came into being with its cumulative rules of origin. See also Francis and Kallummal (2013). According to Hiratsuka (2010), cited in Anukoonwattaka (2011), Japanese automobile assemblers also initially took advantage of ASEAN's region-wide trade liberalisation programmes to consolidate duplicated production facilities in ASEAN countries and facilitated the division of labour within the region, in order to achieve a regional scale of production.
30 See also Patnaik and Rawal (2005).
31 This becomes relevant in the discussion of the pattern of intra-industry trade (IIT) in Indian electronics industry in the next chapter.
32 A study on the employment impact by Banga (2016) has empirically established that growth in forward linkages in GVCs by Indian firms had statistically insignificant impact on employment growth. On the other side, the higher foreign value-added in India's exports was found to have significantly and adversely impacted industry-level employment growth (Banga 2016: 635–636).
33 This refers to the fact that an MNC is moving production activities from abroad back to its home country, as opposed to production

offshoring. As pointed out by Montalvo (2014), backshoring levels need to be analysed always in relation to previous or current relocation/offshoring levels.

34 Some of the policies being adopted by Brazil, China, etc. will be discussed in Chapter 5.

35 Such concerns that have emerged related to the efficiency of offshoring operations include: (i) quality of intermediate components and final products; (ii) lead time for delivery (trans-ocean shipping from Asia to the US, for example, takes at least two weeks); (iii) higher complexity of global operations; (iv) greater environmental and regulatory awareness in host countries; (v) endogenous demand and social stability in host country; etc. (see Montalvo 2014).

36 For instance, China has already become the single largest market for German car manufacturers, larger than the whole European market – and is still rapidly growing (Montalvo 2014).

Chapter 4

Liberalisation sans industrial policy

The experience of the Indian electronics industry

Mis-interpreting the causal interactions between trade and FDI liberalisation, development of indigenous capabilities and participation in GVCs can lead to wrong inferences, and in turn, inappropriate policy formulations, which lead to unsustainable industrial development trajectories. It is therefore important to examine the interactions between trade and FDI liberalisation and other industrial policies as well as the attendant restructuring dynamics of firms in each industry in a systematic manner. This chapter considers these interactive dynamics of GVC engagement by the Indian electronics industry.

The electronics industry – the hardware core of the information and communication technology (ICT) sector – is strategic for any country because of its economy-wide productivity-enhancing impact. Expansion in the cross-sectoral use of digital technologies increases the imperative role of hardware manufacturing capabilities. However, after nearly two decades of trade liberalisation, the gap between country's electronics demand and domestic production capacity has only been widening. Consequently, while India has been considered a 'global super power' in the IT services sector (at least until recently), the electronics industry is one of the top contributors to India's merchandise imports after oil.

Several parallel processes of trade and investment liberalisation have impacted the electronics industry. One of these is the Information Technology Agreement (ITA-1) signed by India in 1996, which is a plurilateral agreement of the WTO. ITA-1 was designed to achieve elimination of all entry barriers on information technology products in six product groups, namely, computers, telecom equipment, semiconductors, semiconductor manufacturing and testing equipment, software and scientific instruments. India also undertook trade liberalisation under its comprehensive free trade agreements (FTAs) with East and Southeast economies such as Singapore, ASEAN, Japan, South Korea and Malaysia. It must be remembered that this has occurred in a context wherein India has been continuously liberalising its foreign direct investment (FDI) policies since 1991. Successive Indian governments have been projecting and attracting FDI as leading to industrial development and export growth. But in addition to unilateral liberalisation of FDI policies towards this, India has dramatically increased her engagement in bilateral and regional FTAs with Southeast and East Asian economies since the mid-2000s. Apart from trade liberalisation, these have involved 'investment' liberalisation, with the purported objective of enabling India's integration into GVCs.

India's participation in FTAs especially with the East and Southeast Asian economies has been argued to offer mutually beneficial linkages through dynamic industrial restructuring within the region leading to greater competition and improved efficiency, as well as gains from greater inter- and intra-industry specialisation, economies of scale and learning-by-doing (see Kumar 2007a; Francois et al. 2009; etc. cited in Francis 2015b). As mentioned, the expectation has been that the reduction/elimination of tariffs and enlargement of markets through these FTAs will help attract export-oriented FDI from MNCs linked to global value chains and enable India to expand exports. As discussed in earlier chapters, the increase in access to competitive imported parts and components through FTAs has also been expected to improve the competitiveness of domestically owned firms and allow them to become part of GVCs.

Analysis in Francis (2011a), based on the Harmonised System (HS) of categorisation of trade flows at the 2-digit level, showed that there has been a significant increase in two-way trade in India's global trade in electrical machinery and non-electrical machinery, apart from others such as petroleum and petroleum products, gems and jewellery, organic chemicals, articles of iron and steel, automobiles, etc. In addition to these sectors, India has witnessed increased two-way trade with Indonesia, Malaysia, Thailand and Singapore in the category of optical, photo, technical and medical apparatus also. It should be noted that the HS chapters of electrical machinery; non-electrical machinery; and optical, photo, technical and medical apparatus together constitute most of the electronics products.

The increase in India's two-way trade with these Southeast economies has been linked to the industrial restructuring being carried out by MNCs in the region, in response to the WTO-plus trade liberalisation that India began undertaking with these countries under the Early Harvest Programme of the Thai-India FTA in 2004 and the Comprehensive Economic Cooperation Agreement (CECA) with Singapore in 2005 (Kumar 2007a; Francis 2009). Francis and Kallummal (2013) further observed that the significant increase seen in India's two-way trade in intermediate products with these countries seems to point towards India's growing involvement with GVCs centred on ASEAN and China. It was also previously argued that the emerging MNC-driven industrial restructuring involving India and the East Asian economies was likely to intensify in particular industries, including the electrical and non-electrical machinery industries, following the entry into force of the overlapping FTAs with ASEAN, South Korea, Japan and Malaysia (Francis 2015b).

The increase in India's two-way trade with Southeast Asian economies seems to offer preliminary evidence of India's integration into electronics industry value chains. However, whether India obtains broad-based productivity benefits from the opportunities for MNC-driven industrial restructuring arising from trade liberalisation (such as greater inter- and intra-industry specialisation, economies of scale and learning-by-doing) depends on India's position in the value chain for particular products (Francis and Kallummal 2013). This is because the division of labour in a specific product is the fundamental determinant of how the value added and profits are distributed among different countries involved in its value chain. As we saw in the discussions in the previous chapter, above all other factors, division of labour in GVCs (particularly under tariff-free trade) is based on countries' relative technological capabilities. Given that trade and FDI have been liberalised in the electronics industry since the 1990s, the nature of participation of the country in the industry's GVCs can be a reasonably good proxy for the level of national technological capabilities in that particular industry.

But rather than using value-added trade data used by the studies discussed in Chapter 3, we follow the intra-industry trade-based methodology used in the literature on vertical specialisation to estimate the extent of India's participation in electronics GVCs and to understand the relative competitive position of the country in the value chains. It should be noted that, while value-added trade data does provide essential information, as pointed out in Baldwin and Lopez-Gonzalez (2013), such data based on inter-country input-output tables suffers from the disadvantage that they involve simultaneous manipulations of all nations' input-output tables. Errors in any of the national IO tables will produce errors in all value-added trade flows (Baldwin and Lopez-Gonzalez 2013: 10).

However, using trade data in goods clearly limits the scope of our analysis to the manufacturing segment of the electronics industry. We do not examine the entire value chain, as the upstream segments of applied R&D and design and the downstream segments of marketing and retailing in the electronics industry are well known to be dominated by developed country firms (with exceptions). Even though the value addition from the manufacturing segment of the value chain is relatively lower compared to these service functions, following the conceptual framework developed in Chapter 2, we attach special significance to accretion in productive employment, build-up and diffusion of technological capabilities and sustainability that accrue from domestic undertaking of manufacturing processes (see also Khan 2010). We also need to take into account inter-sectoral considerations while focusing on the manufacturing segment of the value chain. Sustainability of services competitiveness and its export success require services to generate significant backward linkages in the economy, which in turn requires the existence and continuous upgrading of manufacturing capabilities. In the absence of the latter, the country will not be to avoid unsustainable import dependence. Moreover, despite India's software capabilities, the premium on manufacturing technological capabilities has gone up (and not down) given the emerging trends in advanced manufacturing technologies and automation across sectors including agriculture, driven by growing embedded-ness of software and hardware, digitisation, etc. (see Francis 2018a). Manufacturing sector growth is required from the point of demand for services too.

Thus the objective here is to analyse the extent to which increased two-way trade in the electronics industry reflects India's involvement in the manufacturing segment of electronics industry value chains and explore India's position along the value chain. If India has production capabilities in several product lines, it would help integrate India into the electronics industry value chains. If that is not the case, trade liberalisation under the ITA-1 and FTAs would have only led to increased import dependence in Indian electronics industry. Arguably, the latter would be a clear-cut outcome if there were inadequate attempts on the government's part to develop domestic technological and manufacturing capabilities and to support indigenisation of production by foreign-invested companies prior to and along with tariff liberalisation, using vertical industrial policies.

Underlying the estimation issue of the extent of GVC participation is the major conceptual issue of what part of trade can be categorised as trade under GVCs. India's integration into GVCs would get reflected – according to conventional wisdom – in an increase in intra-industry trade (IIT) at sufficiently disaggregated product levels. Thus clearly, all two-way trade observed at the HS 2-digit level of trade data will not be a reflection of IIT at the product level. Trade flow analysis at a sufficiently disaggregated level is therefore needed to examine the nature of the observed increase in India's electronics two-way trade. Moreover, only a disaggregated level analysis will tell us whether the country's value chain participation is occurring in dynamic sectors with significant increasing returns, which offer sustained productivity growth, rising real wages and externalities through forward and backward linkages. The latter has important implications for the industry's development trajectory as well as national sufficiency in such a strategic industry.

Moreover, given the evolving nature of networks relations involving equity and non-equity engagement of developing country firms with lead firms[1] and the latter's increasingly complex division of labour strategies, network trade must be understood as going beyond the traditional understanding of vertical specialisation based on the idea that countries link sequentially to produce final goods. As opposed to complete vertical specialisation that gets captured by increased IIT at the product level (Hummels et al. 2001; Chen et al. 2005; Banga 2013), we argue that trade between countries involved in a value chain might involve both inter-industry and intra-industry trade at the product level.

Given our focus on trade flows, the analysis of trade flows involved identifying and collating trade data that is available in the HS classification, which is concordant with the International Standard Industrial Classification (ISIC). This study uses trade flow data at the HS 6-digit level available from the WITS website. Data based on the 1996 HS nomenclature is used, for which the time series starts with 1996 data, the year before ITA-1 entered into force. From a total of 5,113 items at the 6-digit level, the final comprehensive list of 372 electronics products at the HS 6-digit level was identified,[2] which also included some products like unrecorded media (see Annexure 4.1).

Before turning towards an analysis of two-way trade in India's electronics industry, the following two sections analyse the post-independent evolution of the industrial policy dynamics in the electronics industry and examine how this has impacted the pattern of trade flows in the electronics industry since the 1990s. In particular, the nature of trade liberalisation under the ITA-1 and the recent FTAs are examined.

Industrial policy dynamics in the electronics industry: an overview

There is a long history of government support to India's IT and related sectors. India was one of the few developing countries that laid stress upon indigenous technological capability development early on in its independent history (Kallummal 2012). The Indian government recognised the importance of computing and electronics for national development and had started building necessary infrastructure and capabilities from the 1950s (see also Sridharan 1996; Chandrasekhar 2005; Kumar and Joseph 2004; Mani 2005; Mathur 2007; Saraswati 2013; Das and Sagara 2017 and the papers cited therein). The country's potential in software exports was also recognised by policymakers early on. By the late 1960s, the concept of IT as an industry had begun to take root as a direct outcome of government-supported programmes and policies (see Kallummal 2012).

In the case of software, one of the industrial policy measures that pushed Indian IT software firms to strive for competitiveness was the fact that these firms were required to export software in the early days of the industry (Saraswati 2013). This arose in the context of a shortage of foreign exchange in India in the 1970s and early 1980s. Software firms that needed imported inputs were required to earn foreign exchange through export of software. The 1972 Software Export Scheme, initiated by the newly established Department of Electronics (DoE), provided 100 per cent loans to management consultancy firms and interested entrepreneurs for the purchase of then expensive computers, with the stipulation that such computers were to be used for exports only and loans were to be repaid using foreign exchange generated by these exports (Saraswati 2013). This specific industrial policy measure enabled them to get a feel of global markets at a very early stage of development. At the same time, the government underwrote their competitiveness by facilitating technological capability building within the sector through investments in public funded R&D institutions, supporting their projects by creating computing facilities and by developing infrastructure for data transfer and networking (Kumar and Joseph 2004: 17; Chandrasekhar 2005; Mathur 2007; Saraswati 2013).

In the electronics hardware sector, while the Indian government had pursued a highly restrictive policy framework for electronics industry in favour of self-reliance in the post-independence period, there was some opening up in the early 1980s, which involved a series of reforms for ensuring a greater play of market forces. The latter had involved liberalisation of component imports, relaxation of capacity constraints for the IT hardware sector and the opening up of the telecommunication sector to private participation (Francis 2018b). As a result, the industry experienced significant growth in the 1980s as compared to the late 1970s (Joseph 1989; Majumdar 2010).

On the other side, the high tariffs and quantitative restrictions for the hardware sector enabled some domestic production of hardware products including PCs, peripherals and components. This was aided by the general reduction in duty on components and liberal import of capital goods for component manufacture under the Components Policy of 1981. During this period, there were three segments in the Indian IT hardware sector: premium producers like Wipro who controlled the upper-end market, large volume retailers like Sterling Computers and HCL who survived on lower per unit margins and, finally, a large number of assemblers catering to the lower-end market (Chandrasekhar 2005: 70).

However, the nature of incentives for software exports due to a myopic policy approach and the absence of vertical industrial policies led to a disconnect between the subsequent boom in software export growth and the domestic IT hardware and telecommunication growth trajectories. This is despite the fact that the Telecommunication Policy of 1984 had opened up telecom equipment (both customer premises and terminal equipment) manufacture to the private sector and the Computer Policy of the same year had allowed all Indian companies to enter all segments of the computer industry without any capacity restrictions (see Mani 2000b; Kumar and Joseph 2004).[3] In fact, Majumdar (2010: 73) observed that the mid-1980s had witnessed the highest number of industrial licences and letters of intent in electrical equipment and telecommunication.

The 1984 Computer Policy had in fact emphasised that planning for software development must be integrally linked with the plan for hardware development and system engineering. However, under the Computer Software Policy of 1986, import of computer systems on a custom duty-free basis was allowed for 100 per cent software export, without reference to indigenous angle clearance.[4] This is a clear reflection of the lack of coherence in the industrial policies of the time.

The disconnect between the growth of the software and hardware segments of the Indian ICT sector got entrenched with the initiation of export-oriented economic reforms in the early 1990s. According to Kumar and Joseph (2004: 7), "an assessment was made by the finance ministry then that apart from the general orientation of all industries towards export markets, India's comparative advantage was in software and not in hardware". With greater thrust consciously given to software exports, new policy measures were initiated to promote them further, which included removal of entry barriers for foreign companies, removal of restrictions on foreign technology transfers, participation of the private sector in policy-making, etc. (see Kumar and Joseph 2004; Chandrasekhar 2005). Further, the DoE created Software Technology Parks of India (STPI) in 1990 to provide infrastructure support for 100 per cent export-oriented software firms through high speed data communication links and built-up space. This scheme with its associated tax incentives for duty-free imports of IT hardware also acted as a counter-productive force for the growth of the domestic hardware sector.

On the one side, while the government laid the foundation and created the facilitating environment with successive steps of proactive intervention for infrastructure provision, capability development and government procurement,[5] which reduced costs, created skills and improved competitiveness of companies, the software industry took off with greater participation by the private sector and increased world demand after the late 1990s *inter alia* on account of the Y2K problem. This was aided in no small measure by a central feature of the global ICT revolution from the late 1990s: acceleration in the outsourcing of IT and IT-enabled services by corporations in the developed countries (Chandrasekhar and Ghosh 2006). Growth in offshore software exports from the country increased from 20–35 per cent during 1991–1992 to more than

70 per cent during 2009–2010. The industry body National Association of Software and Service Companies (Nasscom) also played an important role in lobbying domestically as well as in India's major international markets for rules and regulations favourable to India's software firms. Thus a strong export-oriented software industry emerged in India – during a period characterised by import substitution – due to the concerted efforts on the part of the government through coordinated industrial policy measures and a host of related factors like government-diaspora relationships, private initiatives, public-private partnerships, etc. (Mathur 2007). Therefore, as several other authors have also pointed out, contrary to the popular perception that India's export success in IT services has been an outcome of the free play of market forces and state's 'benign neglect', the Indian software industry is one of the standout examples of prolonged and effective state intervention in India (Saraswati 2013; Kumar and Joseph 2004; Saith and Vijayabaskar 2005; Mathur 2007; etc.).

On the other side, this superb export performance of the IT software and services sector coincided with the debacle of India's IT hardware production capacities in the absence of industrial policy support for domestic electronics manufacturing sector firms. Given that the governments did not seek to link the increase in demand for computers that originated from the growth of software exports to domestic hardware producers through vertical industrial policies, this meant that the local IT hardware and related component producers did not benefit from the growth in software exports- either to realise the economies of scale necessary to make them viable, or by facing the competitive pressure to build up technological capabilities along with advancements in the ICT sector. Arguably, there was inadequate policy focus to push existing domestic producers in computers, telecommunication equipment or parts and components to improve their productivity. This presents a significant contrast to the electronics industry development trajectories in countries such as Singapore, South Korea or Taiwan, where the governments adopted various combinations of vertical industrial policies for production upgrading and skill development in selected industry segments within an overall industrial development strategy, which involved performance-linked incentivisation to induce productivity growth while pursuing simultaneous trade strategies of import substitution and export promotion (see the detailed discussions in Lall 1996; Wade 1990; Sridharan 1996; Amsden 1989, 2001; etc.).

Arguably, the Indian state, which was able to identify the developmental opportunities in the software sector way back in the 1960s and 70s, was myopic when it came to the electronics manufacturing sector. This may be attributed to three factors. Firstly, the government failed to build on the synergies that arise from the integral interconnectedness of the software sector and the ICT hardware sectors through coherent and coordinated industrial policies. Secondly, there was a misreading of the software export success sector. The proponents of economic reforms in 1991 attributed the growing export potential of the software sector to its 'comparative advantage', while paradoxically, the export success that India has had in software exports was based on the 'acquired comparative advantage' developed through explicit and implicit public policy support consistently since the 1950s, along with a strategic alliance between the public and the private sectors (see Kallummal 2012; Saraswati 2013; Mathur 2007; Saith and Vijayabaskar 2005; Kumar and Joseph 2004). Thirdly, from the early 1990s onwards, partly due to balance of payment (BoP) concerns and partly owing to the increased negotiation strength of software firms arising from their export success, the export interests of software firms increasingly came to dominate the policymaking framework and contributed to relegating any erstwhile policy intention of developing national capabilities in the hardware sector to the backburner (Kallummal and Francis 2012; Saraswati 2013).

In the telecom equipment sector, the country had built up considerable capability in the design and manufacture of digital switching equipment domestically – led by public sector research and manufacturing firms and aided by the public procurement policy of the government. However, the lack of "a credible innovation policy and proper technology forecasting" meant that the domestic telecom research sector did not create enough capability in mobile switch technologies, which began gaining prominence in the 1990s (Mani 2005: 315). This can, at least partly, be related to the fact that, while complete de-licensing of all kinds of telecom equipment and removal of public sector reservation was brought into effect from July 1991 (Mani 2000b: 195), the entire telecom equipment manufacturing sector was simultaneously opened to foreign investment up to 51 per cent under the automatic route. Simultaneously, import policies with respect to telecom equipment of all kinds were also relaxed (Mani 2000b: 202). Subsequently, five leading MNCs had set up manufacturing facilities in India in the early 1990s – Alcatel, Lucent Technologies, Ericsson, Siemens and Fujitsu[6] – owing to the public procurement policy of the then main domestic consumer, the Department of Telecom (Mani 2005). Consequently, in the absence of indigenous capability advancement due to the policy failure to strategically re-orient the sectoral system of innovation, when the increase in domestic demand for telecom equipment following the de-licensing of telecom services in 1999 came to be driven by growth in the cellular mobile and internet services segments, the shift away from fixed switches benefited these global players, all of whom have been involved in assembly (see Mani 2005: 287–315 and Mani 2012). Even though local firms also came into the market to benefit from the unprecedented growth in demand for telecom equipment, they were also assemblers of imported parts and components like the MNCs (see Mani 2012). Subsequently, the Indian telecom manufacturing sector came to be dominated by Alcatel and Ericsson, although more recently, the industry has become dominated by the Chinese telecom players Huawei and ZTE (Ernst 2014: 3).

In the case of the consumer electronics industry, although internal liberalisation (relaxation of licensing requirements) took place in 1996 (Ernst 2014: 14) and import liberalisation occurred only later under the FTAs, it may again be argued that the lack of government policies pursuing indigenous capability build-up meant that domestic producers did not invest in scale or new technologies during the period of protection. Thus they could not face the increased competition from foreign investors who had set up local production. Consequently, this segment has also been dominated by Japanese, Korean and Chinese MNCs such as Sony, LG, Samsung, Haier, etc. (see Ernst 2014, 2016).

Similarly, the lack of a strategic policy thrust for developing strong and varied technological capabilities has meant that, while India currently has a strong integrated circuit (IC) design base located within MNCs, Indian chip design engineers lack the breadth and depth in capabilities required for semiconductor fabrication, component manufacturing, as well as in system design and systems manufacturing (Ernst 2014: 24).

Trade liberalisation under the ITA-1 and FTAs

Given the incoherence in industrial policy approach cemented by an understanding of market-led industrialisation that gives credence only to passive industrial policies, India's decision to join the ITA-1 in 1996 was driven by the government's belief that lowering duties on a range of ICT products under the ITA-1 would boost the competitive advantage of India's software exports. The ITA-1 was designed to establish tariff-free trade in a total of 165 products belonging to computers, telecom equipment, semiconductors, semiconductor manufacturing and testing equipment, software and scientific instruments.

Under the mandate of the ITA-1, the participating countries had agreed to eliminate all tariffs as well as other duties and charges on these products in four equal stages in 1997, 1998, 1999, and 2000. But under the Special and Differential Treatment (S&DT) principles, the developing country signatories of ITA-1 – Costa Rica, Indonesia, India, South Korea, Malaysia, Taiwan and Thailand – had flexibility in cutting their tariffs to zero by 2005.

India's 1996 average base duty of 66.4 per cent on the 165 products dropped to 37.8 per cent in March 1997. The average tariff continued to drop at regular intervals to 12 per cent in 2000, and further to about 10 per cent in 2004, and was completely eliminated by 2005 (Kallummal 2012). In fact, the narrow policy focus on IT software export promotion meant that India stood out among developing countries in average applied tariff reduction as well as in terms of the number of tariff lines that were brought under concessions under the ITA-1 (see Figure 4.1). India offered concessions on 66 per cent of its pre-ITA-1 tariff rates. This was far greater than the concessions of even a country like Thailand (30.9 per cent), which was well integrated into electronics production networks and might have stood to gain from the trade liberalisation (Ernst 2014: 19).

However, as shown in Majumdar (2010), tariff liberalisation and increase in foreign investments from the early 1990s or other policies such as decrease in industrial licensing and reduction in excise duties, did not result in greater competition and improved productivity in the electronics hardware industry. This study analysed total factor productivity growth (TFPG) for organised sector electronics firms for two periods 1993–1998 and 1999–2004. As compared to the first period, all the four sub-sectors, computer hardware, consumer electronics, telecommunication and components, had witnessed a significant net decline in TFPG in the second period after external liberalisation was intensified from 1997 onwards under the ITA-1. The poor productivity growth of electronics firms despite liberalisation was explained by the fact that as competition

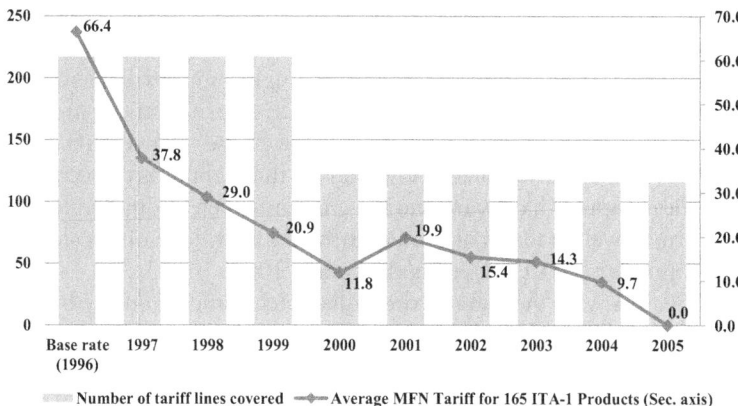

Figure 4.1 India's tariff liberalisation under the ITA-1, 1997–2005

Source: Kallummal (2012).

increased due to liberalisation, R&D per sales witnessed a sharp decline for firms in the industry. R&D expenditure as a percentage of capital imports also decreased substantially for the computer hardware and consumer electronics sub-sectors (Majumdar 2010: 76). This clearly reflected the shift in firms' preference to undertake investments to assimilate imported technology rather than develop in-house technology through R&D, in the absence of any industrial policy emphasis on promoting indigenous technological development.

Owing to their small profit margins, the small computer assemblers were in no position to use the opportunity afforded by protection to build capabilities of a kind that would allow them to compete with large international suppliers (Chandrasekhar 2005). On the other hand, with the government not enforcing any programmes of R&D-based competitive production in the premium segment, the premium producers chose to enjoy their large profit margins and also did not concentrate on developing indigenous sources of supply of components and accessories for reducing costs or on developing innovation capabilities (Chandrasekhar 2005: 71–72). As a result, after liberalisation, many of them moved into trading or other activities. The same was true of the other sub-sectors too. For example, in the telecom equipment industry, printed circuit boards (PCBs) and other components account for around 90 per cent of the product cost. But with the exception of cable harnesses and packaging, no such components have been produced in India (Ernst 2014: 2), which has led to higher import dependence among telecom assemblers. In the absence of productivity growth driven by indigenous capabilities, only those sub-sectors that catered to the market at the low end of the technology spectrum, i.e., the computer hardware and the component electronics industry performed well in terms of production after liberalisation, as shown in Majumdar (2010: 73) using data until 2004.

While this was the state of the Indian electronics industry by the mid-2000s, the impact of ITA-1 was exacerbated by the equally non-strategic tariff liberalisation carried out by India under its FTAs with ASEAN, Japan and South Korea – countries that are already deeply integrated into global electronics value chains.

The India-ASEAN FTA came into force in 2010. Out of the total 216 non-ITA-1 electronics tariff lines (at the HS 6-digit level) for which India made tariff liberalisation commitments to ASEAN, only 11 were kept in the Sensitive Track, and two were excluded.[7] India made 170 non-ITA-1 tariff lines duty-free by 2013 (Normal Track-1) (Table 4.1). For 96 tariff lines, this trade liberalisation was drastic as their MFN tariff in the base year 2007 was 10 per cent, which was reduced to zero over just 3 years between 2010 and 2013. Another 73 products saw their tariffs reduced from 7.5 per cent to zero in 2013.

Importantly, another 33 tariff lines became duty-free in 2016 (Normal Track-2). These include products and parts like loudspeakers and their parts, TV picture tubes of 20", etc. (see Table 4.2).

Table 4.1 Distribution of non-ITA-1 electronics products liberalised under the India-ASEAN FTA

(Number of HS 6-digit tariff lines)

Base MFN rate in 2007 (per cent)	0	7.5	10	Total
Excluded list	0	2	0	2
Normal Track-1	1	73	96	170
Normal Track-2	0	21	12	33
Sensitive Track	0	6	5	11
Total non-ITA tariff lines	**1**	**102**	**113**	**216**

Source: Author's calculation based on India's tariff reduction schedule with ASEAN-5.

Table 4.2 Major non-ITA-1 electronic products that became tariff-free in 2013 under the India-ASEAN FTA

Products with base year (2007) duty of 10 per cent	Products with base year (2007) duty of 7.5 per cent
Professional video tape recorders, radio-broadcast receivers, electric air heaters, cooking devices, personal weighing machines, electrical signalling/traffic control equipment for railways and their parts, other electric sound or visual signalling apparatus and their parts, photographic/cinematographic equipment like cameras, projectors, instant print cameras, etc. and their parts, etc. Microwave tubes (magnetrons, klystrons etc.), parts of cathode-ray tubes, TV camera tubes, vacuum tubes and other valves, etc. Number of products = 96	Radar apparatus, communication jamming equipment, transformers, photocopy machines, office-type offset printing machinery, automatic circuit breakers, navigational instruments, range of equipment used in medical, surgical, dental or veterinary sciences including MRI and X-ray machines and their parts, measuring and checking instruments and their parts, etc. Number of products = 73

Source: Author's compilation based on India's tariff reduction schedule with ASEAN-5.

It is important to note that, while consumer electronics and professional apparatus such as video cameras, photocopiers, medical equipment, etc. were not included under ITA-1 tariff liberalisation, several of them got liberalised under the ITA-1-plus tariff reduction schedules under the FTAs.

In the case of India's CEPA with South Korea, which also came into force in 2010, 8 non-ITA-1 product lines (E0, 2010) that had MFN duty of 12.5 per cent in the base year 2006 came under duty-free trade immediately (Table 4.3). However, in 5 years, that is, from January 2014, another 60 tariff lines (E-5) with MFN duty of 12.5 per cent in 2006 came under duty-free trade (E-5). A further 277 lines (E-8) became tariff-free from January 2016. Only products listed under the excluded category (EXC) are totally exempt from tariff reduction.

Tariffs for products under the Sensitive list (SEN) have been getting reduced in ten equal annual stages from 2010 and will get to half their base rates by January 2019. An important product in

Table 4.3 Distribution of non-ITA-I electronic products liberalised under the India-South Korea CEPA

(Number of HS 6-digit tariff lines)

Base MFN rate in 2007 (per cent)	E-0	E-5	E-8	EXC	RED	SEN	Total non-ITA tariff lines
0	I	0	0	0	0	0	I
12.5	8	60	277	45	21	16	427

Source: Author's calculation based on India's tariff reduction schedule with South Korea.

this category is TV, imports of which were not liberalised under the ITA-1 or the ASEAN FTA. All TV sets (of screen size less than 35 cm up to 105 cm), including LCD TVs (of screen size between 25 cm and 63 cm) had a duty of 12.5 per cent in 2006. These have been getting reduced since 2010. Meanwhile, LCD TV sets of screen size below 25 cm became duty-free from January 2016 (E-8).

India's CEPA with Japan came into force in 2011. Under this, India will bring down the tariffs on 132 non-ITA-1 HS 6-digit lines with 10 per cent base duty to zero in ten equal reductions (B10) by 2020 (Table 4.4). Another 206 product lines with base duty of 7.5 per cent will also become duty-free by 2020. Thirty-six non-ITA-1 tariff lines denoted with 'X' were excluded from any duty reduction or elimination.

It is clear that the margin of preference obtained under these FTAs for imports from ASEAN, South Korea and Japanese firms were as high as 12.5 and 10 per cent in several non-ITA-1 electronics products. Thus the drastic tariff liberalisation of the computer and telecommunications industries under the ITA-1 got broadened by the WTO-plus liberalisation carried out by India under its FTAs with ASEAN, South Korea and Japan, with the latter extending it to several non-ITA-1 electronics products, including consumer electronics and home appliances as well as professional, medical and scientific instruments and their parts.

It should be noted that the 2001 report of the Planning Commission's Working Group on Information Technology for the Formulation of the Tenth Five-Year Plan had recognised the scenario of the IT sector to be grimmer than the other Indian manufacturing sub-sectors and had called for a clear comprehensive national policy for hardware manufacturing industry for making

Table 4.4 Distribution of non-ITA-1 electronic products liberalised under the India-Japan CEPA

(Number of HS 6-digit tariff lines)

Base duty (2007 MFN) (per cent)	Number of non-ITA tariff lines			Total non-ITA tariff lines
	A	B10	X	
7.5	0	206	0	206
10	0	132	0	132
Total	**1**	**341**	**36**	**378**

Note: Duties on tariff lines denoted by A were reduced to zero in 2011.

Source: Author's calculation based on India's tariff reduction schedule with Japan.

the Indian manufacturing sector globally competitive (Kallummal 2012). However, it is clear that, despite the realisation by the early 2000s that output and employment in the domestic electronics industry had been severely affected adversely by the import surge under the ITA-1, the governments continued with deep and non-strategic tariff liberalisation without any attempt to link it with a coherent industrial policy for the long-term development of the industry.

It is notable that India was among the developing country absentees from the ITA-2 agreement, which was adopted by a group of WTO member countries on 24 July 2015, committing tariff-free trade at the multilateral level in a further 155 electronics tariff lines (based on HS 2007 classification). However, this commendable strategic policy decision may have come too late, with India having lost most of her trade policy manoeuvrability with respect to the electronics industry under the FTAs with the GVC-linked economies in East and Southeast Asia.

A trade policy that promotes duty-free imports will clearly reduce incentives for domestic production, particularly in a scenario of absent or ineffective policy push to instil productivity growth at the firm and industry levels. This also meant that trade liberalisation under the FTAs could not help Indian firms to make use of the opportunities to get involved in the electronics industry GVCs. For instance, while domestic production of TVs was being carried out through imported intermediate parts such as picture tubes (despite the relatively high tariffs), there was no attempt during the period of protection to support localisation of such major parts through innovative industrial policy measures as has been done in selected industries by China or Brazil.[8] Currently, imports of TV picture tubes have become duty-free from 2016 under the ASEAN FTA. Simultaneously, imports of the final products, LCD TVs, have also been made duty-free under the South Korean CECA from 2016. This reveals the absence of any strategic intent for the development of the industry. Further, the very fact that such a tariff liberalisation schedule by India became known at least from around 2010 would have definitely influenced the local production decisions of the MNCs which dominate domestic TV production.

Attracting FDI for enabling India's integration into production networks was an avowed policy objective behind the spree of FTAs with East and Southeast Asian countries. However, electronics manufacturing industry has received only a tiny part of the total FDI into India. Based on official data from 1 April 2000 to 30 June 2015, the electronics industry received only $1.68 billion or 0.66 per cent of the total FDI inflow of $258 billion FDI inflow. FDI inflow in electronics in 2014–2015 was $142.9 million and amounted to just 0.42 per cent of the total FDI inflow. Although telecommunications alone received 6 per cent of the total FDI inflow during 2014–2015, this was almost entirely in the provision of telecommunications services (Niti Aayog 2016: 4).

Such low levels of inward FDI into India's electronics industry is in fact related to the liberal FDI policy regime in place since 1991 and the nature of trade liberalisation since the late 1990s, which meant that large foreign original equipment manufacturers (OEMs) and electronics manufacturing service providers have had no incentive to invest in local production in India (Ernst 2014; Saripalle 2015; Francis 2016). As a result, they typically set up only final assembly plants (Ernst 2014: 8).

A comprehensive analysis of what are considered 'real FDI' inflows[9] by Rao and Dhar (2016) also showed that such inflows into the electronics sub-sectors, namely (i) office, accounting and computing machinery; (ii) radio, television and communication equipment; and (iii) medical, precision and optical instruments, watches, were quite small. The low levels of average inflows led Rao and Dhar (2016) also to raise doubts about the extent of localisation of production by these foreign-invested companies. Thus neither the ITA-1 nor the FTAs with ASEAN countries and East

Asian economies helped in attracting substantial inward FDI into the electronics industry.[10]

The resultant adverse impact of the above discussed tariff liberalisation policies enveloped within a liberal FDI policy regime gets reflected in the composition of imports and exports when we analyse changes in electronics industry trade flows in detail.

Changing nature of electronics industry trade flows

Electronics exports constituted 3.2 per cent of India's total manufactured exports in 1996.[11] After growing at an average annual growth rate of just 3.5 per cent during 1996–2000, exports did grow faster from 2001 onwards, at an average of about 22 per cent and 31 per cent during 2001–2005 and 2006–2010, respectively (see Figure 4.2). But subsequently, electronics exports grew at much lower rates (just averaging 2.6 per cent during 2011–2014) than India's total manufactured exports. As a result, their share in manufactured exports declined to 2.7 per cent in 2014, which was lower than that in 1996. Clearly, there was no sustained favourable impact of trade liberalisation on India's electronics export performance.

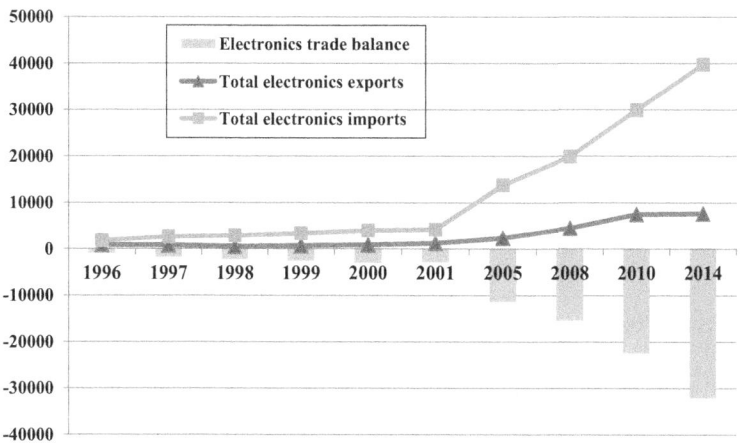

Figure 4.2 Trends in India's overall electronics trade, 1996–2014

Note: Values are in million US dollars.

Source: Author's calculations based on WITS COMTRADE data.

On the other side, the share of electronics imports in India's total manufactured imports, which was at about 5 per cent in 1996, increased continuously and went up to nearly 12 per cent in 2003. Average annual import growth rate for electronics, which was already at about 22 per cent during 1996–2000, went up to about 35 per cent during 2002–2005 and remained strong until 2011.[12] Even though growth in electronics imports became weak after 2011, the share of electronics imports in manufactured imports increased again from 2012 and stood at 9.3 per cent in 2014.

Figure 4.2 shows the rapid increase in electronics industry trade deficit as a result of the huge increase in electronics imports relative to exports from the mid-2000s. The diverging trends in electronics exports and imports after 2012 – when exports declined in value and imports began rising again – is captured in Figure 4.3. It also reveals the loss of importance of electronics exports among total manufactured trade. We will examine the composition of electronics exports and imports in order to understand these shifts.

In 1996, the top three major electronics exports were computer storage units (such as hard disk drives), parts and accessories of computers and automatic circuit breakers. The first two accounted

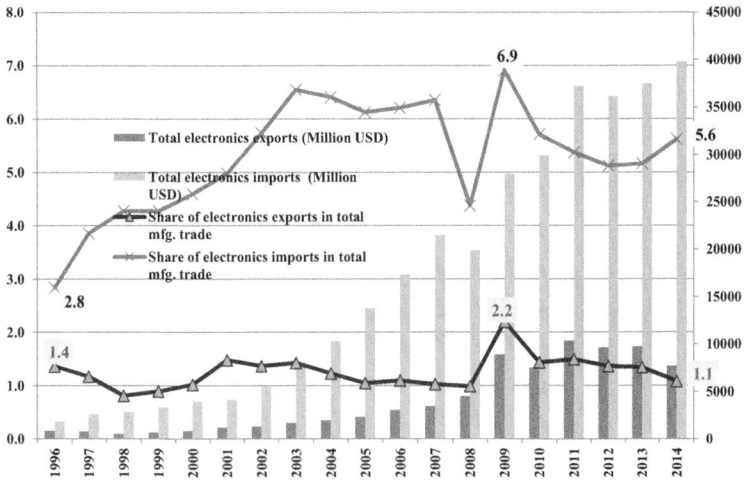

Figure 4.3 Share of Electronics Trade in India's Total Manufactured Goods Trade, 1996–2014

Note: Shares are in per cent.

Source: Author's calculations based on WITS COMTRADE data.

for about 14 per cent each of the total. Other products constituting the top ten exports were colour TVs, hybrid and monolithic integrated circuits (ICs), magnetic tape recorders, etc. By 2001, computer storage devices had moved out of the top ten list. Parts and accessories of computers became the single largest export item with 20 per cent share of the total (see Table 4.5). Other parts of computers had the second largest share of 5 per cent of the total. X-ray tubes, magnetic discs and electro-diagnostic appliances followed with 3 per cent shares each. Photosensitive semiconductor devices and light emitting diodes (LEDs) also registered significant exports.

While the cumulative share of top ten electronics exports declined continuously from about 51 per cent in 1996 to 42 per cent in 2006, there was considerable diversification especially between 2001 and 2006. By 2006, the share of computer parts and accessories came down to just 6.5 per cent although its rank dropped only to the second place. Static converters became India's largest electronics export product, with a share of 11 per cent. A lot of new products had come into the top ten export list, including transformers, medical equipment and their parts, transmit-receive apparatus for radio, telephone, etc. Exports of colour TV and parts of line telephone/telegraph equipment, nes. continued to be significant. In 2010, cell phones (within the category 'transmit-receive apparatus for radio, telephone, etc.' – HS 852520) became the single largest exports with a 20 per cent share of total electronics exports.[13] This was accompanied by significant surges in the shares of printed circuits, photovoltaic devices and LEDs, colour TVs, parts of telecom equipment and other telephonic or telegraphic apparatus (encryption devices, data security equipment, DSL, VPN, etc.). On the contrary, computer parts and accessories registered a major drop in its share after 2006 and dropped out of the top ten list after 2010. While transmit-receive apparatus for radio, telephone, etc. continued to be the top electronics export product, its share dropped significantly after 2010 to 7.5 per cent in 2014.

On the import side, it is seen that concentration has increased significantly. The cumulative share accounted by the top ten imports increased from about 39 per cent in 1996 to 48 per cent in 2001 and further to 58.5 per cent in 2006 (see Table 4.6). Since the mid-2000s, this cumulative share has been sticky around 58 per cent.

In 1996, when domestic production of computers was still significant, India's single largest import item was computer parts and accessories with a share of 9 per cent of the total. The second and

Table 4.5 India's major electronics exports, 1996–2014

S. no.	HS 1996 product code	Product description	Liberalisation category	Ranks (based on percentage share in total electronics exports in each year)					Share (percentage)
				1996	2001	2006	2010		2014
1	852520	Transmit-receive apparatus for radio, telephone, etc.	ITA-1	63	14	5	1		7.5
2	851790	Parts of line telephone/telegraph equipment, nes.	ITA-1	28	46	18	7		6.6
3	850440	Static converters	ITA-1	54	37	1	4		5.9
4	851780	Other telephonic or telegraphic apparatus (encryption devices, data security equipment, DSL, VPN, etc.)	ITA-1	91	179	87	8		3.2
5	852812	Colour TVs	Non-ITA-1	4	12	12	5		2.9
6	901839	Syringes, needles, catheters, cannulae and the like – Other	Non-ITA-1	90	27	16	18		2.9
7	901890	Other instruments and appliances	Non-ITA-1	16	9	11	12		2.7
8	852390	Unrecorded sound recording media except photo/magnetic	ITA-1	29	65	63	11		2.6
9	854140	Photosensitive semiconductor devices; light emitting diodes	ITA-1	40	6	3	3		2.3
10	850490	Parts for transformers, inductors, converters, etc.	ITA-1	24	8	10	15		2.2

11	903289	Regulating or controlling instruments other than thermostats, monostats, hydraulic or pneumatic	Non-ITA-1	25	36	32	38	2.1
12	853400	Printed circuits	ITA-1	9	7	8	2	2.0
13	850423	Liquid dielectric transformers – Having a power handling capacity exceeding 10,000 kVA	Non-ITA-1	33	11	4	6	1.9
14	852990	Other aerials	ITA-1	34	17	6	21	1.7
15	841821	Refrigerators, household type – Compression-type	Non-ITA-1	99	44	21	26	1.7
16	850421	Liquid dielectric transformers – Having a power handling capacity not exceeding 650 kVA	Non-ITA-1	12	25	28	19	1.6
17	847330	Computer parts and accessories	ITA-1	2	1	2	9	1.5
18	853650	Other switches	ITA-1	72	48	17	25	1.5
19	853620	Automatic circuit breakers	Non-ITA-1	64	61	24	34	1.4
20	903300	Parts and accessories (nes.) for machines, appliances, instruments or apparatus of Chapter 90	Non-ITA-1	53	19	50	17	1.4

Note: nes., not elsewhere specified.

Source: Author's calculations based on WITS COMTRADE data.

Table 4.6 India's major electronics imports, 1996–2014

S. no.	HS 1996 product code	Product description	Liberalisation category	Ranks (based on percentage share in total electronics imports in each year)				Share (percentage)
				1996	2001	2006	2010	2014
1	852520	Transmit-receive apparatus for radio, telephone, etc.	ITA-1	10	3	1	1	18.8
2	851780	Other telephonic or telegraphic apparatus (encryption devices, data security equipment, DSL, VPN, etc.)	ITA-1	69	68	22	3	7.8
3	851790	Parts of line telephone/telegraph equipment, n.e.s.	ITA-1	15	9	8	2	6.9
4	847130	Laptops and other portable units	ITA-1	53	19	7	6	5.7
5	854230	Other monolithic integrated circuits	ITA-1	39	27	10	7	3.7
6	847330	Computer parts and accessories	ITA-1	1	1	2	5	3.6
7	852390	Unrecorded sound recording media except photo/magnetic	ITA-1	62	47	59	4	3.0
8	847160	Computer input or output units	ITA-1	12	8	5	12	2.8
9	852812	Colour TVs	Non-ITA-1	109	112	14	10	2.7
10	852990	Other prepared unrecorded media for sound recording	ITA-1	3	5	4	8	2.7
11	847150	Other digital processing units, whether or not containing in the same housing one or two of the following types of unit: storage units, input units, output units	ITA-1	108	16	9	13	2.3

No.	HS Code	Description	ITA					
12	847170	Storage units	ITA-1	8	2	6	9	2.3
13	854140	Photosensitive semiconductor devices, light emitting diodes	ITA-1	73	61	26	18	1.9
14	850440	Static converters	ITA-1	24	20	12	11	1.9
15	901890	Other instruments and appliances	Non-ITA-1	11	6	11	14	1.4
16	852540	Still image video cameras and other video camera recorders	ITA-1	257	94	31	17	1.3
17	903180	Other scientific instruments, appliances and machines	Non-ITA-1	6	11	13	15	1.3
18	854389	Other machines and apparatus:– Other	ITA-1	38	25	15	19	1.1
19	903289	Regulating or controlling instruments other than thermostats, monostats, hydraulic or pneumatic	Non-ITA-1	22	21	17	21	1.0
20	850490	Parts of transformers, converter, inductors, etc.	ITA-1	23	28	38	23	0.8

Source: Author's calculations based on WITS COMTRADE data.

third positions were held by other monolithic digital ICs, as well as parts for radio telephony, TV, radar apparatus, etc. Imports of cathode-ray tubes (CRTs) for colour TVs and video monitors, as well as optical or magnetic readers were also important, which continued to be the case in 2001. However, in 2001, within 5 years of the tariff reduction initiated under the ITA-1, the share of computer parts and accessories went up to 16 per cent of the total, followed by computer storage units in the second rank (Table 4.6). This reflects the increase in domestic assembly of computer sets in this phase using imported parts and components that had become cheaper due to ITA-1. Similarly, there was a huge increase in the shares of telecom imports too.

By 2006, transmit-receive apparatus for radio, telephone, etc. – which had already become the third largest import by 2001 – came to top imports constituting nearly one-fourth of all electronics imports.[14] While computer parts and accessories continued in the second place even in 2006, we also observe a significant increase in the shares of laptops, printers and key boards, computer storage devices and other monolithic ICs. Transmit-receive apparatus for radio, telephone, etc. (HS 852520) continued to be the single largest import in 2010 and 2014 with a share of 18 per cent of the total. Other telephonic or telegraphic apparatus (encryption devices, data security equipment, DSL, VPN, etc.), along with parts of line telephone/telegraph equipment, continued to be the next largest imports. Computer parts and accessories, laptops, printers and key boards and other monolithic digital ICs, other prepared unrecorded media for sound recording, colour TVs, etc. remained the other major imports.

Out of the top twenty imports, the majority were ITA-1 products whose import shares went up significantly following the rapid trade liberalisation under ITA-1. These included telecommunication apparatus and parts, computers, laptops, monolithic ICs, semiconductor devices and LEDs and static converters. Exceptions among ITA-1 products whose import shares dropped were computer parts and accessories, computer storage units and unrecorded media for sound recording. As discussed in the previous section, in the absence of strategic industrial policy support that had failed to domestically link the growth in demand for hardware arising from the success in software exports, Indian computer hardware producers lost out to imports. This got reflected in the decline in the share of computer parts and accessories within exports too. Once India began importing greater volumes of finished computers, laptops, etc., duty-free, it adversely impacted most segments of the domestic computer industry and the need for parts and accessories reduced. However, as expected, import demand for computer input/output units, remained steady. On the other side, imports of cell phone parts also increased to support import-dependent assembly of cell phones ('transmit-receive apparatus for radio, telephone, etc.'), as did other telecom equipment imports that increased in tandem with the huge expansion in the domestic telecom market in the 2000s. In the case of non-ITA-1 products such as transformer parts and scientific instruments too, import demand remained significant. On the other side, import share of colour TVs, a non-ITA-1 product had already begun increasing by 2006, well before TV imports were liberalised under the India-South Korea CEPA from 2016. This, as we saw earlier, reflected the poor competitiveness and technological upgrading capabilities of the domestic TV industry, which despite having built up a few national brands like Videocon could not survive the increased import competition in the absence of productivity growth.

It is clear that, given the domestic electronics industry's development path of the preceding decades without any government-directed effort in creating capabilities and scale, its sudden exposure to severe external competitive pressures with trade liberalisation under the ITA-1 from the late 1990s, which was compounded by trade liberalisation under the FTAs from the mid-2000s has led to a continued surge in imports. It is also clearly seen that tariff liberalisation did not lead to any sustainable expansion in India's electronics exports after the initial surge.

The above analysis also reveals that, while there was some two-way trade in computers along with their parts and accessories as well as ICs in the first period, the nature of two-way trade changed by the mid-2000s. In particular, since 2006, the majority of two-way trade is observed among various kinds of telecommunication apparatus and parts, as well as ICs, static converters, other electronic parts and components along with scientific, measuring instruments. We will examine these changes in detail in the following section. Towards this, it is useful to identify the major trading partners and those with whom there was significant two-way trade.

The cumulative share of top ten markets for Indian electronics exports dropped continuously between 1996 and 2014, falling from 80 per cent in 1996 to 55 per cent in 2014. This was mainly accounted for by the drop in the shares of the US, Singapore and the UK. In the case of electronics exports, the US was the single largest market for India throughout the study period 1996–2014 (see Table 4.7). But its share in India's exports dropped from about 26 per cent to 15 per cent in 2014. The other major markets have been Singapore, Germany, UK and the UAE, which have consistently remained among the next top five markets with varying ranks. The UAE, which was the third largest market from 2001 onwards, became the second largest in 2014.[15] Malaysia was an important market for Indian electronics exports between 1996 and 2001, but dropped out of the top six list subsequently. China, which had moved up to the seventh rank in 2005, went down to the tenth rank in 2010 and climbed up to the fourth rank in 2014. The share of India's electronics exports going to China increased from 0.2 per cent in 1996 to 4.5 per cent in 2014. The odd one out was Austria, which became the second largest market in 1 year alone (2010) with a share of 7 per cent. However, other EU members such as France, Italy and the Netherlands continued to be among the top ten markets.

The sole developing country export market in the early phase was Bangladesh, which dropped in share and rank after 2001. However, Nigeria, followed by Saudi Arabia, Vietnam, Turkey, Indonesia, South Africa, Brazil, Sri Lanka, etc., have become other important developing country markets with increasing shares of electronics exports. Thailand's share shows a minor increase, while that of the Philippines declined. In the case of other major FTA partners such as Japan and South Korea, there was a slight reversal in the declining shares of both these countries between 2010 and 2014. But interestingly, the fastest growing markets during 2005–2010 and 2010–2014 were the African states like Guinea-Bissau, Somalia, Central African Republic, Lesotho, etc. or island states like Aruba, French Polynesia, Cayman Islands, St. Kitts and Nevis, Montserrat and Iceland, as well as some European countries like Portugal, Hungary and Estonia.

It is clear that Indian electronics exports going to developed country markets have all declined in share when compared to those to developing countries. To the extent that there are domestic firms involved in production, this would reflect domestic firms' inability to meet the standards in developed country markets with technologically superior demand. But given that the dominant producers in the Indian electronics industry are MNCs, this is reflective of

Table 4.7 Major markets for India's electronics exports, 1996–2014

S. no.	Country	1996	2001	2005	2008	2010	2014	CAGR (2005–2014)
1	United States	25.7	19.9	23.4	16.0	16.2	14.7	–4.0
2	United Arab Emirates	6.6	6.3	7.4	6.6	6.8	8.6	–0.9
3	Singapore	10.4	5.2	5.8	7.0	6.8	5.0	1.8
4	China	0.2	1.4	2.8	2.2	2.8	4.5	0.2
5	Netherlands	2.8	6.4	3.7	5.5	3.9	4.4	0.4
6	United Kingdom	14.8	3.5	6.0	3.6	2.7	4.4	–8.4
7	Germany	3.6	4.0	8.6	9.3	5.2	4.2	–5.5
8	France	1.0	1.3	1.5	1.6	1.7	3.8	1.1
9	Hong Kong, China	3.0	1.9	1.9	2.3	3.8	2.7	7.9
10	Israel	0.2	0.2	0.9	1.0	0.6	2.5	–4.7
	Total exports (million USD)	879	1246	2360	4502	7507	7652	13.7

Source: Author's calculations based on WITS COMTRADE data.

their market strategy, which in turn is determined by their division of labour across countries. The above trend is reflective of the fact that, because of the lack of national capabilities, MNCs' production strategy in India involves only some exports to developing countries, while being mainly geared towards the large domestic market.

It is relevant to note here that exporting to developed country markets have become more difficult because of their growing use of non-tariff measures in the form of technical barriers to trade (TBT) (Kallummal 2012). Not only did developed countries account for a majority of the total TBT notifications to the WTO, the majority of these were national standards (Kallummal 2012).[16] Current barriers to trade are primarily linked to requirements on product standards, testing and certification, consumer protection and the environment. Further, there are differences between the standards and regulations in the US and the EU. All of these make significantly greater demands on production sophistication in the case of exports to developed country markets. In this sense, the fact that India's export market access in developed countries has not been sustained and that firms have instead taken the low road through increased exports to developing countries is also evidence of the market failure that arises in the absence of strategic industrial policies to develop the national technological base.

When it comes to imports, the US, followed by Singapore and Japan were the top three import suppliers for India until 2001. However, the shares of India's electronics imports originating from all these countries have seen continuous decline. China became the single largest import supplier after 2001 (see Table 4.8). Its share in electronics imports, which increased from 3 per cent in 1996 to 8 per cent in 2001, had shot up to 23 per cent by 2005 and continued to increase further. With a share of about 48 per cent, almost half of all India's electronics imports in 2014 originated from China. Despite the sharp drop in the US share from 22 per cent in 1996 to just 7 per cent in 2014, it has remained the second most important import supplier. Singapore's share dropped from 13 per cent to 4.5 per cent between 1996 and 2014. Japan's share dropped from 12 per cent in 1996 to about 3 per cent in 2014.

South Korea has remained the other major import supplier, with its rank ranging between second and fourth. Germany has been another major supplier with its rank hovering around fifth, even as its share witnessed a drop. Similarly, Malaysia has maintained a rank around sixth position. Meanwhile, Vietnam registered

Table 4.8 India's major suppliers for electronics imports, 1996–2014 (Percentage share in each year's total imports)

S. no.	Country	1996	2001	2005	2010	2014	CAGR (2005–2014)
1	China	3.1	7.9	23.0	41.5	47.5	8.4
2	United States	21.6	16.5	12.3	8.0	7.3	-5.6
3	South Korea	5.1	7.3	12.9	5.8	5.7	-8.6
4	Singapore	13.4	12.7	9.7	6.0	4.5	-8.2
5	Germany	8.7	7.1	5.5	5.2	4.5	-2.3
6	Malaysia	5.0	7.3	5.1	4.1	4.2	-1.9
7	Vietnam	0.0	0.0	0.0	1.2	2.8	78.4
8	Japan	11.6	7.0	4.4	3.5	2.8	-5.2
9	Thailand	1.1	4.3	1.7	1.7	2.4	3.6
10	Other Asia, n.e.s.	4.4	4.1	2.6	2.4	2.3	-1.1
	Total imports (million USD)	1829	4176	13759	29915	39759	

Source: Author's calculations based on WITS COMTRADE data.

nes., not elsewhere specified.

one of the strongest export growth to India in electronics, with its import share jumping from 2010 onwards, the year in which the India-ASEAN FTA came into existence. As a result, Vietnam's rank among India's electronics import suppliers jumped from 221 in 1996 to 16 in 2014. Thailand also moved up from the 18th to the 9th rank between 1996 and 2014. In the 10th rank was other Asia n.e.s., which appears to be Taiwan. While the share of India's imports from most European countries experienced a drop, those of Mexico and Israel increased.

It is important to note that, even though China had joined the ITA-1 only in 2004, it had tariff-free access in ITA-1 products to the Indian market from 1997 when India had begun reducing tariffs.[17] Interestingly, India's overall electronics imports from China were already dominated by ITA-1 products in 1996, reflecting the integration of China into the East Asian electronics value chains by the early 1990s. Parts for sound/video recording and reproducing apparatus as well as parts for radio/TV/transmission apparatus were the largest imports. But cathode-ray colour TV picture tubes, a non-ITA product, were the third largest imports from China in 1996. There were three more non-ITA-1 products with at least a 1 per cent share in imports from China in this phase. However, by 2001, the drastic trade liberalisation that India carried out under the ITA-1 meant that ITA-1 products became more significant and constituted all the top ten imports from China. There was a change in composition of the top ten imports, with an initial sharp increase in the shares of computer parts and accessories, although this declined significantly thereafter. Transmit-receive apparatus for radio and TV became the single largest electronics import from China by 2006 and has remained so. Laptops became the second largest import item by 2010 and were followed by parts of electrical apparatus for line telephony/telegraphy. Another important change that occurred is that the share of colour TVs – a non-ITA product – also began increasing from 2010 onwards. By 2014, India was importing photosensitive semiconductor devices also from China. It is ironic that, while China had not signed the ITA-1 until 2004 nor signed an FTA with India until now, Chinese firms which had matured under strategic guidance from the state were able to gain significant market access in India. The successful latecomer entry by Chinese firms into the global electronics oligopoly market was made possible only as a result of China's extensive and highly interventionist long-term industrial development strategy (Ernst 2014: 26 and 31).

China accounted for nearly 58 per cent of India's total electronics industry trade deficit in 2014. India's electronics trade deficit with South Korea has also increased tremendously, followed by that of Malaysia, Vietnam and Thailand (all FTA partners), while India also continues to have high trade deficit with the US, Germany, Singapore and Japan. Countries with which India has had a consistent trade surplus in electronics trade are all developing countries like the UAE, Nigeria, Saudi Arabia, Bangladesh, Turkey, Kenya, Sri Lanka, Nepal and Myanmar, while South Africa has also emerged recently with trade surplus.

Inter- and intra-industry trade patterns in the electronics industry

Against the backdrop of the observed intra-industry trade (IIT) flows at the HS 6-digit level, an in-depth analysis of bilateral trade flows is carried out in order to understand the extent and nature of India's participation in electronics value chains. Despite considerable advance, misinterpretations abound in the discourse surrounding the use of the term IIT and several authors appear to draw incorrect inferences based on aggregate level IIT estimates. We need to critically consider our understanding of IIT in order to be able to fathom the connections between trade and investment liberalisation, firm strategies and the accompanying production restructuring that occurs within GVCs.

When GVCs boost network trade within a particular industry in the process of fragmenting production processes, this shows up as two-way trade in aggregated trade data. As mentioned earlier, not all increase in two-way trade observed in India's trade in HS chapters 84 (non-electrical machinery) and 85 (electrical machinery) can be considered as IIT. For instance, as we saw above, even as there is significant two-way trade in HS Chapter 84, this is occurring as imports of hard disk drives (HDDs) and exports of computer input or output units. That is, the country is importing the HDDs as an intermediate into the production of a final good, computer, for the domestic market. At the 6-digit level, this shows up as a case of inter-industry trade, which is typically not considered as part of network trade. However, in the broadest sense, this is also part of GVC trade when the import for domestic production is part of an overall division of labour strategy of a foreign-invested firm in the host country. Earlier studies like Fontagné et al. (2006) did not also consider intermediate inputs imported by a firm for assembly into final products for exports as linked to GVCs. This too will get captured under inter-industry trade when the imported intermediate product and the exported final good are represented by different product codes – whether by domestic firms or by foreign-invested firms as part of an MNC's GVC strategy.

Thus analysis using bilateral trade data even at the 6-digit level subsumes four cases, which can be part of a value chain directly or indirectly:

1   when the intermediate product/s imported by a domestically owned firm and the final product exported by it are represented by the same product codes;
2   when the intermediate product/s imported by a domestically owned firm and the final good exported by it are represented by different product codes;
3   when intermediate products imported by a foreign-affiliated firm and the higher value-added intermediate product or final product exported by it are represented by the same product codes; and
4   when intermediate products imported by a foreign-affiliated firm and the higher value added intermediate product or final product exported by it are represented by different product codes.

These various ways of value chain engagement can be examined only at the firm level, through an analysis of sales and sourcing patterns of foreign-invested and domestically owned enterprises.[18]

Several studies that have analysed IIT distinguished between two types of IIT, based on important developments in theoretical literature distinguishing between horizontal and vertical product differentiation. As pointed out by Fontagné et al. (2006), in contrast to the simplistic opposition between inter-industry trade (because of price differences arising from comparative advantage differential that leads to inter-industry specialisation) and intra-industry trade (IIT) – seen as two-way trade of differentiated products within an industry with similar prices – there are both empirical evidence and theoretical arguments in favour of two-way trade of qualitatively differentiated products within an industry.[19] Accordingly, IIT itself has been divided into two parts: IIT in horizontally differentiated (i.e., similar priced) products and IIT in vertically differentiated products (i.e., differing by quality and hence, price).

Horizontal intra-industry trade (HIIT) is largely driven by preference for diversity, while vertical intra-industry trade (VIIT) is seen driven by differing factor endowments. High quality varieties embody larger contents of capital, skilled labour or R&D. Thus intra-industry trade in vertically differentiated goods (VIIT) involves some elements of comparative advantage.[20] That is, VIIT is characterised by differences in factor endowments (including created capabilities), which determines the division of labour in value chains involving vertical specialisation. These differences can be detected empirically only by examining trade flows at a disaggregated (i.e., product) level, rather than at the industry level (Fontagné et al. 2006).[21] At the HS 6-digit level, the possibility of aggregation of different products within one product category is minimised. This justifies the assumption made that differences in prices (unit values) within each product category reflect differences in quality.

We break down India's bilateral trade flows with each of the major trade partners identified earlier, into the three categories, at the HS 6 digit product category level: (i) inter-industry trade (one-way trade), (ii) IIT in horizontally differentiated products and (iii) IIT in vertically differentiated products. First of all, trade in those HS 6-digit products for which the difference between the bilateral export and import values is more than 10 per cent is identified as IIT. Thus products for which imports has an overlap of less than 10 per cent of exports or vice versa (checked by examining whether the minority flows represent at least 10 per cent of the majority flow), are considered as belonging to the inter-industry trade category.

Once we delineate inter-industry trade, a distinction is made between varieties of IIT to capture the nature of vertical specialisation. In order to identify vertical and horizontal IIT, we adopt the methodology used by studies such as Fontagné et al. (2006), Fukao et al. (2003), Hurley (2003), etc. The starting point is the assumption that differences in prices (unit values) within one product category mirror differences in quality.[22] First of all, trade in those HS 6-digit products for which the difference between the bilateral export and import values is more than 10 per cent is identified as IIT. In the next step, unit values (UV) of exports and imports are employed to delineate the two types of IIT.[23] Within IIT, vertical IIT is thus identified as that portion of identified intra-industry trade, which involves products with relative export/import unit values greater than 1.25. For products which exhibit VIIT, we look at the unit value difference with a trading partner to understand whether India is exporting the higher priced, and therefore higher quality, product within a product category or not.[24] While the decomposition of IIT based on unit value dispersion is considered the most comprehensive approach to date, it is important to keep in mind that unusual dispersion of unit values signals a high probability of classification failure due to the heterogeneity of the HS 6-digit heading or due to a measurement error (Fontagné et al. 2006).

The advantage of this method is that it allows us to understand the extent of India's participation in GVCs as well as the nature of its engagement in GVCs in terms of India's relative position vis-à-vis her major trading partners at the product level. We consider both HIIT and VIIT as part of GVC trade given that GVCs increasingly involve complex horizontal and vertical production-sharing strategies. But examination of unit prices in VIIT allows us to analyse the difference in technological capabilities between any two trading partners. This approach may be considered as going beyond the analysis that is done using the Trade-In-Value-Added (TiVA) database.

In this study, we examined the changes in the nature of bilateral IIT in Indian electronics industry trade between 1999 and 2014.[25] The analysis was carried out for all of India's major import suppliers. Table 4.9 summarises the results of the exercise in terms of the

Table 4.9 Change in the relative importance of IIT in India's bilateral two-way trade in electronics

S. no.	Trading partner	Share of IIT in total bilateral trade (percentage)		
		1999	*2014*	*Change, 1999–2014 (percentage points)*
1	China	61.0	98.2	37.2
2	South Korea	17.6	53.5	35.9
3	Singapore	90.0	90.5	0.5
4	Malaysia	91.7	98.4	6.7
5	Thailand	69.9	96.7	26.8
6	US	93.7	99.1	5.4
7	Germany	86.2	94.4	8.2
8	UK	85.3	97.5	12.2
9	Japan	65.0	94.5	29.5
10	Vietnam	3.8	92.3	88.5

Source: Author's calculations based on WITS COMTRADE data.

changes in the levels of bilateral intra-industry trade (IIT) between India and these countries. It is clearly observable that between 1999 and 2014, the levels of IIT within bilateral trade increased across-the-board, with significant increase in seven out of these ten major trading partners. The largest increase was seen in the case of Vietnam, which was followed by China, South Korea, Japan and Thailand.

The further decomposition of India's bilateral IIT with these countries in terms of horizontal and vertical IIT shows interesting results (Table 4.10). In the case of China and South Korea, the share of vertical IIT in total bilateral intra-industry trade showed a drastic decline by 2014. In both these cases, India was therefore trading more in horizontally differentiated products in 2014.

In the case of China, it was seen that, while expansion in horizontal IIT contributed to the increase in IIT between 1999 and 2014, this involved a large number of non-ITA products contrary to the pattern seen in India's overall bilateral trade with China. But as much as 96 per cent of bilateral HIIT was imports. Clearly, the volume of exports from India was very low.

In the US case, despite some increase in VIIT, the high level of IIT continued to be dominated by trade in horizontally differentiated products. But overall, imports dominated HIIT with the US and more non-ITA products than ITA-1 products were involved in this

Table 4.10 Change in the relative importance of vertical IIT in India's bilateral IIT in electronics

S. no.	Trading partner	Share of VIIT in bilateral IIT (percentage)		
		1999	2014	Change, 1999–2014 (percentage points)
1	China	99.0	78.6	−20.4
2	South Korea	100.0	47.5	−52.5
3	Singapore	96.8	96.5	−0.3
4	Malaysia	33.2	99.6	66.4
5	Thailand	77.1	98.3	21.2
6	US	18.7	25.6	6.9
7	Germany	72.3	79.6	7.3
8	UK	84.2	87.8	3.6
9	Japan	88.8	80.9	−7.9
10	Vietnam	32.3	91.0	58.7

Source: Author's calculations based on WITS COMTRADE data.

trade in 2014. India's top most exports involved in HIIT were colour TVs, electro-diagnostic devices, along with other professional instruments and appliances, parts and accessories of professional and scientific appliances, etc., which were all non-ITA products. Two ITA-1 products among the top ten horizontally differentiated exports to the US were photosensitive semiconductors and printed circuits, for which India's exports were greater than imports from the US. On the other side, top HIIT imports from the US were miscellaneous electro-diagnostic apparatus, other electrical machines and apparatus, other computers, other testing/professional appliances, other monolithic ICs, as well as a range of medical appliances and instruments, etc.

The increase in bilateral IIT observed for Germany and the UK was also mostly driven by increased trade in horizontally differentiated products. India had trade deficits with these countries too.

There is significant heterogeneity in India's electronics trade transactions with her major FTA partners. On the one side, as we saw above, in the case of two major partners, China and South Korea, most of the increased bilateral IIT was due to increase in trade in horizontally differentiated products. On the other side, India's trade with Japan continued to be dominated by vertically differentiated products, despite a decline in its share as compared to 1999 (Table 4.10). When it comes to ASEAN partners, India's vertical IIT was always high with Singapore, which is attributable to the latter's entrepot role in the context of the East Asian electronics production networks (that was well established by the early 1990s). However, we observe a significant rise in the relative importance of vertical IIT in the case of Malaysia, Thailand and Vietnam. This would point to an increased degree of trade integration between India and the ASEAN trading partners involving vertical specialisation. However, given that some heterogeneity in products was observed at the 6-digit level categorisation of products (which was also reflected in very high unit value dispersion in certain cases), we have to keep in mind that there could be some overestimation of IIT as well as VIIT.

A comparison of India's bilateral export and import unit values (based on deflated US dollar values) in vertically differentiated products (Table 4.11) helps us to examine the relative quality levels of Indian products involved in observed bilateral IIT. It is observed that, in terms of number of products, a larger proportion of India's VIIT with China in 2014 involved exports with higher unit value

Table 4.11 Status of India vis-à-vis major partners in bilateral VIIT

Bilateral partner	Percentage share of VIIT products in which India had higher unit value in 1999 (based on number of products)	Percentage share of VIIT products in which India had higher unit value in 2014 (based on number of products)	Share in India's electronics imports (2014)	India's electronics trade balance with the partner (2014)
China	73	85	47.5	Deficit
US	38	41	7.3	Deficit
South Korea	75	41	5.7	Deficit
Germany	30	45	4.5	Deficit
Singapore	42	55	4.5	Deficit
Malaysia	47	54	4.2	Deficit
Thailand	45	73	2.4	Deficit
Vietnam	50	65	2.8	Deficit
Japan	43	62	2.8	Deficit

Source: Author's calculations based on WITS COMTRADE data.

vis-à-vis imports when compared with 1999. This was true in the case of India's VIIT with Thailand also and to a lesser extent in the case of Vietnam and Japan. In contrast, in the case of US, Germany and South Korea, India was predominantly importing VIIT products with higher unit values. India's VIIT with Singapore and Malaysia appeared more balanced in terms of numbers.

However, when we analysed the share of import value (based on deflated US dollar value and adjusted to f.o.b. terms) in total bilateral vertical IIT, it is seen that, despite the large proportion of VIIT products in which India had higher unit value, the import share of VIIT products in bilateral VIIT had gone up in the case of China and Vietnam as well as South Korea (Table 4.12). Imports dominated VIIT in the case of Thailand, Malaysia, Japan, Singapore and Germany too. However, in the case of the US, the share of imports in bilateral VIIT showed a dramatic decline.

In order to further understand the relative importance of India's higher unit value exports in VIIT, we analysed their shares in bilateral trade. In the case of China, we examined the VIIT products in which India had higher export unit value bilaterally. It was observed that, in only 11 out of these 175 products, Indian exports

Table 4.12 Share of VIIT imports in total bilateral VIIT

Partner	Percentage share of VIIT imports in total bilateral VIIT	
	1999	*2014*
China	92	97
US	88	59
Germany	87	74
South Korea	53	60
Singapore	90	74
Malaysia	94	83
Thailand	92	87
Vietnam	74	92
Japan	89	84

Source: Author's calculations based on WITS COMTRADE data.

accounted for even a 0.1 per cent share in total bilateral electronics trade in 2014 (see Table 4.13). On the contrary, in 13 of these products Indian imports constituted at least a 1 per cent share in total bilateral trade, with imports of transmit-receive apparatus for radio and TV alone accounting for 32 per cent of total bilateral electronics trade. That is, although there were a large number of products in which India had higher export unit value bilaterally, these products were not significant in bilateral trade value. It was also observed that all major VIIT imports from China, except colour TVs, were ITA-1 products.

Similarly, in the case of Vietnam, not a single product in which India exhibited higher export unit value in VIIT in 2014 had even a 0.5 per cent share in total bilateral trade. As a result, the bilateral trade share of exports of all the VIIT products in which India saw higher export unit value added up to just 1.5 per cent. On the contrary, the bilateral trade share of imports in all these VIIT products (in which India saw higher export unit value) added up to 11 per cent. The top-most vertically integrated products were again the ITA-1 product, transmit-receive apparatus for radio and TV with an import share of 48 per cent in bilateral trade in 2014, followed by parts of electrical apparatus for line telephony with an import share of 14 per cent. Interestingly, all the top ten products involved in VIIT with Vietnam in 2014 were ITA-1 products. But wherever products that got liberalised under normal Track-1 or Normal

Table 4.13 Major products involved in India's bilateral VIIT with China, 2014

S. no.	Product	ITA-I product	Share of India's exports in bilateral trade	Share of India's imports in bilateral trade	Unit value difference (X unit value-M unit value)
1	Transmit-receive apparatus for radio, telephone, etc.	ITA-I	0.02	31.9	Positive
2	Other telephonic or telegraphic apparatus (encryption devices, data security equipment, DSL, VPN, etc.)	ITA-I	0.05	5.6	Positive
3	Input or output units, whether or not containing storage units in the same housing	ITA-I	0.01	3.9	Positive
4	Parts and accessories of the machines of heading No. 84.71	ITA-I	0.16	3.7	Positive
5	Other	ITA-I	0.09	3.3	Positive
6	Photosensitive semiconductor devices, including photovoltaic cells whether or not assembled in modules or made up into panels; light emitting diodes	ITA-I	0.01	2.6	Positive
7	Reception apparatus for television, whether or not incorporating radio-broadcast receivers or sound or video recording or reproducing apparatus:– Colour	Non-ITA	0.0	2.1	Positive

(Continued)

Table 4.13 (Continued)

S. no.	Product	ITA-1 product	Share of India's exports in bilateral trade	Share of India's imports in bilateral trade	Unit value difference (X unit value-M unit value)
8	Other monolithic integrated circuits	ITA-1	0.1	1.9	Positive
9	Static converters	ITA-1	0.3	1.7	Positive
10	Storage units	ITA-1	0.0	1.6	Positive
11	Digital processing units other than those of sub-headings 8471.41 and 8471.49, whether or not containing in the same housing one or two of the following types of unit: storage units, input units, output units	ITA-1	0.0	1.4	Positive
12	Still image video cameras and other video camera recorders	ITA-1	0.0	1.3	Positive
13	Other devices, appliances and instruments	ITA-1	0.0	1.2	Positive

Source: Author's calculations based on WITS COMTRADE data.

Track-2 of India-ASEAN FTA came into the top thirty list, imports clearly dominated over exports.

In the case of Thailand, out of the 107 VIIT products in which India had higher unit value exports, there were just two products with more than 1 per cent share in total bilateral trade. These were lighting and signalling equipment as well as other medical/dental apparatus. But only in the case of the latter did Indian exports hold a greater share in bilateral trade as compared to imports. In all the other products, India's imports from Thailand significantly outweighed India's exports to that country. Within these, imports of computer storage devices constituted as much as 21 per cent of total bilateral trade value, even when India showed a higher unit export value.

Among the 91 products in VIIT with Malaysia in which India exhibited higher export unit values, significant exports happened only in three products. Among these the export share was greater than import share only in two products. These were: liquid dielectric transformers and parts for burglar/fire alarms and similar apparatus. On the other side, top imports were colour TVs (with 22 per cent share – non-ITA product), followed by computer parts and accessories as well as other telephonic or telegraphic apparatus (encryption devices, data security equipment, DSL, VPN, etc.).

In VIIT trade with Singapore, India's exports were even a little bit significant in bilateral trade (with shares ranging between 0.5 per cent and 2 per cent) only in 8 out of 115 products in which India was exporting products with higher unit value. In the remaining majority of such products, imports dominated over exports. Overall, imports were more diversified compared to the cases above, with top import among VIIT products having a share of 13 per cent in bilateral trade ('other computers').

Evidently, even though India exported an increased number of higher value-added products in observed vertical IIT with most of the major trade partners (except the US, South Korea and Germany) in 2014 when compared to 1999, they involved insignificant shares in bilateral trade. Within the vast majority of vertically traded products in which India showed higher unit export value, volume of imports far outweighed that of exports. At one level, this means that, while India appears to have export capabilities in some higher value-added products, the scale of such export production is abysmally low to have a significant impact on broader productivity growth. These export capabilities could be of the 'enclave' sort, limited to some MNCs' production facilities. The dominance of imports evident from the detailed analysis of aggregate as well as bilateral intra-industry trade flows makes it clear that, even the small level of the FDI inflows that came into the electronics sector did not result in developing substantial production capabilities for exports. This, as we discussed earlier, is due to the fact that incentives for domestic production were negated by the non-strategic trade liberalisation which created larger markets for duty-free trade in electronics products and the absence of industrial policies promoting domestic linkages or technological development.

At another level, the above finding could also mean that only a small proportion of the imported intermediates got used in export production, which in turn points towards significantly increased import intensity of domestic production. The continuing growth in India's total electronics imports despite the declining trend in electronics exports would also point to this. The reason why this is not getting captured in higher inter-industry trade levels could be because of the inclusion of different types of products under the same 6-digit category. This is possible in such an industry with very rapid technological changes, owing to the rise of new products. This might have resulted in some classification errors[26] and could lead to an overestimation of IIT and VIIT even at the 6-digit level. This would point to an underestimation of inter-industry trade in electronics even at the 6-digit level. It is also evident that the individual bilateral IIT results presented above should be interpreted only within the context of the value of bilateral exports and imports.

Clearly, the rapid trade liberalisation under the ITA-1 and the subsequent WTO-plus liberalisation under India's comprehensive FTAs with the East and Southeast Asian countries have significantly changed the incentives facing producers in the Indian electronics industry. At one level, in the context of a liberal investment policy regime that had nil or ineffective industrial policy measures in place to develop competitive indigenous production and technological capability build-up,[27] deep trade liberalisation under overlapping FTAs – while enlarging the market – removes the tariff-hopping and other policy-driven incentives for MNCs to maintain parallel operations in India along with other countries for the same product lines. This leads them to rationalise their operations to exploit 'locational advantages'. That is, MNCs can meet the demand in specific regional or even global markets in particular products through affiliates in particular countries and choose to close similar production facilities in others (Kumar 2007a; Francis and Kallummal 2013;

Francis 2015b). Apart from foreign MNCs, industry-level restructuring in response to trade liberalisation clearly involves consequent changes in domestic firms' business strategies too. Thus at another level, deep and broad trade liberalisation – in the absence of industrial policies to build up national technological capabilities and a competitive domestic production base, increases domestic firms' incentives also for importing raw materials and intermediate products from FTA partners to carry out local assembly of final products or may completely remove their incentive to undertake any local production/assembly and lead to increased trading in electronics. As a result, production restructuring undertaken by the latter also contributes to changes in the industry's trade pattern.

Conclusion

This chapter examined the interplay between trade and FDI liberalisation and other industrial policies and its implications for India's electronics industry restructuring, towards understanding how these have influenced India's engagement in GVCs. It is observed that, given the domestic electronics industry's development path of the preceding decades without adequate government-directed effort for creating technological capabilities and scale in domestic firms, the industry's exposure to severe external competitive pressures with rapid trade liberalisation under the ITA-1 from the late 1990s created a major obstacle in its development trajectory. The tariff liberalisation of the computer and telecommunications industries under the ITA-1 was worsened by the rapid and deep tariff liberalisation under India's overlapping FTAs with East and Southeast Asian countries, with the latter extending it to several non-ITA-1 products, including consumer electronics and home appliances as well as professional, medical and scientific instruments and their parts.

A trade policy that promotes duty-free imports will clearly reduce incentives for domestic production in the absence of other policies that support the development and upgrading of indigenous capabilities for promoting domestic production. Moreover, the fact that there was no industrial strategy guiding tariff liberalisation in any strategic manner led to many final products becoming duty-free, while several components had to be imported paying tariffs. Despite having the advantage of a large domestic market, this became an adverse factor influencing producers' incentives even for domestic assembly, in the absence of a sufficiently developed domestic parts and components supply base. Despite its history of illustrious manufacturing and engineering capability development, Indian firms were not able to withstand the competition thrown open by the ITA-1.

This clearly reveals that access to liberalised markets do not remove the well-known market failures related to technological learning and upgrading (Joseph and Parayil 2006). If productivity were simply a function of the type of machinery and intermediate goods used, then the availability and accumulation of machinery and intermediate inputs following trade liberalisation under the ITA-1 should have helped India to be a manufacturer of quality electronic products, especially given that many of the operating technologies may be freely available. What is missing is the mix of organisational, operational and technological capabilities and skills that can only be developed through actual experience (see Khan 2010 for a detailed discussion) and accumulated through policy-induced learning efforts. Apart from creating disincentives for domestic production and displacing it, trade liberalisation leads to a disruption of this learning process when direct imports take over. The fact that a country like Vietnam which did not join the ITA managed to develop a rather successful ICT production base[28] while the Indian production base withered away, is revealing of the impact of using tariff liberalisation as a policy to bring about technology development and diffusion.

On the other side, successive governments' friendly policies towards FDI with a hands-off approach meant that there were also no policies linking foreign-invested firms and the domestic supply base (unlike, for instance, the indigenisation policy in the automobile industry), which could have let to vertical spillage effects and technological upgrading among domestic firms. Consequently, trade liberalisation has only seen India's growing demand for electronics products leading to high import dependence. The underlying reason behind the erosion of electronics manufacturing capabilities appears to be the absence of a visionary state with a long-term industrial development strategy, which guides trade liberalisation and ensures focused implementation of structural support policies that push firms to be productive and innovative as well as ensure backward linkages from foreign-invested companies to the domestic supplier base, as was the case in South Korea, Taiwan and, more recently, in China.

The consequences are reflected in the nature of the observed increase in India's two-way trade in electronics products. The trade analysis undisputedly establish that the observed rise in over-all intra-industry trade, whether it involved horizontal or vertical product differentiation, has only contributed to India's rising trade deficit with all her major electronics trading partners. While analysis at the 6-digit level of trade data could have led to some overestimation of IIT and VIIT, it was clearly observed that, within IIT, irrespective of whether horizontal IIT or vertical IIT dominated bilateral IIT, imports outweighed exports. Wherever there was an increase in vertical trade integration between India and the ASEAN trading partners, India's exports involved insignificant volumes compared to imports. This development trajectory has made the country's production lines and consumption dependent on other countries' production systems, in particular, China. Although there was evidence of relatively higher value-added production in a few product categories, it was seen that the Indian electronics industry's vertical trade integration could not lead to productivity-enhancing structural transformation in the industry (of the kind witnessed in South Korea, Taiwan or China) due to limited domestic backward linkages and productivity externalities leading to limited economies of scope and scale in local production. Lack of domestic linkages even in parts and components where India previously had capabilities is also relatable to the disincentive for local production due to the increased incentive to import final products under FTAs in the absence of vertical industrial policy support. This adds to the evidence we saw in Chapter 3 that developing countries' participation and upgrading in GVCs cannot take place without active industrial policy interventions to build up national technological capabilities and promote domestic linkages, while guiding investments towards increasing returns activities in order to generate domestic value addition in a sustainable manner.

The development trajectory of the Indian electronics industry clearly shows that, in the absence of coherent and coordinated industrial policy support to effectuate the firm-level, industry-level and economy-wide productivity conditions by upgrading indigenous capabilities, trade and investment policy liberalisation diluted and negated incentives for domestic production for both Indian and foreign producers in the electronics industry.

The huge increase in aggregate import dependence that has been experienced by the Indian electronics industry, the low level of FDI into the electronics industry and the evidence in import growth revealed by the analysis of bilateral inter-industry and intra-industry trade are all stark reflections of the impact of the interplay between the trade (and investment) liberalisation that has been carried out by India and the market failures associated with non-strategic trade and investment liberalisation in the absence of industrial policy support. This clearly points to the need to re-evaluate the premises underlying India's current trade and industrial policies, including those pursued with the purported objective of promoting GVC engagement.

As discussed already, one of the major policy offshoots of the interpretation that trade and FDI liberalisation (along with horizontal industrial policies) are sufficient to enable the manufacturing sector to get integrated into GVCs was seen in the policy shift to free trade agreements (FTAs). The next chapter shows that, even as the dynamics of GVCs, climate change and emerging trends in advanced manufacturing technologies increases the imperative for industrial policies of the selective or vertical kind, the use of many such policy instruments are getting further constrained under the FTAs.

Annexure 4.1 Concordance table for electronics products across ISIC revised classifications

ISIC (R1)	ISIC (R2)	ISIC (R3)	ISIC (R3.1)	ISIC (R4)	Industry segment
360	3825	2919	2919		Manufacture of weighing machines
		3000	3000		Manufacture of office, accounting and computing machinery
	3829	2930	2930		Manufacture of domestic appliances n.e.c. (domestic cooking ranges, refrigerators, laundry machines)
370	3832	3110	3110		Manufacture of radio transformers
		3120	3120		Manufacture of semiconductor circuits
		3190	3190		Manufacture of visual and sound signalling and traffic control apparatus
		3210	3210		Manufacture of electronic valves and tubes and other electronic components including fixed and variable electronic capacitors

ISIC (R1)	ISIC (R2)	ISIC (R3)	ISIC (R3.1)	ISIC (R4)	Industry segment
		3220	3220		Manufacture of television and radio transmitters and apparatus for line telephony and line telegraphy
		3230	3230		Manufacture of television and radio receivers, sound or video recording or reproducing apparatus and associated goods and radio transmitters and apparatus for line telephony and line telegraphy
		3311	3311		Manufacture of X-ray apparatus; electrotherapeutic apparatus
		3312	3312		Manufacture of radar equipment, radio remote control apparatus
		3530	Not included		Manufacture of communication satellites
391	3851	3311	3311		Manufacture of surgical, medical, dental equipment, instruments and supplies; orthopaedic and prosthetic appliances
		3312	3312		Manufacture of instruments and appliances for measuring and controlling equipment, except industrial process control equipment
		3313	3313		Manufacture of industrial process control equipment
	3852	3000	3000		Manufacture of photo-copying machines (R3)
		3311	3311		Manufacture of ophthalmic instruments
		3312	3312		Manufacture of scientific measuring instruments
392		3320	3320		Manufacture of optical instruments and photographic equipment
393	3853	3330	3330		Manufacture of watches and clocks
395	3902	3692	3692		Manufacture of musical instruments

Source: Author's own compilation based on ISIC classifications.

nes., not elsewhere specified.

Notes

1 Milberg and Winkler (2013) has established that, despite the expansion of GVCs, the share of intermediate trade that occurs in the form of arms-length transactions (as opposed to intra-firm trade between MNC divisions) has not declined – because of the proliferation of non-equity modes of internationalised production linkages between lead firms and their suppliers. See the analysis of intra-firm trade data between the US and its trading partners in Milberg and Winkler (2013: 41–42).
2 Under the HS 1996 nomenclature, there are a total of 5,113 items at the 6-digit level. Starting from the ISIC Rev.1 categories of non-electrical machinery and electrical machinery, we used concordance tables between various ISIC revised classifications to arrive at ISIC Rev.3 categories (at the 4-digit level) representing electronics sub-sectors. Subsequently, we used concordance between ISIC Rev. 3 and HS 1996 to arrive at a list of HS products belonging to the electronics industry. A definition guide to the electronics industry from the World Electronics Yearbook that gives HS 4-digit level product groups of electronics industry sub-sectors (that are concordant with SITC Revision 3) was also used while finalising the list of HS 1996 products chosen as belonging to the electronics industry.
3 According to Mani (2000b: 193–194), the terminal equipment industry and the cable manufacturing industry were deregulated in 1984 and accordingly, terminal equipment like electronic push button telephone instruments and facsimile machines were manufactured in the private sector since 1984. The switching equipment industry was also deregulated in 1985 allowing the private sector to invest in these industries, but large local switches continued to be a monopoly of the state-owned undertaking, ITI Ltd. (Mani 2000b: 195).
4 See Table 1 on p. 5 in Kumar and Joseph (2004): 4–6.
5 The government helped in the development of software industry also by generating large and complex assignments that gave confidence and management experience to the local firms. These include automation of railways reservation and bank automation, among others. See Kumar and Joseph (2004).
6 Some of these were joint ventures. See Mani (2005).
7 Interestingly, one of these already had an MFN duty of zero in 2007.
8 See UNCTAD (2014, 2016) for the use of WTO-compatible industrial policy measures by these and other countries.
9 Rao and Dhar (2016) consider foreign investors as belonging to two broad categories: one, who merely seek return on their investments and the other perceiving the host country operations as integral to their global operations. The first category essentially comprises a host of financial investors. It is the second category, which is considered as real FDI (RFDI).
10 Further, Verma (2015) found a persistent and overall rising negative net impact of foreign affiliates operating in high-technology manufacturing sub-sectors on the current account and the trade account of India's balance of payment (BoP) over the 1993–2013 period. This analysis

included 29 listed firms belonging to the electrical and non-electrical machinery industries, with foreign promoters' equity shareholding of 10 per cent share or more.

11 In the ensuing analysis, we consider the following major break points in the time series data for the 19 years covering 1996–2014: (i) 1996 (the year prior to the beginning of tariff reduction under the ITA-1), (ii) 2001 (the year immediately after the ITA-1 was implemented by all developed countries), (iii) 2005 (the year by which tariffs were eliminated on all ITA-1 products by India and also the year in which the India-Singapore CECA came into being), (iv) 2010 (the year in which the FTAs with ASEAN and South Korea took effect) and (v) 2014.

12 These averages exclude 2001 and 2008 with negative growth rates due to global slowdown in those years.

13 This had led to an increase in the top ten cumulative share from 42 per cent in 2006 to 55 per cent in 2010.

14 Given that the WITS COMTRADE data does not provide 8-digit level data, we examined the 8-digit level data for India's exports and imports for the product category HS 852520 using DGCIS data. It was clearly seen that, while imports of two-way radio communication equipment and other radio communication equipment (like VHF, UHF and microwave equipment) dominated imports until 2001, cell phones have been the dominant import product in this category since then.

15 This is mainly explained by the fact that the UAE, particularly Dubai, is a major import hub for the Middle East region aided by the Free Zones created in Dubai. A majority of the African market is also served through the re-export route (Ernst et al. 2015).

16 National standards are specific legislations that need to be adhered to by foreign producers to operate or sell in those markets. These may be different from the internationally harmonised standards by the International Standards Organisation (ISO). For details, see Kallummal (2012).

17 This is because the ITA-1 signatories had to extend the trade liberalisation to the non-ITA members of the WTO also following the most-favoured-nation (MFN) principle.

18 The author has commenced such a firm-level study of domestic and foreign-invested firms in the Indian electronics industry, with the support of the Indian Council for Social Science Research (ICSSR).

19 See Fontagné et al. (2006) for a review.

20 Vertical product differentiation is, therefore, related more to the traditional theory of international trade and its modified versions, while horizontal product differentiation is related to the new theories of international trade, which supposes horizontal product differentiation. *Ibid.*

21 The United Nation's classification of Broad Economic Categories (BEC), which defines the main end-use of products (primary, intermediate, capital or consumption goods), is especially useful in delineating these categories. Alternatively, one may rely on the import content of intermediate consumption, using input-output tables (Fontagné et al. 2006).

22 This assumption is only acceptable with the most detailed trade data, where aggregation of different products within one product category is minimised (Fontagné et al. 2006). Since relying on national tariff line data would restrict international comparisons, we have used HS 6-digit trade data.

23 As a result, we had to leave out products for which unit value data was unavailable.

24 However, as Fontagne et al. (2006) pointed out, unusual dispersion of unit values signals a high probability of classification failure due to the heterogeneity of the HS 6-digit heading or due to a measurement error.

25 The starting year had to be taken as 1999 as the relevant series of RBI's export and import price indices – used for deflating export-import values – has a base of 1999–2000 = 100. This however means that we do not have the opportunity to estimate the IIT values for 1996, to examine the pre-ITA-1 pattern. Following accepted international practice prescribed by the IMF, import values in cost, insurance and freight (CIF) terms were discounted by 10 per cent to obtain the corresponding free on board (FOB) values.

26 The very high unit value dispersion observed in some products categorised under VIIT could also be a reflection of this.

27 Here the reference is clearly to vertical industrial policies.

28 Vietnam joined the ITA only in 2006, with its tariff reduction schedule likely beginning in 2008 – this clearly gave the country a significantly long period to prepare the domestic production base.

Chapter 5

Industrial policy constraints in Indian FTAs

Introduction

One of the economic arguments behind the promotion of FTAs in Asia has been that increased trade liberalisation under FTAs would lead to dynamic and efficient industrial restructuring within the region led by MNCs. The previous chapter analysed the impact of WTO-plus FTA-driven tariff liberalisation on the Indian electronics industry against the backdrop of passive industrial policies. It was seen that rapid and deep trade liberalisation through overlapping FTAs generated disincentives for foreign and domestic producers to carry out domestic electronics manufacturing and led to India's increased import dependence despite the increase in two-way trade apparently reflecting the industry's participation in value chains. This adds to the evidence we saw in Chapter 3 that developing countries' participation in GVCs (let alone upgrading within them) cannot take place without active industrial policy interventions to build up national technological capabilities, while guiding investments towards increasing returns activities.

This requires India to create and continuously upgrade indigenous capabilities to manufacture products that lead to productivity growth and externalities required for generating virtuous cycles of growth. This imperative is further enhanced by the urgency to respond to the growing challenges arising from climate change, rapidly evolving digital technologies as well as emerging 're-localisation' or 'backshoring' trends in manufacturing industries. However, India faces significant challenges in formulating such vertical industrial policies under the FTAs signed since the mid-2000s.

As discussed elsewhere (Francis 2015b),[1] while the 'Look East' policy announced by the Indian government in 1992 is acknowledged to have played a role in India's move towards East Asian regionalism, both multilateral and regional factors have been important catalysts that accelerated India's trade policy shift involving FTAs. The literature on the rationale for the surge in India's preferential trade agreements (PTAs) thus mirror those found in the wider literature explaining the increased drive towards deep integration across countries, which are inter-linked aspects in the canvas of 'new regionalism'. Some of these describe 'the successful experiences' with regional economic integration in the industrialised countries since the mid-1980s, namely, the European Union (EU) and the North American Free Trade Agreement (NAFTA), as having prompted Southeast and South Asian countries (including India) to adopt or accelerate economic integration strategies from the late-1990s. This discussion ignores the severe problems faced by the East European developing economies in their rapid FDI-led industrial restructuring strategies during and after the integration with the EU, or by Mexico in the case of the NAFTA.[2] This explanation is also blind to the fact that (unlike popularly perceived and argued in sections of the literature) *de facto* regional integration was already relatively high in East and Southeast Asia by the late 1980s due to their involvement in MNC-driven production networks in several industries. The latter has been due to historical economic factors (going back to the political economy of the 1960s the 1985 Plaza Accord) and critical domestic policy initiatives that created entrenched capacities and interests that contributed to the attraction of MNCs to invest in and export from those economies. As argued in Francis and Kallummal (2009), state-led initiatives for regional integration centred on the Association of Southeast Asian Nations (ASEAN) in the 1990s are more appropriately analysed as a defensive strategy aimed at consolidating the existing regional trade-investment links between these small economies, in order to compete with the diversion of export-oriented foreign investments to other countries/regions in the wake of NAFTA and the liberalisation of China's FDI policies.[3] Subsequently, China's entry into the WTO in 2001 drove ASEAN members – many of which feared competition with China in third-country markets on MFN basis – to pursue various bilateral FTA initiatives at the individual and the bloc levels concurrently, in order to seek preferential access to their major markets. For instance, while Singapore, Thailand, Malaysia, Vietnam, etc. have bilateral FTAs with Japan, the EU, South Korea and India (among many others), ASEAN as a regional grouping also has FTAs with Japan, South Korea, the EU, India, etc.

The misconceptions tied to the causalities between liberalisation of trade and FDI policies and ASEAN and China's GVC participation and manufactured goods export expansion have significantly influenced India's policy approach towards FTAs. As more and more countries become members of multiple RTAs, the desire of the Indian government to avoid the perceived negative effects in terms of marginalisation in the export markets has played an important role, as the country feared exclusion from the perceived benefits of belonging to the RTAs.[4] With the ASEAN-China Free Trade Area (ACFTA) coming into being in 2004, competitive regionalism[5] also has played a role.[6] Despite its huge domestic market and a tradition of domestic manufacturing capabilities that called for a different approach, India drew wrong lessons from the East and Southeast Asian economies' varying development experiences.

Under these agreements, India, like several other developing countries, has made binding policy commitments that are stricter or more liberalising than those under the WTO. These go beyond greater tariff liberalisation (as they must be 'WTO plus' by definition under the WTO rules) to include regulatory aspects that severely impinge on national policymaking sovereignty. While ASEAN's initial regional market initiatives had focused only on investment liberalisation (apart from consolidating regional free trade), the FTAs that came into force in the region subsequently have been 'disciplining' national investment/industrial policies (Francis 2015b). Provisions in some FTAs on trade-related investment measures (TRIMs), intellectual property rights (IPR), agriculture, services, public procurement, etc. are examples for WTO-plus requirements. Many FTAs have also expanded their coverage to areas *beyond* those covered under the WTO such as investment protection, competition, environment, labour, human rights, etc. These have been referred to as WTO-extra provisions (Berger et al. 2016). Given that most of the WTO-plus deeper commitments relating to investment, IPR, services, etc. have been included in the FTAs mainly through the incorporation of what have been referred to as WTO-extra provisions (mostly through the investment chapter), we refer to all the above as WTO-plus provisions in this book.

Investment chapters or investment provisions are a major WTO-plus feature of several FTAs in the sense of having both broader and deeper regulatory commitments restricting industrial policy autonomy. Two major inter-related aspects of investment chapters in FTAs are of utmost importance in the context of the discussion

in the previous chapters. The first one relates to the broad definition of investment employed by them, and the second relates to an
expanding set of binding regulatory commitments, which restrict
FTA members' ability to apply policies related to the operations
of foreign investors (termed 'treatment of investment') and other
commitments that oblige members to guarantee protection of the
investments that come under the purview of the FTA. Another
WTO-plus constraint that has crept into some FTAs, which has significant implications for vertical industrial policies, is the definition
of expropriation to include indirect expropriation (Francis 2017).
Evidence shows that North-South agreements, in particular, those
with the United States (US), generally contain a larger number of
enforceable WTO-plus commitments than either North-North or
South-South agreements (see, for example, Thrasher and Gallagher
2008; WTO 2011; Kohl et al. 2013; UNCTAD 2014: 86–87). However, South-South FTAs also have increasingly included WTO-plus
provisions (Kumar 2007a; Sauve 2007; Kohl et al. 2013; Francis
2015b; etc.).

While several countries have been using the remaining policy
space available under the WTO ingeniously, WTO-plus provisions
in FTAs reduce policy sovereignty and heighten the risk of policy
failures by limiting the possibilities to redesign industrial development trajectories towards more sustainable paths. India is currently involved in 18 bilateral and regional FTAs.[7] India's major
bilateral and regional FTAs include those with Sri Lanka, Thailand,
the South Asian Association for Regional Cooperation (SAARC)
and ASEAN countries; the Asia-Pacific Preferential Trade Agreement (APTA) (involving Bangladesh, Sri Lanka, South Korea, Laos
and China); the India-MERCOSUR Preferential Trade Agreement
(PTA); the PTA with Chile; the Comprehensive Economic Cooperation Agreements (CECAs) with Singapore and Malaysia; and the
Comprehensive Economic Partnership Agreements (CEPAs) with
South Korea and Japan. All of India's FTAs since 2005 contain
WTO-plus provisions in many areas.

As known, India has entered into bilateral investment treaties
called Bilateral Investment Promotion & Protection Agreements
(BIPAs) with a number of countries in order to promote and protect bilateral investments on a reciprocal basis. India has so far
signed BIPAs with 82 countries, out of which 72 have been in
force. Although India's FDI policy has been progressively liberalised especially since the 1991 Industrial Policy and several BIPAs

with broad investment definitions have been in force,[8] the country still has the flexibility to change its industrial policy framework when the circumstances change or when the need for fine tuning it to meet industrial policy objectives is recognised (Francis 2015b). Much of this sovereignty has been surrendered by making BIT-plus and WTO-plus commitments on 'disciplining' different investment-related industrial policies and measures in the comprehensive trade agreements with Japan, South Korea, Malaysia, etc.[9]

This chapter provides a discussion of WTO-plus provisions in the last four major FTAs signed by India involving investment chapters or separate investment agreement (namely, India-Singapore CECA 2005, India-South Korea CEPA 2010, India-Japan CEPA 2011 and India-Malaysia CECA), which impinge most directly on the policy space for vertical industrial policies; their possible implications that ought to be kept in mind while planning any future trade agreements; and the industrial policy options that can still be exercised within a strategic industrial development framework.

WTO-plus tariff liberalisation in FTAs

For applying vertical industrial policies, countries should have the option of using tariffs on a selective basis, as and when needed for industrial upgrading, while remaining subject to multilateral disciplines (Akyuz 2007: 11). As mentioned in Chapter 2, even if a WTO developing country member has brought down its applied tariff levels in several industries through unilateral liberalisation as India has done, it still has the flexibility to raise its applied tariffs in any industry/product to the level at which it has bound multilaterally at the WTO if the need arises. It is only for raising tariff rates above their MFN bound levels that countries have to abide by rules on applying safeguard measures that relate to compensation to injured parties.[10] In principle, this means that developing countries can still use tariffs as an industrial policy tool if they want, in all those product lines where there is sufficient gap between the applied and MFN bound rates.

However, increase in market access through WTO-plus tariff liberalisation is one of the cornerstones of all FTAs. FTAs members have to reduce tariffs on 'substantially all' goods traded between them to be allowed an exception from the WTO's most-favoured-nation (MFN) treatment.[11] Consequently, under their bilateral or regional FTAs, developing countries have brought down duties on several tariff lines below the MFN bound levels and eliminated them or fixed them at significantly lower levels (often in the 0–5 per cent range).[12] This is one of the important ways in which policy flexibility has been lost for promoting particular manufacturing industries in developing countries. Liberalisation of agricultural tariffs in developing countries also has adverse impacts on sustainable industrial development trajectories by weakening the domestic inter-sectoral linkages between the production of local raw material and intermediate products and the manufacturing sector, apart from its adverse impact on farm livelihoods and food security.[13]

According to the Department of Commerce Annual Report (2009–2010), more than 31 per cent of India's non-agricultural tariff lines were unbound at the multilateral level at the commencement of the WTO's Doha Round in 2001. Further, despite the autonomous tariff liberalisation carried out by India since 1995 which brought down India's average applied tariff (for all non-agricultural tariff lines) to around 11 per cent in 2015, her average MFN bound tariff was 34 per cent (Dhar and Das 2015: 261). However, in its FTAs with ASEAN, Japan and South Korea, India committed to reducing or eliminating tariffs in almost all consumer goods, capital goods and intermediate goods. These include products belonging to industries such as organic and inorganic chemicals, metal and metal products, electrical and non-electrical machinery industries, etc., which have gone far beyond the country's commitments under the WTO, including under the Information Technology Agreement (ITA-1) as we saw in the previous chapter.

Another fallout of India's WTO-plus tariff liberalisation commitments under bilateral or regional FTAs is found in the inverted duty structures faced by several domestic end-product manufacturers. As a result of the fact that tariff liberalisation under FTAs has not been undertaken within a strategic industrial policy framework, India is facing higher duties on several parts and components whereas the end products are being imported duty-free (see Francis 2015b). Apart from tying up the government's hands under the tariff reduction schedules of the FTAs, such duty structures have incentivised end-product imports and dis-incentivised intermediate imports. This has compounded the post-WTO problems facing local manufacturing sector producers. Ironically, this feature of India's FTA tariff liberalisation was in fact, contradictory to the theoretical argument in favour of FTAs that increased preferential market access to intermediate products from partners will increase the competitiveness of India's final goods exports.

Overall, pursuant to such WTO-plus tariff liberalisation, the combined market share of 25 FTA partners in India's imports increased from 28.4 per cent in 2007 to 30.4 per cent in 2014. On the other side, even among 13 major FTA partners,[14] India's share in an FTA partner's imports increased in a stable manner between 2007 and 2014 only in three countries, namely, Brazil, Japan and Nepal. In fact, as a result of the higher degree of market penetration in India by FTA partners, India has experienced a higher level of import dependence on her FTA partners, as compared to world at large (see Figure 5.1).

By giving up the tariff flexibility that remained under her WTO commitments and thus reducing her industrial policy space under the recent FTAs, India's manufactured exports have been adversely impacted. The current policy focus is on reducing tariffs on intermediate goods to increase the competitiveness of final products exports. The dilemma here that, if the government brings down tariffs on parts and components significantly to improve the competitiveness of end-product manufacturers, it will reduce whatever possibilities exist for promoting domestic production of parts and components (Francis 2015a). As argued in Chapter 4, the central objective should be to ensure that locally produced intermediate

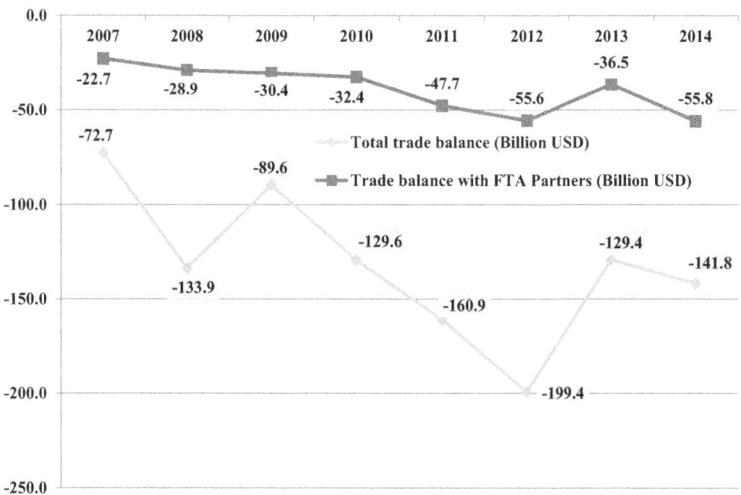

Figure 5.1 Trends in India's trade deficit with FTA partners, 2007–2014

Source: Author's calculations based on WITS COMTRADE data.

products achieve the necessary productivity increase to become competitive against imported intermediates; or else, the country will become progressively more import-dependent with adverse medium- and long-term consequences. It may be useful to allow manufacturers to access imported parts and components at reduced rates in a time-bound fashion conditional upon their establishing local manufacturing of such parts and components within a stipulated time frame, which is one way of ensuring that such foreign investments lead to technological spillovers in the local economy. Simultaneously, the government has to undertake public investments in R&D and industry-specific infrastructure development and financial support for improving technological capabilities necessary to sustain the process. Thus it will be critical to employ vertical industrial policy measures to simultaneously promote employment-generating domestic production and improve its productivity at the sectoral level, while mindful of the need to move away from carbon-intensive technologies. The scope for these kinds of policies has to be seen against the backdrop of the available space for vertical industrial policies under the WTO and FTAs.

WTO-plus investment policy constraints under FTAs

Investment chapters and provisions are a major WTO-plus feature of several FTAs in the sense of having both broader and deeper regulatory commitments.[15] While several bilateral investment treaties (BITs) have been in existence to protect foreign investments into developing countries, there is no evidence to confirm any direct relationship between a country signing BITs and foreign investment inflows into that country (Francis 2013a; Singh and Ilge 2016). Despite this, many recent FTAs have involved detailed provisions to liberalise and protect all kinds of investments, all of which impinge upon the space for industrial policies.

While the US was the trailblazer in putting in place WTO-plus investment provisions in its agreements with developing countries beginning with NAFTA, the failure of developed countries' attempt to incorporate investment in the 2003 WTO Cancun Ministerial through a Multilateral Framework on Investment seemed to drive the entry of investment provisions into other North-South and South-South FTAs from around the mid-2000s. This approach was also promoted by a segment of the mainstream academia analysing the potential dynamic effects of FTAs.[16] According to Ali and

Perez (2006), this approach argues that the dynamics effects of an FTA can increase economic growth rate through its effects on factor accumulation (investments) and this justifies the introduction of free capital mobility into FTAs (Francis 2015b).

This offered a rationale to the 'nuanced' argument behind the promotion of FTAs in Asia (and as we saw, particularly in the context of India) that increasing India's participation in preferential trade agreements, especially involving the East and Southeast Asian economies, would lead to dynamic and efficient industrial restructuring within the region driven by increased FDI inflows, given the diversity in the levels of economic development, economic structure and capabilities of the countries in the region (Kumar 2007a, 2007b). Furthermore, it was argued that India would also gain from the greater specialisation, economies of scale and learning-by-doing that will accrue from being part of global production networks/global value chains (see Kumar and Joseph 2004; Batra 2006; Francois et al. 2009; Das 2009; and Park et al. cited in Francis and Kallummal 2013). However, these predictions on dynamic gains from FTAs through GVC-driven industrial restructuring have not factored in the implications of tariff liberalisation on incentives for local production and in turn on MNCs' incentives.

As argued in Chapter 3, MNCs' location decisions are crucially influenced by the technological capabilities of the host country for the particular production process that they plan to relocate. Given that broader FTAs with cumulative rules of origin enhance the possibility of sourcing inputs from the larger region at preferential rates or duty-free (Francis and Kallummal 2013; Francis 2015b) to improve their cost competitiveness, this shifts the nature of incentives facing foreign producers against undertaking domestic production in countries without the required capabilities. Deep and broad trade liberalisation also increases domestic firms' incentives for importing raw materials and intermediate products from FTA partners. 'In some industries, inverted duty structures have lead to increased incentives for directly importing the final products'. All of these would lead to an eventual decline in output and employment as well as domestic value addition in particular countries,[17] even as there might be an increase in the volume of exports and imports involving the FTA partners. This was established in Chapter 4, which analysed the experience of the Indian electronics industry with drastic trade liberalisation under the ITA-1 and the FTAs with ASEAN, South Korea and Japan. Furthermore, India's overall export performance (Francis 2015a) also clearly shows that an increase in export competitiveness that is mainly attributable to greater access to cheaper imports from FTA partners has not been sustainable.

While the above points to the challenges of maintaining local production by domestic and foreign producers under region-wide tariff liberalisation, investment chapters in FTAs compound this problem by restricting the space for vertical industrial policies, which are required for creating other 'policy-driven incentives for domestic value generation' (e.g., through the imposition of performance requirements on foreign investors).

Two major inter-related aspects of investment chapters in FTAs are important. The first one relates to the broad definition of investment employed by them and the associated problems. The second relates to an expanding set of binding regulatory commitments that restrict FTA members' ability to apply policies related to the operations of foreign investors (termed 'treatment of investment') and other commitments that oblige members to guarantee protection of the investments that come under the purview of the FTA (that is, 'covered investments'). It is important to note that commitments under investment chapters are also applicable to investments in the services sectors, even if they are not liberalised under the WTO's General Agreement on Trade in Services (GATS).[18] Otherwise, services sectors must be explicitly listed in the investment chapter as exemptions from national treatment[19] and MFN treatment[20] at the time of signing the FTAs/investment agreements. This is important for keeping ample space for adopting vertical industrial policies, as we will discuss subsequently.

One of the major problems with the investment chapters in FTAs has been the asset-based definition of investment adopted by them, which typically states that 'investment means every kind of asset'. This means that all the policy commitments that a government undertakes in such an investment chapter is binding upon all kinds of foreign investments in a developing country, irrespective of whether they are FDI, portfolio investments, lending, investments in derivatives or investments in government debt instruments (sovereign debt), etc. Moreover, most of these investment definitions often cover a broad range of non-financial assets (called 'intangible assets') owned by foreign investors, such as intellectual property rights, business concessions, leases and mortgages on real property, etc.

Given that foreign and domestic enterprises cannot be discriminated, such broad investment definitions – together with the more stringent provisions in those FTA chapters related to the treatment of investments and protection of investments – mean that there are at least three WTO-plus levels at which they impact developing countries' policy space in the context of this study:

- They adversely affect developing countries' ability to attract and regulate FDI in order to maximise their benefits to the host economy in a sustainable way.
- They impact upon the host country regulatory autonomy for technology policies with implications for sustainable development strategies.
- They also impact the host country's ability to regulate non-FDI types of foreign investments, with adverse implications for financial/macroeconomic stability required for sustainable development.

Performance requirements have been an integral part of the FDI regulatory framework and industrial policies in the countries which have effectively utilised FDI for successful industrial restructuring, precisely because the contributions of FDI that enable faster catching-up by countries do not occur automatically. An illustrative list of traditional performance requirements that were binding on foreign investors is as follows (Lall 1996; Amsden 2001; Thrasher and Gallagher 2008; Francis and Kallummal 2013; Francis 2015b):

- joint venture requirements,
- export obligations,
- restriction on domestic sale of goods and services,
- restrictions on exports,
- local procurement/purchase of goods and services,
- transfer of technology or other proprietary knowledge,
- performing a given level of R&D in the host party,
- upper bounds on royalties expressed as a percentage of sales,
- prohibition of property rights over local adaptations,
- hiring of employees or managers of the host party nationality,
- training of professionals and workers,
- location of regional or global headquarters in the host country, etc.

It has been understood since long that it is easier for developing countries to prescribe such general legal and economic requirements than it is to effectively monitor the true terms of technology transfer associated with a particular foreign direct investment or the 'quality' of that which is acquired in a particular instance of FDI (Helleiner 1989: 1460).[21] This is also why governments used to establish screening procedures for their monitoring and control. Such non-price terms were crucial in facilitating the development of local technological capabilities, export promotion and regional or global economic integration. Several such interventions were used by all the successful late industrialisers (starting with Japan and followed by South Korea, Taiwan, etc. in their earlier stages of development and China subsequently) in order to maximise the impact of FDI on local productive capabilities, employment and industrial upgrading by:

• simultaneously regulating competition in the domestic market and pushing for export competitiveness of domestic producers at different phases of an industry's development;
• ensuring the creation of local backward and forward linkages; and
• facilitating direct and indirect modes of technology transfer between foreign-invested firms and local firms in myriad ways.

Against the backdrop of the arguments in Chapter 3, it is evident that these are ever more useful industrial policy tools for countries that seek to enter GVCs while engaging with MNCs.

The Trade-Related Investment Measures (TRIMs) Agreement under the WTO rules out the use of many performance requirements including local content requirements, trade balancing requirements and foreign exchange restrictions through quantitative restrictions on imports or exports as well as measures that violate national treatment by favouring domestic firms over foreign firms (Shadlen 2005; Wade 2006; Akyuz 2007). The TRIMs Agreement prohibits the use of such performance requirements in general as well as when they are attached as conditions for the receipt of investment incentives offered by the government (Francis and Kallummal 2013). Yet as Shadlen (2005) observed, "beyond these measures explicitly included in the appendix, TRIMS leaves developing countries with the right to determine what is and what is not a 'trade-related investment measure', and thus what they are obligated to report to the WTO" (UNDP 2003 cited in Shadlen 2005: 259).

Thus for example, WTO members can still promote domestic producers of specific locally manufactured products with positive externalities, which require support to reap scale economies or improve productivity, by formulating policies that promote end user demand through government procurement and combine them with measures (including incentives) to raise technological standards in local production. It is known that the application of ICT in sectors as diverse as education, health, agriculture, environment, taxation, governance, etc., increases the aggregate demand for ICT-related products, viz. electronics products. Thus inclusion of preference for locally produced goods in government procurement can be utilised to achieve desirable environment-friendly technological upgrading objectives in particular industries. As suggested in Francis (2015a), the application of suitable standards in government procurement contracts (for example, those related to energy efficiency or other environmental standards) in combination with technology upgrading incentives can help generate the necessary economies of scale to make locally manufactured products competitive vis-à-vis imports.

End user demand for domestic products can be expanded through government procurement as practised by Brazil also. The Buy Brazil Act (2010) establishes price preference for Brazilian goods and services in government contracts, limited to a maximum of 25 per cent above the price of foreign goods and services (Stephenson 2013: 25). Notably, in the case of goods, India had attempted to utilise this policy space while liberalising the foreign equity cap in the retail sector. However, it was diluted subsequently.[22] However, the government procurement route to promoting local goods and services is still available because India remains only an observer to the WTO's Government Procurement Agreement (GPA). Similarly, governments can mandate the use of local services by foreign investors. It is possible for countries to apply local content requirements for the procurement of services, including technology and data flows, unless they have been prohibited because of the country's commitments in the GATS schedule (UNCTAD 2014: 82–83). This is in fact a policy space that can be used to improve domestic services firms' ability to take part in the upstream and downstream service sector activities of GVCs. Again, in Brazil's government procurement contracts for strategic IT and communications technology, tenders are restricted to goods and services developed with national technology (Stephenson 2013: 25).

What is crucial, however, in utilising this industrial policy space is that countries should not have bound their foreign investment policies in such service sectors under the GATS or should have listed them as limitations to national treatment in their GATS schedule of commitments. Also, it requires that India should not enter into any FTA committing to liberalise government procurement.

Clearly, it is also important for India to not make any commitments in FTAs in the service sectors which remain unbound under the GATS, so that they can utilise the available flexibility for vertical industrial policy measures. It is instructive to consider Vietnam's approach in its bilateral/regional trade and investment agreements. Although the country's services sector has undergone extensive liberalisation, most of Vietnam's current bilateral agreements follow a positive-list approach, as in the GATS. Under the latter, FTA signatories list only the sectors they wish to liberalise. This gives autonomy to the country to flexibly change policies related to all other sectors not listed for liberalisation. This is in contrast to a negative list approach, wherein only those sectors that are to be protected are listed, and all others are, by their absence, considered liberalised. Once a service sector is liberalised, it automatically comes under the national treatment obligation, due to which the country cannot apply preferential treatment for local services. Further, change in policies related to any non-listed sector/activity can become subject to costly disputes under the ISDS provision of investment provisions. ISDS provisions grant rights to foreign investors to sue host country governments at international tribunals for treaty violations (detailed discussion on ISDS follows later). In the above example, Vietnam has been able to maintain foreign ownership ceilings in telecommunication services, impose higher fees on foreign firms in shipping and require an economic-needs test for foreign-owned retail outlets beyond the first ones already established – all because it has followed a positive-list approach (UNCTAD 2014: 98).

Crucially, the prohibitions under the TRIMs agreement apply only after foreign investments have been allowed in any sector and the national treatment obligation kicks in. Depending on changing industrial structure and impacts of domestic or external factors on domestic industries and economy, it may be necessary for host governments to regulate foreign investors' entry and establishment in the context of employment effects, technology transfer, environmental impacts, defence capabilities, cultural impacts or other developmental concerns (Francis 2011b; Francis and Kallummal 2013; UNCTAD 2014: 82). This requires that policymakers should have the flexibility to impose industry-specific entry conditions or limitations on foreign investors.

This flexibility is retained under the WTO despite the TRIMs agreement. Although the latter imposes restrictions on certain performance requirements on foreign investors, it does not regulate host country policies related to the *entry* of FDI. This would have required countries to commit to what is called the pre-establishment stage of investments.[23] This means that, despite the TRIMs agreement, WTO members can demand joint ventures in particular sectors, require foreign firms to transfer technology to local firms, etc. (Shadlen 2005: 759).

Retaining this ability to screen foreign investments before approving their entry is especially crucial, given that countries have already lost the policy space to impose several kinds of performance requirements on foreign investors *after* they have set up investments in a host country. Remember that traditionally, foreign investors have been expected to accept various performance requirements in exchange for cost-offsetting advantages such as privileged market access (protection against competing imports) or subsidisation (e.g., corporate tax breaks) (Low and Tijaja 2013: 13). Therefore, legally committing (open) market access in investments under FTAs erodes government's ability to even conceptualise WTO-compatible performance requirements on foreign investors in exchange for allowing FDI into a particular sector that is otherwise closed to FDI. This has been one of the most important policies utilised by China (see Francis 2018b).

Thus in the post-WTO era – after the 5-year transitional period for developing countries to abide by the TRIMs agreement came to an end in 2000,[24] maintaining the policy space for prior approval for foreign investments is a crucial component of a strategic industrial policy framework. But in the India-Singapore CECA, the coverage of the investment definition is TRIMs-plus, as it covers the pre-establishment stage or admission of investment. This curtails India's right to regulate entry of FDI from Singapore, by binding investment liberalisation in both goods and services sectors at the levels committed under the FTA.

Such regulatory freedom for FDI continues to be maintained and utilised as an industrial policy measure by countries such as China and Brazil. Zarsky (2010: 19) shows how China has been explicitly targeting FDI in low-carbon and other sustainable industries and technologies. For example, in December 2007, China announced a "dramatic revision" of its foreign investment strategy, the "keystone" of which is an "emphasis on quality over quantity". The second of five new policies is:

encouragement of investment in sustainable resources and environmental protection. Foreign investors are encouraged to support the newly implemented Circular Economy (i.e. sustainable development) and Cleaner Production policies, as well as invest in the area of environmental protection, sustainable resources and anti-pollution. The 2007 catalog greatly expands the list of encouraged investments in this area. On the other hand, foreign investment in high resource-use, high energy-use and high-pollution enterprises is restricted or prohibited.

(Quoted in Zarsky 2010: 19)

A serious problem is that members of FTAs which liberalise foreign investors' entry under their investment or service chapter provisions risk facing costly disputes under the investor-state dispute settlement (ISDS) mechanism when they make policy changes in the liberalised sectors. For the same reason, even when countries have carried out unilateral liberalisation of their national FDI policies, such as India has, committing such liberalisation (or binding them) under FTAs will severely curtail countries' policy space.

Under the agreements with Japan and South Korea, India has bound its liberalisation of FDI norms at the 2010 level, wherein 100 per cent FDI is allowed without screening (through the automatic route) in most manufacturing and services sectors, except in a few areas like single-brand retail trading, atomic energy, etc. It is true that India has been undertaking autonomous liberalisation of FDI policies. However, with the binding of such liberalisation under these FTAs any changes in FDI policy can make the government liable to face investor-state disputes and compensation claims from investors covered under this FTA for alleged violation of its provisions. This will restrict government flexibility to change policies to suit changing policy priorities in tune with changing economic dynamics of specific industries at different stages of development.

Given the inability to treat foreign and domestic investors differentially once industries/sectors are liberalised for entry of foreign investments under FTAs (due to the national treatment clause), it is therefore crucial for India to keep her policy sovereignty over her FDI regulatory regime in order to ensure coordination with other development objectives like domestic technological capability building, employment generation and environmental protection that underlie sustainable development. Furthermore, as in the case of tariff liberalisation, investment liberalisation commitments in agriculture also have to recognise the inter-linkages between agricultural and industrial development as well as the national imperative to support domestic agriculture production for ensuring livelihood, food security and environmental protection (see detailed discussion in Francis and Kallummal 2013). Thus it is crucial to limit the coverage of FTAs to post-establishment treatment of investments.

In addition to retaining a WTO member country's FDI regulatory space in the pre-entry phase, TRIMs also does not limit the use of several post-entry regulatory measures historically applied on foreign investments to promote sustainable development through technological capability building in the host economy. Among those mentioned in the illustrative list above, these include requirements on foreign-invested firms to employ or train local labour, transfer technology, undertake local R&D, etc. But investment chapters in FTAs such as India-South Korea and India-Japan CEPAs are TRIMs-plus, as they prohibit performance requirements relating to technology transfer and nationality of senior management board of directors. They also prohibit export obligations for services (Francis and Kallummal 2013). In general, any such performance requirements can be maintained only as conditions to be met for the receipt of government's investment incentives.

Furthermore, in India's CEPA with Japan, India has given up its right to adopt any new policy measures on foreign investments that do not conform to its obligations on national treatment, MFN treatment and the prohibition of performance requirements under that FTA (Francis and Kallummal 2013). Except in the manufacture of a short list of products listed in an annex, the government can introduce new performance requirements on investments covered under this FTA only when they are tied to the grant of investment incentives.

In a context of low or zero tariff protection, subsidisation becomes the only carrot that can be offered while putting performance requirements in place. This obviously places a burden on the exchequer.

At the same time, new laws and regulations (unattached to investment incentives) to ensure maximum long-term benefits from foreign investments can be employed by states and other sub-national governments.[25] Given that state, provincial or other local governments can also pursue industrial policy measures, it is important for India to preserve the right to adopt investment-related measures as per the laws and regulations framed at sub-federal government levels. This is critical from the perspective of maintaining the remaining autonomy for industrial policy.

In this context, it is relevant to note that the WTO's Agreement on Subsidies and Countervailing Measures (ASCM) prohibits the use of subsidies either for export promotion or for supporting domestic production by subsidising locally made goods (Wade 2006: 3; Akyuz 2007: 13; UNCTAD 2014: 84). Prohibited subsidies relate to any financial transfers from, or revenue foregone by, government bodies (federal or sub-federal) for income or price support that confers a benefit, as well as to indirect subsidies provided through concessional credit (preferential credit) from the banking sector to specific sectors.[26] Prohibited subsidies can be subject to disputes under the WTO's Dispute Settlement Body (DSB) and need to be reversed if they are found to be WTO non-compatible. But specific subsidies are also 'actionable'. Specific subsidies are defined in terms of access to them being explicitly limited in some way to specific sectors, industries or firms (either in terms of design or possible outcome). In this case, however, the complaining WTO member has to prove the injury caused by those subsidies to its domestic sector before imposing countervailing duties (CVD). However, India has been able to use sector-specific export incentives because of the provision that LDCs and countries with a per capita income less than $1000 (Annex VII countries) can use export subsidies until their graduation from this category. India graduated out of this category in 2017 and is now considering re-formulating these subsidies.

Further, subsidies for research and development (R&D), human capital formation, backward region development and environmental purposes are allowed. Thus governments can grant tax rebates to firms for new capital equipment and R&D investments towards technological upgrading as well as for skill development in technology-intensive activities and industries (Francis 2015a). Subsidies may also be channelled through non-banking financial intermediaries, including specialised technology funds, start-up funds, venture capital funds, etc. Countries can also include support for disadvantaged communities as exemptions to national treatment commitments. As suggested by UNCTAD (2014), if specific industries which do not have an export market yet are located in backward regions, governments can promote their development through regional subsidies.

As mentioned, the prohibited subsidies are those that involve an element of government financial transfer or revenue foregone. But instead of foregoing revenue through tax rebates, the government can support industries by offering infrastructural and other services. Apart from for general infrastructural services such as power, fuel, water, etc., such support can also be provided by setting up specialised processing zones, technology parks, etc. where the facilities and infrastructure are provided by the government to support the growth of particular industries. As we saw, this has been extensively utilised by several countries in their EPZs and by India in its SEZs. Importantly, this will become increasingly more important in emerging advanced technology industries as well as in existing employment-intensive industries such as agro-processing, textiles, leather, etc. There are also important challenges related to social inclusion and environmental protection that can be ensured by governments through specialised infrastructural provision. Furthermore, support may also be channelled through sub-national agencies. This discussion clearly reveals that it is of critical importance not to restrict such policy space under FTAs at either the federal or sub-federal levels.

This is also crucial from the point of view of retaining the flexibility to put in place locality-specific climate change adaptation and mitigation measures (Francis 2017). There is ample evidence that proactive industry policies can be effective in promoting climate-friendly industrial growth. Zarsky (2010: 10–11) points out that China's industry support policies have propelled its emergence as a leader in solar photovoltaic and wind technology, as well as in 'clean coal' technologies such as direct coal liquefaction. Similarly, Brazil's support for the development and deployment of a domestic sugar-based ethanol industry allowed it to capture a vibrant export market in the burgeoning global bio-fuels sector (*ibid.*).

It is important to note that, while subsidies for production are not prohibited under this WTO agreement, they are 'actionable'. They can be challenged through the WTO's Dispute Settlement Mechanism (DSM) or be subject to countervailing action by an importing country if subsidised imports are shown to cause injury to domestic producers. However, there are some exemptions here too. Production subsidies are not questionable as long as subsidisation of a product does not exceed 5 per cent of its total estimated value or when one-time measures to cover operating losses sustained by an enterprise are offered (UNCTAD 2014: 109).

However, whether subsidies are considered illegal or not, they may be subject to countervailing or anti-dumping duties. This possibility clearly reduces any security that countries might otherwise enjoy in terms of legally sanctioned access to certain subsidy practices (Low and Tijaja 2013: 14).

WTO-plus constraints on technological progress under FTAs

While the WTO's TRIMs Agreement and TRIMs-plus provisions in FTAs related to performance requirements restrict the use of several proactive industrial policies for enabling technological progress and technology transfer in developing countries, another set of constraints on technological development and diffusion have arisen from the Agreement on Trade-Related Intellectual Property Rights (TRIPs) in the WTO. The TRIPs agreement has established binding rules on minimum standards for intellectual property protection regimes for WTO member countries with the aim of recognising and enforcing the rights of innovators. These standards for protecting the use of intellectual property rights (IPRs) such as patents, copyrights and trademarks have tilted the balance between technology creation and technology diffusion in favour of established knowledge exporters in the developed countries, disadvantaging follower developing countries who are net technology importers.

Parties to the TRIPs agreement are obliged to offer patents in almost all fields, give protection to owners of IPRs no less than the level provided in the agreement, apply national treatment to foreign owners of IPRs registered with them and observe non-discrimination among foreign holders of IPRs (Akyuz 2007). The agreement has already severely restricted reverse engineering and other forms of imitative innovation previously used by many countries, including the now-developed ones, for their industrial upgrading and structural transformation processes (UNCTAD 2014: 83. See also Correa 2016).

While the proponents of the TRIPs Agreement operated on the premise that minimum standards of protection would be equally beneficial for countries with diverse levels of socio-economic and technological development, the dominant view flowing from decades of academic and other analyses strongly reject that premise (Correa 2016: 8). There is very little evidence supporting its claimed benefits, including acceleration of innovation in developing countries and greater spillovers of technology from developed to developing countries through increased FDI. This is supported by the fact the global map of research and development (R&D) does not show a general improvement of R&D capabilities in developing countries in the last 20 years, with a few exceptions, notably in the case of China (Correa 2016: 3).[27] This is a clear reflection of the fact that the strict enforcement of the patent system leads to legal barriers to the use of inventions for follow-on innovations, apart from high prices for products (Love 2014). Furthermore, as seen in Chapter 3, even after their entry into GVCs, effective absorption of the technologies disseminated by lead MNCs by domestic firms in developing countries occurs only if they have developed their own technological capabilities. All these point to the ineffectiveness of the emphasis on patents and their enforceability in driving technological capability development.

In fact, developed countries such as the US, which has been a major proponent of tightening IPR rules in developing countries, continue to depend heavily on government funds for financing innovation. The United States National Science Board's 2012 edition of *Science and Engineering Indicators* breaks down R&D expenditures into three categories, basic, applied and development. Data provided in Love (2014: 10) shows that for 2009, governments and other non-profit entities performed more than 80 per cent of basic research, 42.4 per cent of applied research and 10.5 per cent of research in final product development stages. This should be read together with the information that, in the case of all entities (public, private and non-profit) performing research, 19 per cent was spent on basic research, 17.8 per cent on applied research and 63.2 per cent on later stages of product development.

The impact of the TRIPs regime has been particularly telling for developing countries in the experience of the pharmaceutical industry, as many studies have shown (Correa 2016; Kallummal and Bugalya 2012; Abrol 2014; etc.). The cost of healthcare has also increased manifold across countries due to the shift from process patents to product patents in countries like India, which had successfully developed a domestic generic pharmaceutical industry under the national process patent regime until 2005. India has thus been a major supplier of low-cost medicines to other developing countries. On the other side, low investment in R&D by the pharmaceutical industry continues to be a concern (Correa 2016). The extension of a product patent regime and test data protection under TRIPs has not helped developing countries address the diseases prevalent in those countries (often referred to as 'neglected diseases') because of the lack of interest (Correa 2016).

However, given that patents provide profits for their owners (Correa 2016: 5), the patent regime has adversely affected competitive conditions in many industries. It has been found that patents "are increasingly used as strategic assets to influence the conditions of competition rather than as a defensive means to protect research and development outcomes" (UNCTAD 2014: 83). Thus the shift to strict enforcement of the patent regimes, which increases the pricing power of innovating firms, has contributed to the consolidation of market power across GVC segments. This has led to growing consolidation, especially in industries such as electronics and pharmaceuticals, but also in several other industries. Since industrial upgrading becomes more demanding, and imitation and adaptation of foreign technology gain added importance at intermediate stages of industrialisation, the TRIPs agreement has been found to place greater constraint particularly on technical progress in middle-income countries (Akyuz 2007).

Yet, some flexibility is available in the TRIPs Agreement to take care of developing country's technological development requirements through its mechanisms of compulsory licensing and parallel imports (Gopakumar 2010).[28] Compulsory licensing is when a government allows someone else to produce the patented product or process without the consent of the patent owner. The Doha Declaration on the TRIPs Agreement and Public Health, which was adopted at the WTO Ministerial Meeting in 2001, clarified some of these flexibilities in the context of the pharmaceutical industry. Many of its clauses have broader implications and concern IP in any field of technology and may also be used to promote domestic production (Correa 2014, cited in UNCTAD 2014: 83). For instance, varying patentability standards, such as the granting of narrow patents for incremental innovations that build on more fundamental discoveries, may be useful for adapting imported technologies to local conditions.

The current Indian Patent Act contains all the TRIPs flexibilities and can be used for ensuring availability of patented medicines at affordable prices with further fine tuning of the relevant provisions, institutional capacity-building, etc. (Gopakumar 2010). For instance, Section 3(d) of the Indian Patent Act bans the patentability of minor/incremental modifications to pharmaceutical formulations and other incremental developments relating to existing drugs. This provision has been put in place to prevent the granting of extended patent protection through 'secondary' patents in India beyond the normal 20 years (to obtain what is known as the 'ever-greening' of patents). India has come under tremendous pressure under its FTA negotiations with developed countries to exclude this provision. While countries such as the US, EU and Japan have been major proponents of strict implementation of patents in developing countries through TRIPs and have been including and advocating for TRIPs-plus provisions in their FTAs with developing countries, a wide range of research- and innovation-related tasks in these countries have since long been financed through public research grants and contracts (Love 2014: 4). These governments, which invest heavily in research grants and contracts in sectors such as energy, informatics, biotechnology, nanotechnology or agriculture, often do so to advance science, address a social concern and/or to develop domestic industrial capacities. This has been in clear recognition of the limited value of the patent system for certain research and development activities, such as that for the development of products with small commercial market potential (including pre-commercial research and development), research outcomes that cannot be successfully monopolised and monetised and particularly risky development projects (Love 2014: 4–6). This discussion clearly brings out the necessity for developing country governments to increase their public spending on national R&D activities.

At the same time, India needs to resist any TRIPs-plus provision in FTAs. The inclusion of IPR in the broad definitions of investment in FTAs (discussed in the earlier sub-section) may be interpreted as eliminating the scope for flexible implementation of TRIPs-compatible IPR policies by developing countries. The broad open-ended investment definition commits a host country to granting additional protection to IPRs that may not be consistent with the country's socio-economic development needs. It is thus critical that intangible assets like intellectual property not be covered under the scope of investment in FTAs. Further, India should never trade off the hard-won flexibilities under TRIPs under any trade agreements. TRIPs-plus IPR protections will serve to strengthen the trends in market consolidation seen among MNCs within and outside GVCs.

WTO-plus constraints on managing macroeconomic instability

It is notable that the TRIMs agreement prohibits host country restrictions on payments and transfers abroad only for those related to FDI. However, the provision for guarantee of free transfer of all funds associated with broad investment definitions in FTAs liberalise outflows related to non-FDI foreign investment categories also. This is because broad investment definitions rule out the distinction between direct and portfolio investments and thus lead to the liberalisation of both current account and capital account transactions.

Comprehensive trade agreements require all transfers 'relating to investment' from the contracting parties to be allowed freely and without delay into and out of the host Parties. An analysis of the capital transfer provisions in the 72 Indian BIPAs in force and the four major comprehensive trade agreements (India-Singapore CECA, India-South Korea CEPA, India-Japan CEPA and India-Malaysia CECA) revealed that all of them contain the relevant article. On the contrary, the new model BIT brought out by India in 2015 specifies a narrow investment definition.[29]

However, under the above major FTAs, India has committed to offering free capital repatriation, which is usually offered to foreign direct investors, to other classes of investors like private equity (PE) and venture capital (VC) funds (apart from foreign portfolio investors),[30] who neither bring in FDI-type ownership advantages to the host companies nor contribute to national investments even in the medium term, as they are known to sell and move out (Francis 2015b). The freedom for capital repatriation guaranteed to non-FDI investors under FTAs can have serious consequences for member countries' policy space related to the use of capital controls.

The broad investment definitions in the investment provisions under FTAs erode the national policy space to regulate different forms of capital flows and, therefore, autonomous macroeconomic policies. Typically, the use of capital controls is allowed only as defined under the safeguard measures in the FTAs – that is, only under emergency situations in case of 'serious difficulties' with monetary policy, exchange rate policy or balance of payments, and that, too, only temporarily.[31] In India's FTAs with Singapore, Japan, South Korea and Malaysia, all the capital account regulatory measures allowed as exceptions must not only go beyond what is necessary to remedy the specific situation being addressed (Francis 2013b), but must also avoid unnecessary damage to the commercial, economic and financial interests of the investor. Such provisions with a very broad scope of interpretation prevent developing countries from making use of different kinds of capital account regulations in order to *prevent* 'serious difficulties' in a manner required for sustainable development. Moreover, as

Argentina's experience with its bilateral investment treaties with an investor-state dispute settlement (ISDS) provision amply established, once a country includes ISDS provisions in an FTA, it may be faced with international arbitration by affected foreign investors even for currency controls applied during a financial crisis (Williams 2016: 31).[32]

It has been widely recognised that, in countries integrated with international financial markets and open capital accounts, dynamic capital account regulations are necessary to: improve macroeconomic stability; provide the policy space for counter-cyclical monetary policy management; limit speculative activity; and guide the composition of capital flows toward more long term, less debt-creating and productive types of foreign investments for realising sustainable development objectives (see the detailed discussion in Francis 2013a: 72; Epstein et al. 2003; Epstein 2012; Ghosh 2010; Gallagher, Griffith-Jones and Ocampo 2012). Furthermore, as the 2008 global financial crisis showed, all countries with open financial sectors will be affected by the volatile functioning of unregulated financial markets elsewhere. This emphasises the need for national governments to flexibly regulate capital flows to prevent macroeconomic instability, which has adverse implications on productive investments in the economy.

Investment policy coherence for productive capacity-building therefore calls for coherence with financial sector policies too because financial fragility, which blows up in a financial crisis, can completely derail a country off its development trajectory. As experiences in other countries have shown, short-run macroeconomic adjustment problems triggered by a BoP or financial crisis often severely limit the policy options available for pursuing industrial growth and diversification needs and can also truncate indigenously driven industrial development trajectories (Francis 2013a: 73; Kallummal and Dhar 2002).

One option to reclaim this policy space, as discussed in Francis (2011a), is the inclusion of financial stability in the preamble of IIA as one of the explicit public policy objectives that could warrant regulatory measures on the part of the signatory host state/s. Another option would be to bring in public measures 'necessary to ensure financial stability' under the general exceptions article of agreements, similar to the objectives of public order and health objectives, and make the general exceptions non-justiciable, or justiciable only under domestic legal processes.

Other WTO-plus constraints in FTAs

Another major WTO-plus constraint that has crept into some FTAs with significant implications for industrial policies is the definition of expropriation to include indirect expropriation. Direct expropriation refers to the nationalisation, transfer of title or seizure of private property by the host government. Typically, protection provisions in bilateral investment treaties (BITs) and FTAs state that expropriation of investment is not allowed except when carried out for public purpose in a non-discriminatory manner. Given that provisions on investment protection provide for fair and equitable compensation to foreign investors in the event of an expropriation, it is crucial to define the terms of coverage of expropriation to include only direct expropriation.

In India's CEPAs with South Korea and Japan, expropriation is both direct and indirect. Under these FTAs, the determination of what types of government actions/measures will be interpreted to constitute an indirect expropriation is to be based on a case-by-case inquiry (Annex 10-A), which includes "the extent to which the government action interferes with distinct, reasonable investment-backed expectations" (Francis and Kallummal 2013: 119). The manner in which the latter is defined in the agreement implies that, if any new regulatory policy is introduced in a sector that was not previously regulated when the treaty came into force, it will be considered as expropriation and the government can be subjected to disputes and costly compensation claims.

This is severely problematic, given that the inclusion of investor-state dispute settlement (ISDS) provisions in the FTAs' investment chapters has heightened the risk of international arbitration of states by foreign private corporations.[33] ISDS provisions allow foreign investors in a host country to sue a host government at international arbitral forums (private courts that remain totally outside national jurisdiction), if they interpret host country measures or laws as leading to a reduction in their business profitability or even future prospects. Within the WTO, the flexibility is clear: a country may not bring a suit under the Dispute Settlement Understanding (DSU) unless the benefits inured to them under the agreement have been "nullified or impaired" by the other country's actions (Art. 3.8; see Thrasher and Gallagher 2008). However, ISDS provisions in several FTAs have been used by corporations around the world to force governments to use taxpayer money to compensate them for perfectly legitimate regulations to protect public health, environment and other public interests, including industrial development, employment generation and financial stability. ISDS thus poses serious risks to industrial policies.

While the state-to-state dispute settlement procedure under the WTO's Dispute Settlement Body (DSB) remains a democratic institution in principle, the international arbitration system under ISDS has been found to be anti-democratic,[34] totally non-transparent, as well as ridden with serious procedural drawbacks and conflicts of interests among the panel members and legal practitioners arguing for the big multinationals (Eberhardt et al. 2016). As pointed out in UNCTAD (2013), repeated instances of inconsistent awards and interpretations by panels deepen the uncertainty about the meaning of key obligations and compound the problem of the unpredictability of arbitral awards.

Furthermore, recent studies have shown that the very presence of the risk of litigation for compensatory claims by foreign investors under the ISDS provision has begun to create disincentives for states to avoid or modify their regulatory decisions. Referred to as 'regulatory chill', this fear is usually linked to the breadth of foreign investor protections in ISDS, the inability of states to bring claims against foreign investors, the weaknesses of exceptions to protect the state's right to regulate, the ability of foreign investors to receive uncapped amounts of compensation from the state, the international enforceability of ISDS awards, exclusive access of foreign investors to ISDS (leaving no similar option for domestic investors) or the absence of conventional judicial safeguards in ISDS (Van Harten and Scott 2015).[35]

These problems associated with investor-state disputes raise the development costs of policy failures relating to the absence or non-implementation of policy measures that would be needed to ensure socially, economically and ecologically sustainable trajectories of structural transformation needed for sustainable development. Singh and Ilge (2016) also point out that the risk of regulatory chill is very real given that a wide range of policy and regulatory measures – from taxation to the plain packaging of tobacco products to the disposal of hazardous waste – have all been challenged by foreign investors in the recent past.[36]

But developing countries including India can learn from the several alternatives that have been put forth recently, which include, among others: state-state dispute settlement (SSDS) mechanisms

(Nathalie Bernasconi-Osterwalder 2016); limiting investors' access to ISDS; introducing an appeals facility; and creating a standing international investment court (Zhan 2016). Furthermore, as pointed out by Dumberry (2016), nothing in international law prevents countries from signing investment agreements imposing human rights obligations upon private corporations. This is an area where the UN has begun discussions.

It should be remembered that the exercise to revise India's model act governing bilateral investment treaties (BITs) was undertaken after India faced a number of international arbitration cases wherein foreign investors invoked the ISDS provisions in existing BITs for enforcing their rights in India.[37] It is a welcome change that India's new Model Bilateral Investment Treaty (December 2015) requires investors to exhaust local judicial remedies before commencing international arbitration against the host state. However, it still retains the clause on investor-state arbitration.

The way forward in FTA negotiations

While several countries have been using the policy space available under the WTO ingeniously, the WTO-plus provisions in FTAs reduce policy sovereignty and heighten the risk of policy failures by limiting the possibilities to redesign industrial development trajectories in developing countries towards more sustainable paths. While the discussion in the preceding sections pointed to several policies that can be adopted by India, these involve strategic choices to be made while negotiating FTAs.

In the context of the ongoing negotiations on Regional Comprehensive Economic Partnership (RCEP),[38] it is important to note that the increased integration of Asian developing countries into GVCs is an important factor behind the changing political economy of FTA negotiations in the region to involve investment provisions. With greater integration of these economies into GVCs (and associated benefits from increased access to cheaper imports), there are larger domestic constituencies in individual countries that become interested in maintaining and locking-in a liberal trade policy regime. However, for achieving sustainable development, states have to rise above sectoral interests and possible short-term geo-political gains. Only competent bureaucracies can steer the fundamental shift required – negotiating different stakeholder segments' interests – and move away from transient export benefits that may arise, to the longer-term gains to be obtained from safe-guarding countries' remaining policy space for guiding industrial development and structural transformation along sustainable trajectories.

Given the common imperative to meet the challenges arising from the constantly evolving GVC dynamics amidst digitalisation and advanced manufacturing technologies, as well as the need to take care of climate-resilient development strategies and social inclusion and cohesion, all RCEP members, including lead industrialisers Japan and South Korea, as well as Australia and New Zealand, have similar interests as ASEAN, India and China, to bring an alternative agenda to the negotiating table that maintain the space for selective industrial policies. The discussion in this chapter shows that a central component of such a strategy would particularly involve rethinking FTA provisions on investments. This is the opportunity to move away from investment provisions that have become 'templates' in ASEAN's existing bilateral/regional FTAs with other negotiating members by default. This would be a rational decision to be a made given that governments have found their policy sovereignty constrained in so many unanticipated ways because of provisions in the WTO and bilateral/regional investment treaties and agreements.

Overall, the RCEP negotiating countries should strive for coherence between the inter-related aspects of selective industrial policies, such as trade, investment, intellectual property protection, taxation, capital controls, etc. in order to retain maximum industrial policy space that remains WTO-compatible. Some suggestions towards this are the following:

- Tariff elimination commitments should be undertaken on the least number of products beyond the exiting FTAs.
- India should not make any binding commitments in the service sector, which remains unbound under GATS so that it can utilise the available policy space as part of a strategic industrial policy.
- There should be no pre-establishment investment commitments and no indirect expropriation clauses.
- There should be neither TRIPs-plus nor TRIMs-plus commitments. This requires narrow definitions of investments as well as clarifying that compulsory licences granted in relation to intellectual property rights in accordance with the Agreement on TRIPs do not come under the purview of expropriation.

Given the uncertainties facing the global economy and the rapid technological changes occurring in several industries inside and outside GVCs, RCEP countries should also agree on a re-negotiation clause, which will enable all the member countries to review the agreement within an agreed number of years of its coming into force.

At a time when several WTO-plus provisions have been recognised as severely encroaching upon the sovereign policy space of developing countries and international investment agreements are being reformed (or terminated) with alternative approaches already being implemented by some countries, it will be a huge disservice to the progress made so far if RCEP goes ahead with an investment chapter including a broad investment definition, ISDS and indirect appropriation. Against the backdrop of the analysis presented in the previous chapters, taking care of these considerations is critical for India if the RCEP negotiations go forward.

Failing to factor in the industrial policy causalities involved in indigenous technology development, the many barriers to GVC entry and upgrading erected by monopolistic lead firms, the assessments of the impact of existing FTAs and FDI liberalisation on firm-level incentives for undertaking domestic production and the industrial policy constraints imposed by FTAs can prove costly for India. This is a particular challenge given that a systematic and comprehensive review of India's existing FTAs has still not been carried out. These issues assume critical significance in the context of India's proposed trade negotiations with developed countries.

Notes

1 This chapter includes portions from the essay previously published as Smitha Francis (2015b), 'Preferential Trade Agreements: An Exploration into Emerging Issues in India's Changing Trade Policy Landscape', in Jayati Ghosh (ed.), *India and the World Economy*, ICSSR Research Surveys and Explorations (New Delhi: Oxford University Press). The extracts have been reproduced with the permission of Oxford University Press India © Oxford University Press 2015.

2 Some of the problems they faced were discussed in Chapter 3. Very detailed discussions of the experiences of the developing countries involved in these regional integration agreements can be found in Kattel et al. (2009) for Central and Eastern European countries; Puyana (2007, 2011) and Gallagher and Zarsky (2007) for Mexico's experience under NAFTA; and Palma (2010) for Latin American countries in general. See also the country case studies cited in UNCTAD 2016: 118–119.

3 For a detailed discussion on the evolution of regional integration in Southeast Asia through market-led integration and regionalism, see Francis and Kallummal (2009).

4 See, for instance, the argument in Kumar (2005).

5 Competitive regionalism, wherein countries seek "to secure their trade interests as well as establish spheres of influence that include but also go beyond trade policy", was originally conceived as driving developed countries' preferential trade agreements. See Majluf (2004: 1).

6 See the detailed discussion on rationale behind India's FTAs in Francis (2015b).

7 See http://commerce.gov.in/InnerContent.aspx?Type=International Trademenu&Id=32.

8 See the detailed discussion in Francis (2013b).

9 Additionally, the Asia-Pacific Trade Agreement (APTA) and the SAARC Agreement on Trade in Services also contain investment clauses. These have not been covered here.

10 See Thrasher and Gallagher (2008: 21–23) for a discussion on safeguards.

11 There is no agreement at the WTO as to what constitutes 'substantially all trade'. However, the European Union has interpreted it as requiring 80 per cent of tariffs to be removed. US FTAs often require the developing country partner to remove all of its tariffs on US products (Smith 2009).

12 For instance, in the ASEAN-China FTA, trade was liberalised in 98 per cent of all tariff lines, including trade in agricultural products (Sauve 2007).

13 See the detailed discussion on inter-sectoral impacts of tariff liberalisation under FTAs in Francis (2015b).

14 Major FTA partners are defined here as those partners holding at least a 1 per cent share in India's total exports.

15 This discussion on investment provisions in FTAs builds on the conceptual framework in Francis (2015b) and the analysis in Francis and Kallummal (2013). The extracts have been used here with the permission of Oxford University Press, India © Oxford University Press 2015 and *Economic and Political Weekly*.

16 This is in contrast to the static effects, which are due to the greater efficiency that arises because FTA members can import more from 'lower-cost' producers in their partners instead of from 'higher-cost' domestic producers. See Francis (2015b) for a critique of the mainstream theoretical treatment of the impact of FTAs.

17 The net impact of the division of labour under production networks on productivity and output growth as well as job creation will depend on a number of factors. See the discussion in Francis and Kallummal (2013).

18 Foreign investment in services sector is covered under the GATS Agreement of the WTO because of the ingenious inclusion of the 'commercial presence' delivery mode of trade in services, that is, Mode 3. Thus if a country has committed to liberalise Mode 3 in a particular sector without limitations, then it gives up the flexibility to change its foreign investment policies for that sector.

19 This means that government policy cannot treat foreign and domestic investments differentially.
20 This means that investments from all foreign countries have to be given the same treatment under government policies.
21 This is precisely because developing countries are often scarce in the necessary skills for bargaining the terms of technology transfer in individual cases of direct foreign investment (Helleiner 1989).
22 See Rao and Dhar (2016) for a discussion on the political economy dynamics that led to the dilution of this domestic content requirement.
23 This is sometimes referred to in the literature as 'market access' for investments.
24 The transitional period for LDCs was 7 years.
25 See page 1066, Annex 9, India-Japan CEPA.
26 Although offering concessional credit to domestic firms in export or import-substituting industries is not allowed, there is a major exception in the WTO Agreement on Subsidies and Countervailing Measures through a safe-haven clause. The latter allows export credit practices which are in conformity with the interest rate provisions of the Arrangement on Officially Supported Export Credits of the OECD. The OECD arrangement involves publicly supported export credits relating to exports of goods and/or services and to financial leases with a repayment term of 2 or more years. In fact, Brazil successfully claimed in the WTO Dispute Settlement Panel set up by Canada that a financing programme supporting its aircraft industry was in accordance with the SCM's safe-haven provision (UNCTAD 2014: 84–85).
27 In the case of China, this has been the outcome of significant efforts and funding from the government for research and development (R&D) as we saw earlier.
28 Parallel imports refer to imports of a non-counterfeit product from another country by independent traders outside the manufacturer's distribution system without the permission of the intellectual property owner/manufacturer.
29 It has also taken out the MFN clause totally and also narrowed down the scope of the national treatment and FET clauses significantly. Equally importantly, the new BIT only covers the post-establishment phase of the covered investments. See the detailed discussions in Singh (2015a, 2015b).
30 Covered investments also include those in sovereign debt, where government securities are not explicitly excluded in the investment definition.
31 See also the other papers in Gallagher (2013).
32 According to Williams (2016), almost all the ISDS cases faced by Argentina were related to the 'pesofication' law passed by the country's parliament during the financial crisis in 2002.
33 See Williams (2016) for a global discussion.
34 The power of extra-jurisdictional legal procedures over constitutions and national legislation has been repeatedly warned against, even in developed countries. The German Magistrates Association, for instance, clearly stated that TTIP investment courts would 'deprive courts of member states of their power' and be therefore illegal (Jachnow 2017: 5).

35 See also the analysis of the impact of the NAFTA Chapter 11 on Canadian policymaking in Van Harten and Scott (2015). It is relevant to note that out of the 17 ISDS suits brought under the NAFTA, the US has lost none so far.

36 Most recently, in the first case of its kind, two multinational oil companies have launched a pre-emptive legal strike against Vietnam under the UK-Vietnam BIT to stop the country's government from collecting taxes amounting to USD 179 million on the profits made in a major deal involving Vietnam's oil assets (see Tuner 2018).

37 So far, India has faced ISDS cases only under its bilateral investment treaties (BITs). India faced an ISDS case on expropriation involving an Australian firm, White Industries Limited (WIL), and India's largest state-owned enterprise in the coal mining sector, Coal India Limited. In this case, Indian courts' delay in dealing with a WIL application for enforcing an International Chamber of Commerce Award in favour of WIL was argued to be tantamount to expropriation (and a violation of Article 7 of the Australia-India BIT). The firm claimed compensation for this expropriation (see the detailed discussion in Dhar 2015: 3).

38 RCEP is one of the two mega-FTAs aiming at greater integration in the Asia-Pacific region, the other being the Comprehensive and Progressive Trans-Pacific Partnership (CPTPP or TPP-11) – a trade pact among 11 Pacific Rim nations (after the US, which was among the original proposers, dropped out). Beginning in May 2013, the RCEP negotiations are being undertaken between Australia, China, India, Japan, New Zealand, South Korea and the ten members of ASEAN. While seven of these (Australia, Brunei Darussalam, Japan, Malaysia, New Zealand, Singapore and Vietnam) are members of the TPP-11, RCEP involves another major BRICS economy, China, and another major Asian lead industrialised economy, South Korea.

Chapter 6

Conclusion

Indian policymakers have been grappling with domestic industrial slowdown, growing import dependence and slowdown in its manufactured export growth in recent years without acknowledging their integral inter-linkages. In trying to untangle this puzzle, we need to understand the various interactions between trade policy, foreign investment policies and other industrial policies and examine how these dynamic interactions impact firm-level strategies. The series of FTAs that India signed from the early 2000s has altered the incentives for domestic production in different ways. The ability of Indian firms to engage with GVCs and obtain developmental benefits from such engagement, with or without FDI, needs to be understood within this framework.

But in seeking to formulate revival strategies for its stagnant manufacturing sector, India has been severely constrained by the neoliberal analytical framework underlying export-led and market-oriented growth paradigm since 1991. Grossly misunderstood and maligned, industrial policy has been anathema in this framework. Industrial policy as understood in early development literature – with the goal of advancing specific sectors that bring economy-wide productivity gains required to sustain a dynamic development process – had been discredited and shunned by neoliberalism since the 1980s. Subsequently, the international financial institutions and the mainstream of development economics have promoted only functional or horizontal industrial policies. The latter accept existing comparative advantages and mainly aim to reduce the costs of doing business, while the greater play of market forces brought about through trade and financial liberalisation is believed to lead to the desirable structural change. However, successful late industrialisers (like China and Brazil) are the ones that have seen through the irrationality and inadequacy of the 'economic framework role of the state' (as Wade 2012 referred to it) and combine functional and selective (or vertical) policy measures in ingenious ways to practise industrial policy in its 'wholeness'. The inability to acknowledge the role of learning-by-doing and knowledge accumulation in indigenous technological development lie behind the artificial dichotomy constructed by neoliberalism between horizontal and vertical industrial policies.

Consequently, as in the mis-interpretation of East Asian development successes as 'FDI-driven export-led growth under passive industrial policies', the mainstream narratives on GVCs and FTAs since the 2000s have been constructed as if signing FTAs and getting integrated into GVCs are substitutes for industrial policy for developing countries. The underlying framework of an FDI-led industrial upgrading strategy through GVCs also falls prey to the 'flying geese syndrome' in that it draws an automatic causation flowing from a country's openness to FDI to the participation of its firms in GVCs and to sustainable industrial development in a simplistic manner, without factoring in indigenous technological capabilities as necessary conditions. The acquisitive, operative, adaptive and innovative capabilities of the domestic economy agents play a critical role in bringing out the dynamic gains and positive spillovers from their international interactions, whether through trade or through FDI. Misconceiving this crucial role of indigenous capabilities has been a crucial reason for the failure of mainstream academia and policy analysts to appreciate the import of different industrial policy measures on firm-level strategies while analysing the implications of GVC participation by developing country firms. Thus the theoretical and empirical bases for the mainstream claims that GVCs will enable developing countries to leapfrog are found to be untenable.

Once tariffs are no longer a significant factor subsequent to liberalisation, production costs become the more dominant deciding factor that determine the division of labour between potential host countries participating in fragmented tasks and processes within GVCs. While this is the conclusion arrived at by mainstream literature also, the similarity with heterodox analysis stops there. The significant evidence on the low value-added nature of participation of developing country firms and their limited upgrading within GVCs show that production costs which determine the location advantage of a country within vertical division of labour, are not determined solely by factor price differences – that is, unit labour costs alone. Technological considerations are intrinsic to the cost competitiveness calculations relevant for efficiency-seeking or vertical FDI by MNCs involved in GVCs. The fact that GVCs are characterised by highly asymmetric governance relations controlled centrally by monopolistic technology-owning lead firms accentuate the pressures on competing suppliers across low-income countries and minimise their shares in total value addition. Only technological strength and its continuous upgrading will help domestic firms to engage beneficially with firms within GVC, whether with lead firms or tier one suppliers, and to achieve upgrading in a dynamic sense. This may or may not involve FDI.

As summarised effectively by Chandrasekhar (2013: 75):

> Differences in knowledge embodied in production are seen to be a crucial determinant of productivity differentials across sectors and nations . . . (and therefore affect the value added associated with a particular distribution of the value chain). But transmission of these intangibles from the pure knowledge domain to commodities must be mediated by the application – in different stages stretching from the acquisition of knowledge, through innovation, to the different segments of production – of knowledge labour of different kinds. Labour at each of these stages must acquire the necessary intangibles. Hence any successful transition to knowledge-economy status requires investment geared to the production and dissemination of knowledge of various kinds (i.e. education, R&D, information and coordination, and in training).

In the absence of industrial policy support that help build up such indigenous capabilities, extensive trade and investment liberalisation leads to an erosion of the incentives for local production by both foreign and domestic investors on the one side. On the other hand, whatever local production is carried out by foreign and domestic investors become increasingly dependent on input procurement from producers abroad. Such interactive dynamics between trade and investment liberalisation and other industrial policies have implications for the nature of developing country participation in and their gains from GVCs. They also have implications for wage growth, domestic demand and sustained productive investment in the GVC participating developing country. This was clearly seen in the case study of the electronics industry. The huge increase in aggregate import dependence experienced by the Indian electronics industry, the evidence in import growth revealed by the detailed analysis of bilateral inter-industry and intra-industry trade, as well as the very low level of FDI inflows into the electronics industry, are all stark reflections of the impact of the interplay between the trade and investment liberalisation carried out by India and the market failures associated with non-strategic trade and investment liberalisation in the absence of industrial policy support.

Therefore, the important role of industrial policy for enabling indigenous technology development assumes greater critical significance in the absence of tariff protection in the context of GVCs. While MNC location decisions are being sought to be influenced by Indian governments using investment incentives at the central and state levels as a way to lower input costs, none of the medium- and long-term benefits that India expects from participating in GVCs will accrue in the absence of indigenous technological capabilities required in different processes/activities. The latter is an integral part of the overall ecosystem that needs to be created within India to offer an overall 'incentive' for localising production as well as to draw long-term benefits from such production.

This is again related to our central argument – that is, there is a heightened need for vertical industrial policies to support developing countries' participation in GVCs in increasing returns activities. This first requires India to create and continuously upgrade indigenous capabilities to manufacture products that lead to productivity growth and externalities required for generating virtuous cycles of growth. This is further enhanced by the urgency to respond to the growing challenges arising from climate change, emergence of advanced manufacturing technologies and rapidly evolving digital technologies as well as 're-localisation' or 'backshoring' trends in manufacturing industries.

It is sometimes argued that, given that India has missed the industrialisation bus by at least two decades, and given that the gap with technological frontrunners is enormous, India will not be able to catch up without relying on foreign technology. We contend that whether India is to catch up with or without FDI, the ability to catch up depends on indigenous technological capability build-up.

However, while India faces humongous challenges in maintaining and upgrading local production by domestic and foreign producers under region-wide tariff liberalisation, investment chapters in FTAs compound this problem by restricting the space for many industrial policies, which are required for creating other 'policy-driven incentives for domestic value generation'. The trade-off that was put before developing countries by the WTO between enhanced market access and constraints on industrial policies has intensified under the FTAs that have been in place in India since the mid-2000s.

Although India's FDI policy has been progressively liberalised since the 1991 Industrial Policy and several BITs with broad investment definitions have been in force, the country still had the flexibility to change its industrial policy framework when the circumstances changed or when the need for fine tuning it to meet industrial policy objectives was recognised. Much of this sovereignty has been surrendered by making BIT-plus commitments on 'disciplining' different investment-related industrial policies and measures in the comprehensive trade agreements with Japan, South Korea, Malaysia, etc. The recent trade agreements, by locking in liberalisation at exiting levels and restricting the use of a range of policies and instruments, reduce the policy space to implement several industrial policy tools for building and upgrading domestic capabilities. The following inter-related aspects of investment chapters in FTAs are of utmost importance in this context:

- the broad definition of investment,
- an expanded set of binding regulatory commitments that restrict India's ability to apply policies related to the operations of foreign investors,
- other commitments that oblige India to guarantee protection of all kinds investments that come under the purview of the FTA,
- the definition of expropriation to include indirect expropriation, and
- the ISDS mechanism.

As a result, these agreements have served not only to undermine the purported objectives of RTAs, namely, increased investments and greater exports, but have also undermined India's long-term development prospects.

Domestic and foreign interests formed by the outcomes of previous liberalisation policies in the production and financial sector spheres also form constraints on strategic industrial policymaking. But as argued elsewhere, the interests of exporters and outward investors need to be contextualised within a strategic national development framework that balances the interest of different sections of the society. Further, the sustainability of outward investments (and exports) itself depends crucially on developing and maintaining the dynamic competitiveness of domestic entrepreneurs.

What we mean by industrial policy goes beyond a role of the government in focusing its resources in *stimulating* the private sector to produce new products and services in new ways. A strategic use of industrial policy tools aimed at improving domestic firms' manufacturing and technological capabilities and addressing the market failures in inter-sectoral coordination to foster forward and backward linkages domestically is called for. It is in figuring out the combination of policies that create this overall incentive ingeniously that a developing country like India's greater possibility for GVC engagement lies in. This needs to begin with the acknowledgement that strategic industrial and technological development policies are incompatible with fully liberalised trade, FDI and financial sector regimes. Trade, investment, fiscal and financial sector policies and policies for skill and technology development across sectors have to be coordinated within a strategic framework to achieve sustainable industrial development. Fragmentation of industrial policy initiatives must be avoided. This also requires that along with specific policies geared towards upgrading firm-level, industry-level and economy-wide productivity from a long-term perspective (and not solely import-driven productivity growth), trade and FDI policies should not negate incentives for domestic production, whether in agriculture, industry or services. To the extent that this requires re-formulating the FTAs, the government should explore the ways and means.

Once we are able to move beyond the constraint imposed by the neoliberal framework in terms of the state-market dichotomised debate on policy choices, we can discuss the appropriate state intervention. There is no argument or policy space to return to industrial policies of the kind that were in existence in the 1970s, 80s or 90s. What is appropriate at a point in time will necessarily depend on the kind of industry, its current stage of development and domestic and international economic and political factors, and this necessarily changes with the needs of changing circumstances. "It could variously mean leading or following the market, handmaidenly support, traditional selective protection, state enterprise and so forth" (Sridharan 1996: 8). This could be the role of facilitating and participating in the growth of industrial network structures (Breznitz 2006; Nawrot 2014), of being the entrepreneurial state (Mazzucato 2013) or of market-steering, 'societal mission roles' (Wade 2018;

Kattel 2018; Mazzucato 2017). In practice, it will clearly have to be a combination of these various roles in different areas.

Given the legal constraints in certain areas, what is required for coordinating sectoral policies and technology development policies is to think of new ingenious ways of linking up upstream and downstream demand in several industries and sectors. Moreover, linked to technological abilities is the fact that standards increasingly play a critical role in coordinating cross-country production sharing within GVCs. Therefore, concerted efforts to improve the standards compliance capacity of firms and infrastructural support are crucial for increasing Indian firms' competitiveness across the agricultural, manufacturing and services sectors. This has to go hand-in-hand with ways to build up indigenous capabilities through massive public investments in secondary and higher education as well as science and technology and R&D.

It is pertinent to note that the emphasis of the IFIs is shifting to services sector liberalisation as the way forward to increasing engagement in GVCs – again, within the framework of increasing manufacturing firms' productivity by reducing input costs, this time of services. This is clearly observable in World Bank's recent study:

> For developing countries wishing to participate more in GVCs and to move up the value chain, one obvious measure is to open services to import competition and direct foreign investment. Improved access to finance, communications, transport, and other services, through reform in general, foreign direct investment in particular, enhances manufacturing firms' productivity and other aspects of the performance of downstream firms.
>
> (World Bank 2017: 12)

We have shown the contradictions between the policy objective of increasing India's integration with GVCs by attracting vertical FDI and the policy tools of trade and financial liberalisation within the neoliberal framework. Further, the evidence that MNC/foreign subsidiaries tend to employ more import-intensive techniques and that even domestic producers shift to import-intensive production contradict the objective of creating large-scale employment through participation in simple consumer/capital goods production within GVCs. These need to be factored in while framing policies to promote GVCs.

An assessment of recent government initiatives need to be carried out within this analytical framework by examining how the interfaces and interactions between various vertical and horizontal industrial policies impact firm-level incentives for undertaking domestically based activities. This is beyond the scope of the current work. However, what must be mentioned is that the continuing emphasis on the 'ease of doing business' including at the state level (because they feed into the international 'ease of doing business' ranking of the country) will be effective only to the extent that other policies to build up capabilities and capacities take place simultaneously. Just creating an 'enabling' start-up ecosystem or further easing of horizontal constraints will not be sufficient to attract FDI in higher technological activities and to get the medium- and long-term benefits from FDI.

It would be timely for a new industrial policy document to dissociate both state support for industrial development and public sector institutions – industrial, scientific and technological as well as financial – from the legacy of the excesses that were part of import-substitution industrialisation and grant them the rightful place in financing long-term investment and technological change. However, financing mechanisms must be designed in ways that preclude political leverage to avoid rent-seeking behaviour and inefficiencies. Moreover, any government support must be time bound and periodically modified based on performance monitoring. The advanced countries and the late industrialisers in East Asia and elsewhere have set varied examples; India will need to chart its own course.

New laws and regulations (unattached to investment incentives) to ensure maximum long-term benefits from foreign investments can be employed by states and other sub-national governments. Given that state, provincial or other local governments can also pursue active industrial policy measures, it is important for India (from the perspective of maintaining autonomy for industrial policy) to preserve the right to adopt investment-related measures as per the laws and regulations framed at the sub-federal government level. This is critical from the perspective of maintaining autonomy for industrial policy. This is also crucial from the point of view of retaining the flexibility to put in place locality-specific climate change adaptation and mitigation measures. If competition among states for attracting foreign investors is not to lead to a race-to-the-bottom in labour and environmental protection rights, investment incentives offered at the sub-national levels must be coordinated by a central agency to avoid investors from 'shopping around'. This would be important to prevent the build-up of undue fiscal burden too.

In the rapidly changing global environment that has impacted foreign capital flows into the economy, policymakers might soon push for the pending comprehensive trade agreements with the EU, EFTA and the US under the belief that they will help to bring in more foreign investment into debt-ridden enterprises that help them survive. However, signing more and more legally binding trade and investment agreements with inadequate understanding of the interconnectedness of industrial and trade policies to the macroeconomic growth dynamics through employment, value addition and technological development, will lead to further adverse impacts on India's development prospects.

As the digital phase of the ICT techno-economic revolution throws up new and emerging windows of opportunity (see Perez 2002; and other papers cited in Francis 2018a), the question is about India's capabilities to make use of the existing and emerging windows of opportunities. The strategic nature of electronics industry in the sense of its competitiveness being critical to competitiveness in other industries cannot be over-emphasised as we have moved into the digital era.

Business strategies are being revolutionised in an unprecedented manner in the digital age. Digitisation will transform the way products and services are made, procured, sold and traded. It will also change the way business processes are carried out, as well as how products and services are combined. All these in turn have significant implications for GVC dynamics. The top end of the GVCs in a number of sectors is likely to be controlled by businesses owning digital platforms and data. As seen in the digital platforms and globalised oligopolistic competition in several other industries/segments, the objective of private firms to appropriate the maximum rents from their investment in R&D suggests that, generally, they will concentrate on developing techniques that cannot be easily replicated. All these create significant hurdles for developing country firms. Meanwhile, there are ongoing attempts by developed countries as well as China to forge new regulations in e-commerce at the WTO and through free trade agreements (FTAs). These need to be considered by India with extreme caution.

Currently, there is significant optimism in India surrounding the innovation capabilities observed among the numerable services and other start-ups. However, if India has to create the conditions for a major structural transformation mediated through entrepreneurial and innovative dynamism, it needs to upgrade its manufacturing capabilities to a significantly higher level so as not to end up in an even higher import-dependency from the emerging digitalised production and consumption patterns. This needs a multi-pronged and multi-layered approach. The country has to formulate strategies that build on and dynamically grow the synergies between different activities across industries. Such strategies have to be a combination involving the following:

- economy-wide efficiency enhancing measures involving heavy public investments for improving social and physical infrastructure (The former will necessitate large public investments in particular, higher and technical education, health and skill levels and minimum social protection);
- policies aimed at improving the competitive and innovative strengths of particular industries such as pharmaceuticals, automobiles, textiles and garments, electronics hardware, software, chemicals, metal products, etc.;
- policies aimed at developing and building on intra-industry and cross-sectoral synergies to stimulate network effects and agglomeration externalities in productive activities; and
- a big push from the government in terms of public R&D in selective advanced and emerging technologies, in collaboration with private sector, which might allow India to leapfrog into frontier technologies.

The magnitude of the challenge before India to increase investments for improving productive capacities and capabilities on a large enough scale to improve its manufacturing sector competitiveness globally is humungous. The level of government expenditure commitments required can only be supported by following prudent counter-cyclical macroeconomic and financial sector policies for ensuring the financing of productive investments and financial stability as well as by having in place progressive taxation policies that do not erode the government's revenue base.

There is no denying that it is not always the case that industrial policy formulation is being held back by a lack of policy space. This takes us to the discussion in the literature related to the required strategic capacity of the state to 'reconstruct' the appropriate forms of the intervention required. The concept of strategic capacity of the state as determined by the autonomy and implementation capacity of state institutions (credited to Deyo, Evans, Wade, etc.) is useful to understand the path dependence of the industrial development trajectory and to explore whether this may be overcome. Analyses of the Indian state's regulatory capacity by Chibber (2004) and Das Gupta (2016) broadly follow this framework. Chibber (2004: 254) observed that *independently of the effects of corruption and clientelism* (emphasis in the original), effective industrial policy in India had been crippled by the fragmentation of the policy apparatus and the inability to discipline capital. This argument is complemented by Das Gupta (2016: 259), who showed that "state power has become so entangled with big capitalist interests that even feeble attempts at establishing discipline or control over the accumulation process have been abdicated".

It may be acknowledged in some policy circles that the creation of internationally competitive indigenous firms is vital to sustain economic growth and self-reliance, instead of successive rounds of foreign capital-dependent acquisition of technology and capital goods that lead to ever increasing levels of foreign dependence and spiralling of debt. But for various reasons as observed above, the former might not be the priority of any particular government. Ultimately, as Sridharan (1996) argued, the more fundamental question of "what sort of strategy the state *will* decide to adopt and implement" (emphasis in the original) can be answered only by situating strategic capacity within the framework of the political-economic grand strategy of the state elite, which is in turn determined by their "strategic priorities" (Sridharan 1996: 200).

The emerging picture thus necessarily involves complex interactions between multiple socio-political and economic factors. But what is evident is that failing to factor in the industrial policy causalities involved in indigenous technology development, the many barriers to GVC entry and upgrading erected by monopolistic lead firms, the assessments of the impact of existing FTAs and FDI liberalisation on firm-level incentives for undertaking domestic production and the industrial policy constraints imposed by FTAs will prove costly for India.

Bibliography

Abrol, Dinesh (2014) 'Technological Upgrading, Manufacturing and Innovation: Lessons from Indian Pharmaceuticals', *ISID Working Paper No. 162*, Institute for Studies in Industrial Development (ISID), New Delhi.

Abrol, Dinesh (2016) 'Who Will Gain from the National IPRs Policy?' *ISID Policy Brief No. 1*, Institute for Studies in Industrial Development (ISID), New Delhi, pp. 1–4.

Aghion, P., D. Hemous, and R. Veugelers (2009) *No Green Growth Without Innovation*, Policy Brief, Bruegel, Brussels.

Akamatsu, Kaname (1961) 'A Theory of Unbalanced Growth in the World Economy', *Weltwirtschaftliches Archiv*, Vol. 82 (2), pp. 196–217.

Akamatsu, Kaname (1962) 'A Historical Pattern of Economic Growth in Developing Countries', *Journal of Developing Economies*, Vol. 1 (1), pp. 3–25.

Akyuz, Yilmaz (2005) *The WTO Negotiations on Industrial Tariffs: What Is at Stake for Developing Countries?* TWN Trade and Development Series No. 24, Third World Network (TWN), Malaysia.

Akyuz, Yilmaz (2007) 'Global Rules and Markets: Constraints Over Policy Autonomy in Developing Countries', *Paper Prepared for the International Institute for Labour Studies of the ILO.*

Alcorta, Ludovico (2014) 'Strategic Specialization: Policy Responses to a Changing Global Manufacturing Landscape', in Annelieke van der Giessen, Claire Stolwijk, and Jos Leijten (eds.), *Can Policy Follow the Dynamics of Global Innovation Platforms? Collection of Conference Papers*, The Innovation Network 6CP, Delft.

Aldonas, Grant (2013) '*Trade Policy in a Global Age*', International Centre for Trade and Sustainable Development (ICTSD), Geneva.

Ali, Anesa, and Perez Caldentey Esteban (2006) 'Regional Trade Agreements: The Mainstream Approach and an Alternative Treatment', Available at www.networkideas.org/featart/aug2006/Trade_Agreements.pdf

Amiti, M., and J. Konings (2007) 'Trade Liberalization, Intermediate Products and Productivity: Evidence from Indonesia', *The American Economic Review*, Vol. 97, pp. 1611–1638.

Amsden, Alice H. (1989) *Asia's Next Giant: South Korea and Late Indus-trialization*, Oxford University Press, Oxford.

Amsden, Alice H. (2001) *The Rise of "The Rest": Challenges to the West from Late-Industrializing Economies*, Oxford University Press, New York.

Ando, Mitsuyo, and Fukunari Kimura (2003) 'The Formation of Interna-tional Production and Distribution Networks in East Asia', *Paper Pre-sented at the Fourteenth NBER Annual East Asian Seminar on Economics*, 'International Trade', Held in Taipei, Taiwan, September, pp. 5–7.

Anukoonwattaka, Witada (2011) 'Introduction', in Witada Anukoonwat-taka, and Mia Mikic (eds.), *India: A New Player in Asian Production Networks?* ESCAP-ARTNeT Studies in Trade and Investment 75, UN, Bangkok.

Asian Development Bank (2008) *Emerging Asian Regionalism: A Partner-ship for Shared Prosperity*, ADB, Manila.

Athukorala, Prema-chandra (2003) 'Product Fragmentation and Trade Pat-terns in East Asia', *Trade and Development Discussion Paper 2003/21*, Division of Economics, Research School of Pacific and Asian Studies, The Australian National University, Canberra.

Athukorala, Prema-chandra (2007) 'Singapore and ASEAN in the New Regional Division of Labour', *Revised Version of a Paper Presented at the Workshop, 'Production Networks and Changing Trade and Invest-ment Patterns: The Economic Emergence of China and India and Impli-cations for Asia and Singapore'*, September, pp. 14–15, 2006, Singapore Centre for Applied and Policy Economics, University of Singapore.

Athukorala, Prema-chandra (2011) 'Production Networks and Trade Pat-terns in East Asia: Regionalization or Globalization?' *Asian Economic Papers*, Vol. 10 (1), 65–95.

Athukorala, Prema-chandra (2016) 'Global Production Sharing and Export Expansion: Emerging Opportunities and the Indian Experience', in C. Veeramani, and R. Nagaraj (eds.), *International Trade and Industrial Development in India: Emerging Trends, Patterns and Issues*, Orient BlackSwan, New Delhi.

Athukorala, Prema-chandra, and Nobuaki Yamashita (2006) 'Production Fragmentation and Trade Integration: East Asia in a Global Context', Available at http://ideas.repec.org/p/pas/papers/2005-07.html

Balakrishnan, Pulapre (2011) (ed.) *Economic Reforms and Growth in India, Essays from Economic and Political Weekly*, Orient Blackswan Pvt. Ltd, New Delhi.

Baldwin, Richard (2013) 'Global Supply Chains: Why They Emerged, Why They Matter and Where They Are Going', in D. K. Elms, and P. Low (eds.), *Global Value Chains in a Changing World*, World Trade Organi-zation (WTO), Geneva.

Baldwin, Richard, and Anthony Venables (2010) 'Relocating the Value Chain: Offshoring and Agglomeration in the Global Economy', *NBER Working Paper 16611*, Cambridge.

Baldwin, Richard and Javier Lopez-Gonzalez (2013) 'Supply-Chain Trade: A Portrait of Global Patterns and Several Testable Hypotheses', *OCED Working Paper 18957*, OECD, Massachusetts.

Baldwin, Richard, and Toshihiro Okubo (2012) 'Networked FDI: Sales and Sourcing Patterns of Japanese Foreign Affiliates', *NBER Working Papers No. 18083*, The National Bureau of Economic Research (NBER), Cambridge.

Banga, Karishma (2016) 'Impact of Global Value Chains on Employment in India', *Journal of Economic Integration*, Vol. 31 (3), pp. 631–73.

Banga, Rashmi (2013) 'Measuring Value in Global Value Chains', *UNCTAD Background Paper No. RVC-8*, UNCTAD, Geneva.

Batra, Amita (2006), 'Asian Economic Integration- ASEAN+3+1 or ASEAN+1s?', ICRIER Working Paper No. 186, ICRIER, New Delhi.

Beltramello, A., K. De Backer, and L. Moussiegt (2012) 'The Export Performance of Countries Within Global Value Chains (GVCs)', *OECD Science, Technology and Industry Working Paper No. 2012/02*, OECD.

Berger, Axel, Clara Brandi, and Dominique Bruhn (2016) '*Environmental Provisions in Preferential Trade Agreements: Comparing the European and Emerging Markets' Approach*', January 15, Version, German Development Institute, Available at www.oefse.at/fileadmin/content/Down loads/tradeconference/BergerBrandiBruhn_Green_PTAs_Jan_16.pdf

Bernasconi-Osterwalder, Nathalie (2016) 'State: State Dispute Settlement in Investment Treaties', in Kavaljit Singh, and Burghard Ilge (eds.), *Rethinking Bilateral Investment Treaties, Critical Issues, and Policy Choices*, Both Ends and SOMO, Amsterdam and Madhyam, New Delhi.

Bhaduri, Amit (2007) 'Alternatives in Industrialisation', *Economic and Political Weekly*, April, pp. 1597–1601.

Borrus, Michael, Dieter Ernst, and Stephan Haggard (2000) *International Production Networks in Asia: Rivalry or Riches*, Routledge, London and New York.

Bose, Ahana, and Parthapratim Pal (2018) 'External Commercial Borrowings: Is It a Boon or a Bane?' *Economic and Political Weekly*, Vol. LIII (30), pp. 19–22.

Brandt, Philipp, and Josh Whitford (2017) 'Fixing Network Failures? The Contested Case of the American Manufacturing Extension Partnership', *Socio Economic Review*, Vol. 15 (2), pp. 331–357.

Breznitz, Dan (2006) 'Innovation and the State: Development Strategies for High Technology Industries in a World of Fragmented Production: Israel, Ireland, and Taiwan', *Enterprise & Society*, pp. 675–85, Oxford University Press on behalf of the Business History Conference.

Casini, Paolo, and Neil Kay (2014) 'Competing in Global Value Chains', in Annelieke van der Giessen, Claire Stolwijk, and Jos Leijten (eds.), *Can Policy Follow the Dynamics of Global Innovation Platforms? Collection of Conference Papers*, 6CP, Delft.

Chandra, Vandana, and Sashi Kolavalli (2006) 'Technology, Adaptation, and Exports: How Some Countries Got it Right', in Vandana Chandra (ed.) *Technology, Adaptation and Exports*, World Bank Publications.

Chandrasekhar, C. P. (1994a) 'Aspects of Growth and Structural Change in Indian Industry', in Deepak Nayyar (ed.), *Industrial Growth and Stagnation: The Debate in India*, Oxford University Press, New Delhi.

Chandrasekhar, C. P. (1994b) 'The Macroeconomics of Imbalance and Adjustment', in Prabhat Patnaik (ed.), *Themes in Economics: Macroeconomics*, Oxford University Press, New Delhi.

Chandrasekhar, C. P. (2005) 'The Diffusion of Information Technology and Implications for Development: A Perspective Based on the Indian Experience', in Ashwani Saith, and M. Vijayabasker (eds.), *ICTs and Indian Economic Development*, Sage Publications, New Delhi.

Chandrasekhar, C. P. (2013) 'Knowledge and the Asian Challenge', in Nobuharu Yokokawa, Jayati Ghosh, and Robert Rowthorn (eds.), *Industrialization of China and India: Their Impacts on the World Economy*, Routledge, London and New York.

Chandrasekhar, C. P. (2015) 'Promise Belied: India's Post-independence Industrialisation Experience', in C. P. Chandrasekhar (ed.), *Indian Industrialization*, ICSSR Research Surveys and Explorations, Oxford University Press, New Delhi.

Chandrasekhar, C. P., and Jayati Ghosh (2002) *The Market That Failed: A Decade of Neoliberal Economic Reforms in India*, Leftword Books, New Delhi.

Chandrasekhar, C. P. and Jayati Ghosh (2006) 'IT-driven Offshoring: The Exaggerated "Development Opportunity"', Available at http://net workideas.org/featart/jan2006/Driven_Offshoring.pdf

Chandrasekhar, C. P., and Jayati Ghosh (2007) 'IT-driven Offshoring: The Exaggerated Development Opportunity', *IDEAs Working Paper No. 03/2007*, International Development Economics Associates (IDEAs), New Delhi.

Chandrasekhar, C. P., and Jayati Ghosh (2017) 'Lopsided Industrialisation', *The Business Line*, May 8.

Chang, Ha-Joon (2002) 'Kicking Away the Ladder: An Unofficial History of Capitalism, Especially in Britain and the United States', *Challenge*, Vol. 45 (5), pp. 63–97.

Chaudhuri, Sudip (2013) 'Manufacturing Trade Deficit and Industrial Policy in India', *Economic and Political Weekly*, Vol. 48 (8), pp. 41–50.

Chaudhuri, Sudip (2015) 'Import Liberalisation and Premature Deindustrialisation in India', *Economic and Political Weekly*, Vol. 50 (43), pp. 60–69.

Chibber, Vivek (2004) Locked in Place: State Building and Late Industrialisation in India, Tulika Books, New Delhi.

Contractor, F. J., et al. (2011) Global Outsourcing and Offshoring: An integrated approach to Theory and Corporate Strategy, Cambridge University Press, Cambridge.

Correa, Carlos M. (2016) 'Innovation and the Global Expansion of Intellectual Property Rights: Unfulfilled Promises', *Research Paper No. 70*, South Centre, Geneva.

Dachs, B., and S. Kinkel (2013) 'Backshoring of Production Activities in European Manufacturing – Evidence from a Large-Scale Survey', *Proceedings 20th Annual Conference of the of the European Operations Management Association (EurOMA)*, EurOMA, Dublin.

Damodaran, Sumangala (2016) 'New Strategies of Industrial Organization and Labour in the Mobile Telecom Sector in India', in Dev Nathan, Meenu Tiwari, and Sandip Sarkar (eds.), *Labour in Global Value Chains in Asia*, Cambridge University Press, New York.

Das, Abhijit, and Zaki Hussain (2017) 'Global Value Chains: Asymmetries, Realities and Risks', *Centre for WTO Studies Working Paper No. 36*, Indian Institute of Foreign Trade, New Delhi.

Das Gupta, Chirashree (2016) State and Capital in Independent India: Institutions and Accumulation, Cambridge University Press, Delhi.

Das, Keshab, and Hastimal Sagara (2017) 'State and the IT Industry in India: An Overview', *Economic & Political Weekly*, Vol. LII (41), pp. 56–64.

Dash, Ankita, and Rupa Chanda (2017) 'Indian Firms in Automotive Global Value Chains: A Sectoral Analysis', *CWS Working Paper No. 40*, Indian Institute of Foreign Trade, New Delhi.

Dastidar, Ananya Ghosh (2015) 'India's Experience with Export-led Growth', in Jayati Ghosh (ed.), *India and the World Economy*, ICSSR Research Surveys and Explorations, Oxford University Press, New Delhi.

D&B Analysis (2012) 'IT Hardware and Electronics: Productivity and Efficiency Benchmarking', Government of India, Ministry of Science and Technology, Department of Scientific and Industrial Research (DSIR).

De Backer, Koen De, and Norihiko Yamano (2010) *International Comparative Evidence on Global Value Chains, Directorate for Science*, Technology and Industry, OECD.

DEITy (2012) *DEITy, Report of the Working Group on Information Technology Sector, Twelfth Five Year Plan (2012–2017)*, Ministry of Communications and Information Technology, Government of India.

Department of Industrial Policy and Promotion (DIPP 2011) 'National Manufacturing Policy', 2011, Press, Note no. 2 (2011 Series), Ministry of Commerce & Industry, Government of India.

Devlin, R. and Graciela Moguillansky (2012) 'What's New in the New Industrial Policy in Latin America?', Policy Research Working Paper 6191, World Bank, Washington, D.C.

Dhar, Biswajit (2014) 'Industrial Policy: Its Relevance and Currency', *ISID Working Paper No. 174*, Institute for Studies in Industrial Development (ISID), New Delhi.

Dhar, Biswajit (2015) 'India's Experience with BITs: Highlights from Recent ISDS Cases', *Investment Policy Brief*, South Centre, Geneva.

Dhar, Biswajit, and Kasturi Das (2015) 'Negotiations in the Doha Round: Critical Issues for India', in Jayati Ghosh (ed.), *India and the World Economy*, ICSSR Research Survey Vol., Oxford University Press, New Delhi, pp. 225–286.

Dhar, Biswajit, and Murali Kallummal (2002) 'Capital Inflows and Effects of Market-driven Investments: A Focus on Southeast Asian Crisis', *RIS Occasional Paper No 66*, RIS, New Delhi.

Dhar, Biswajit, and Murali Kallummal (2007) 'Trade Policy Off the Hook: The Making of Indian Trade Policy Since the Uruguay Round', in Mark Halle, and Robert Wolfe (eds.), *Process Matters: Sustainable Development and Domestic Trade Transparency*, IISD, Manitoba.

Dicken, Peter (1998) *The Global Shift: Transforming the World Economy*, Paul Chapman Publishing Ltd., London.

Dobson, Wendy, and Chia Siow Yue (eds.) (1997) *Multinationals and East Asian Integration*, IDRC, Canada and ISEAS, Singapore.

Dobson, Wendy, and Frank Flatters (eds.) (1994) Pacific Trade and Investment: Options for the 90s, *Proceedings of a Conference Held in Toronto*, June, pp. 6–8.

Draper, Peter, and Andreas Freytag (2014) *Who Captures the Value in the Global Value Chain? High Level Implications for the World Trade Organization*, E15Initiative, International Centre for Trade and Sustainable Development (ICTSD), Geneva.

Dumberry, Patrick (2016) 'Suggestions for Incorporating Human Rights Obligations into BITs', in Kavaljit Singh, and Burghard Ilge (eds.), *Rethinking Bilateral Investment Treaties, Critical Issues, and Policy Choices*, Both Ends and SOMO, Amsterdam and Madhyam, New Delhi.

Dunning, J. H. (1980) 'Towards an Eclectic Theory of International Production: Some Empirical Tests', *Journal of International Business Studies*, Vol. 11 (1), pp. 9–31.

Dunning, J. H. (1988) *Explaining International Production*, Harper Collins, London.

Dutt, Amitava K. (2005) 'International Trade in Early Development Economics', in K. S. Jomo, and Erik S. Reinert (eds.), *The Origins of Development Economics*, Tulika Books, New Delhi.

Eberhardt, Pia, and Cecilia Olivet (2016) 'Profiting from Injustice: Tracing the Rise of Investment Arbitration Industry', in Kavaljit Singh, and Burghard Ilge (eds.), *Rethinking Bilateral Investment Treaties, Critical Issues, and Policy Choices*, Both Ends and SOMO, Amsterdam and Madhyam, New Delhi.

ECA (2016) *Transformative Industrial Policy for Africa*, UN Economic Commission for Africa (ECA), Addis Ababa.

Epstein, Gerald (2012) 'Capital Outflow Regulation: Economic Management, Development and Transformation', in Kevin P. Gallagher, Stephany Griffith-Jones, and José Antonio Ocampo (eds.), *Regulating Global Capital Flows for Long-Run Development*, Pardee Center Task Force Report, Boston University, MA.

Epstein, Gerald, Ilene Grabel, and K. S. Jomo (2003) 'Capital Management Techniques in Developing Countries', in Ariel Buira (ed.), *Challenges to the World Bank and the IMF: Developing Country Perspectives*, Anthem Press, London.

Ernst, Dieter (1997) 'Partners for the China Circle? The Asian Production Networks of Japanese Electronics Firms', DRUID Working Paper No. 97-3, 7-3, DRUID, Copenhagen Business School, Department of Industrial Economics and Strategy/Aalborg University, Department of Business Studies.

Ernst, Dieter (2009) 'A New Geography of Knowledge in the Electronics Industry? Asia's Role in Global Innovation Networks', *East West Center Policy Studies, No 54*, East-West Centre, Honolulu.

Ernst, Dieter (2014) 'Trade and innovation in global networks regional policy implications: A think piece', in Annelieke van der Giessen, Claire Stolwijk, and Jos Leijten (eds.), *Can Policy Follow the Dynamics of Global Innovation Platforms? Collection of Conference Papers*, The Innovation Policy Network Six Countries Programme (6CP), Delft.

Ernst, Dieter (2014) *Upgrading India's Electronics Manufacturing Industry: Regulatory Reform and Industrial Policy*, A Special Study, East-West Centre, Honolulu.

Ernst, Dieter (2015) 'From Catching up to Forging Ahead: China's Policies for Semiconductors', East-West Centre Working Papers, East-West Centre, Honolulu.

Ernst, Dieter, and Barry Naughton (2008) 'China's Emerging Industrial Economy: Insights from the IT Industry', in Christopher A. McNally (ed.), *China's Emergent Political Economy – Capitalism in the Dragon's Lair*, Routledge, London and New York, pp. 39–59.

Ernst & Young and FICCI (2015) Study on Indian Electronics and Consumer Durables Segment, Ernst and Young, Available at https://www.ey.com/Publication/vwLUAssets/EY-study-on-indian-electronics-and-consumer-durables/%24FILE/EY-study-on-indian-electronics-and-consumer-durables.pdf.

Felipe, Jesus, Arnelyn Abdon, and Utsav Kumar (2012) 'Tracking the Middle-income Trap: What Is It, Who Is in It, and Why?' *The Levi Economic Institute Working Paper No. 715*, Levy Economics Institute of Bard College, New York.

Felipe, Jesus, Utsav Kumar, Norio Usui, and Arnelyn Abdon (2010a) 'Why Has China Succeeded: And Why It Will Continue to Do So', *The Levi*

Economic Institute Working Paper No. 611, Levy Economics Institute of Bard College, New York.

Felipe, Jesus, Utsav Kumar, Norio Usui, and Arnelyn Abdon (2010b) 'Exports, Capabilities, and Industrial Policy in India', *The Levi Economic Institute Working Paper No. 638*, Levy Economics Institute of Bard College, New York.

Findlay, C. and M. Pangestu (2001) 'Regional Trade Arrangements in Asia-Pacific: Where are they taking us?', Paper presented at the Trade Policy Forum 'Regional Trade Arrangements', 12–13 June, Bangkok.

Fine, Ben, Jyoti Saraswati, and Daniela Tavasci (eds.) (2013) *Beyond the Developmental State – Industrial Policy into the Twentieth Century*, Pluto Press, London.

Fine, Ben, and K. S. Jomo (eds.) (2006) *The New Development Economics: After the Washington Consensus*, Tulika, New Delhi.

Fontagné, Lionel, Michael Freudenberg, and Guillaume Gaulier (2005) 'Disentangling Horizontal and Vertical Intra-Industry Trade', *CEPII Working Paper No. 2005–2010*, CEPII, Paris.

Fontagné, Lionel, Michael Freudenberg, and Guillaume Gaulier (2006) 'A Systematic Decomposition of World Trade into Horizontal and Vertical IIT', *Weltwirtschaftliches Archives*, Vol. 142 (3), pp. 459–475.

Francis, Smitha (2003) *'Foreign Direct Investment Flows and Industrial Restructuring in South East Asia: A Case Study of Thailand (1987–1998)'*, Ph.D. Thesis, Centre for Economic Studies and Planning, Jawaharlal Nehru University (J.N.U.), New Delhi.

Francis, Smitha (2004) 'Fluid Finances, Systemic Risk and the IMF's SDRM Proposal', in K. S. Jomo (ed.), *After the Storm: Crisis, Recovery and Sustaining Development in Four Asian Economies*, Singapore University Press, Co-authored with C. P. Chandrasekhar and Jayati Ghosh, pp. 75–97.

Francis, Smitha (2010) 'Foreign Direct Investment Concepts: Implications for Negotiations', *Economic & Political Weekly*, May 29, Vol. XLV (22), pp. 31–36.

Francis, Smitha (2011a) 'The ASEAN-India Free Trade Agreement: A Sectoral Impact Analysis of Increased Trade Integration in Goods', *Economic & Political Weekly*, Vol. XIVI (2), pp. 46–55.

Francis, Smitha (2011b) 'Rethinking Investment Provisions in Free Trade Agreements', IDEAs Policy Note, Available at www.networkideas.org/alt/may2011/alt09_Investment_Policy_Note.htm

Francis, Smitha (2013a) 'Changing the Investment Policy Menu', *Economic and Political Weekly*, Vol. XLVIIL (5), pp. 68–73.

Francis, Smitha (2013b) 'Capital Account Regulatory Space Under India's Investment and Trade Agreements', in Kevin Gallagher (ed.), *Compatibility Review of the Trade Regime and Capital Account Regulations*, Pardee Centre Taskforce Report, Frederick S. Pardee Centre for the Study of the Longer-Range Future, Boston University, MA, pp. 109–120.

Francis, Smitha (2015a) 'India's Manufacturing Sector Export Perfor-
mance: A Focus on Missing Domestic Inter-sectoral Linkages', *ISID
Working Paper No. 182*, Institute for Studies in Industrial Development
(ISID), New Delhi.
Francis, Smitha (2015b) 'Preferential Trade Agreements: An Exploration
into Emerging Issues in India's Changing Trade Policy Landscape', in
Jayati Ghosh (ed.), *India and the World Economy*, ICSSR Research Sur-
veys and Explorations, Oxford University Press, New Delhi.
Francis, Smitha (2016) 'Impact of Trade Liberalisation on the Indian Elec-
tronics Industry: Some Aspects of the Industrial Policy Dynamics in
Global Value Chain Engagement', *ISID Working Paper No. 192*, ISID,
New Delhi.
Francis, Smitha (2017) *Towards a Progressive Industrial Policy in the Time
of GVCs and FTAs: An Overview with a Focus on India*, Rosa Luxem-
burg Stiftung (RLS), Brussels.
Francis, Smitha (2018a) 'Evolution of Technologies in the Digital Arena:
Theories, Firm Strategies and Policies', *Working Paper No. CWS/
WP/200/47*, Centre for WTO Studies, New Delhi.
Francis, Smitha (2018b) 'India's Electronics Manufacturing Sector: Get-
ting the Diagnosis Right', *Economic and Political Weekly*, Vol. LIII (34),
pp. 112–117.
Francis, Smitha and Murali Kallummal (2009), The New Regionalism
in Southeast Asian Trade Policy and Issues in Market Access and
Industrial Development: An Analysis of the ASEAN-China Free Trade
Agreement', *Journal of Economic Policy and Research*, Vol.4 (2),
pp. 82–136.
Francis, Smitha, and Murali Kallummal (2013) 'India's Comprehensive
Trade Agreements: Implications for Development Trajectory', *Eco-
nomic & Political Weekly*, Vol. XLVIII (31), August, pp. 109–122.
Francois, J., P. B. Rana, and G. Wignaraja (eds.) (2009) *Pan-Asian Integra-
tion: Linking East and South Asia*, ADB, Palgrave Macmillan, Hampshire.
Fu, Xiaolan, Carlo Pietrobelli, and Luc Soete (2010) 'The Role of Foreign
Technology and Indigenous Innovation in Emerging Economies: Tech-
nological Change and Catching Up', *Technical Notes No. IDB-TN-166*,
Inter-American Development Bank, Washington, DC.
Fukao, Kyoji, Hikari Ishido, and Keiko Ito (2003) 'Vertical Intra-Indus-
try Trade and Foreign Direct Investment in East Asia', *Hitotsubashi
University Discussion Paper Series*, No. 434, Hitotsubashi University,
Tokyo.
Fuller, Douglas B. (2016) *Paper Tigers, Hidden Dragons: Firms and the
Political Economy of China's Technological Development*, Oxford Uni-
versity Press, New York.
Gallagher, Kevin P., and L. Zarsky (2007) *The Enclave Economy: Foreign
Investment and Sustainable Development in Mexico's Silicon Valley*,
MIT Press, Cambridge, MA.

Gallagher, Kevin P., and Mehdi Shafaeddin (2009) 'Policies for Industrial Learning in China and Mexico', *RIS-DP No. 150*, Research and Information System for the Non-Aligned Countries (RIS), New Delhi.

Gallagher, Kevin P, Stephany Griffi th-Jones and José Antonio Ocampo ed. (2012): *Regulating Global Capital Flows for Long-Run Development*, Pardee Center Task Force Report.

Gallagher, Kevin P. and Leonardo E. Stanley (2013) 'Capital Account Regulations and the Trading System: The Need for Reconciliation', in Kevin Gallagher (ed.), *Compatibility Review of the Trade Regime and Capital Account Regulations*, Pardee Centre Taskforce Report, Frederick S. Pardee Centre for the Study of the Longer-Range Future, Boston University, MA, pp. 1–11.

Gereffi, G., and M. Korzeniewicz (eds.) (1994) *Commodity Chains and Global Capitalism*, Praeger, Westport, CT.

Gereffi, Gari (1995) 'Global Commodity Chains and Third World Development', *Paper Presented in the Conference 'Regionalisation and Labour Market Interdependence in East and South-East Asia'*, Bangkok, January, pp. 23–26.

Gereffi, Gari (2014) 'Global value chains in a post-Washington Consensus world', *Review of International Political Economy*, Vol. 21 (1), pp. 9–37.

Gereffi, Gari and T. Sturgeon (2013) 'Global Value Chain-Oriented Industrial Policy: The role of emerging economies', in Deborah Elms and Patrick Low (eds.) *Supply Chains in a Changing World*, WTO, Geneva.

Gereffi, Gari, J. Humphrey, and T. Sturgeon (2005) 'The Governance of Global Value Chains', *Review of International Political Economy*, Vol. 12 (1), pp. 7–104.

Gereffi, Gari, J. Humphrey, R. Kaplinsky, and T. Sturgeon (2001) 'Introduction: Globalisation, Value Chains and Development', *IDS Bulletin*, 32 (3), pp. 1–8.

Gerschenkron, A. (1962) *Economic Backwardness in Historical Perspective*, Belknap Press of Harvard University Press, Cambridge, MA.

Ghosh, Jayati (2005) 'Michal Kalecki and the Economics of Development', in K. S. Jomo (ed.), *Pioneers of Development Economics*, Zed Books, London.

Ghosh, Jayati (2009) 'Growth, Macroeconomic Policies and Structural Change', *Thematic Paper Prepared for UNRISD (2010)*, Combating Poverty and Inequality, UNRISD Flagship Report, Geneva.

Ghosh, Jayati (2010) 'The Economic and Social Effects of Financial Liberalisation: A Primer for Developing Countries', Available at www.net workideas.org/featart/sep2005/Financial_Liberalisation.pdf

Ghosh, Jayati (2013) 'Growth and Emergent Constraints in the Indian Economy in the Context of Global Uncertainty', in Nobuharu Yokokawa, Jayati Ghosh, and Bob Rowthorn (eds.), *Industrialization of China and*

India: Their Impacts on the World Economy, Routledge, London and New York.

Gopakumar, K. M. (2010) 'Product Patents and Access to Medicines in India: A Critical Review of the Implementation of TRIPS Patent Regime', *The Law and Development Review*, Vol. 3 (2).

Government of India (2017) *Industrial Policy 2017: A Discussion Paper, Department of Industrial Policy and Promotion (DIPP)*, Ministry of Commerce and Industry, New Delhi.

Grossman, G., and E. Helpman (1991) *Innovation and Growth in the Global Economy*, The MIT Press, Cambridge, MA.

Grossman, G., and E. Rossi-Hansberg (2006) 'Trading Tasks: A Simple Theory of Offshoring', *National Bureau of Economic Research Working Paper, No. 12721*, MA, United States.

Gunther, Tillman, and Ludovico Alcorta (2011) 'Industrial Policy for Prosperity: Reasoning and approach', *Working Paper 02/2011*, Development Policy, Statistics and Research Branch, UNIDO, Vienna.

Gupta, Neha (2016) 'Domestic Value-added Growth Is Vital: Are Indian Industries Gaining by Linking into Value Chains?' *South Asia Economic Journal*, Vol. 17 (2), pp. 1–24.

Haddad, Mona (2007) 'Trade Integration in East Asia: The role of China and production networks', *World Bank Policy Research Working Paper 4160*, World Bank, Washington D. C.

Harrison, Ann, and Andrés Rodríguez-Clare (2009) 'Trade, Foreign Investment and Industrial Policy for Developing Countries', *NBER Working Paper No. 15261*, NBER, Cambridge.

Harvie, C., D. Narjoko, and S. Oum (2010) 'Firm Characteristic Determinants of SME Participation in Production Networks', *ERIA Discussion Paper Series 2010–2011*, Economic Research Institute for ASEAN and East Asia, Jakarta.

Hatekar, Neeraj, and Ambrish Dongre (2005) 'Structural Breaks in India's Growth: Revisiting the Debate with a Longer Perspective', *Economic and Political Weekly*, Vol. 40 (14), pp. 1432–1435.

Hausmann, Ricardo, and Bailey Klinger (2006) 'Structural Transformation and Patterns of Comparative Advantage in the Product Space', *CID Working Paper No. 128*, Centre for International Development, Harvard University.

Hausmann, Ricardo, Jason Hwang, and Dani Rodrik (2007) 'What You Export Matters', *Journal of Economic Growth*, Vol. 12, pp. 1–25.

Helleiner, G. K. (1989) 'Transnational Corporations and Direct Foreign Investment', in H. Chenery, and T. N. Srinivasan (eds.), *Handbook of Development Economics*, Vol. II, Elsevier Science Publishers B. V.

Helpman, Elhanan (1984) 'A Simple Theory of International Trade with Multinational Corporations,' *Journal of Political Economy*, 92(3), pp. 451–71.

Hidalgo, C., and R. Hausmann (2009) 'The building blocks of economic complexity', *Proceedings of the National Academy of Sciences of the United States of America*, Vol. 106 (26), pp. 10570–75.

Hidalgo, C., B. Klinger, A. L. Barabasi, and R. Hausmann (2007) 'The Product Space Conditions the Development of Nations', *Science*, Vol. 317, pp. 482–87.

Hidalgo, César A. (2009) 'The Dynamics of Economic Complexity and the Product Space over a 42-year period', *CID Working Paper No. 189*, Centre for International Development, Harvard University.

Hill, Hal, and Prema-Chandra Athukorala (1998) 'Foreign Investment in East Asia: A Survey', *Asian Pacific Economic Literature*, Vol. 12 (2).

Hobday, Michael (2001) 'The Electronics Industries of the Asia-Pacific: Exploring International Production Networks for Economic Development', *Asian-Pacific Economic Literature*, Vol. 15 (1), pp. 13–29.

Hobday, Michael (2009) 'Asian Innovation Experiences and Latin American Visions: Exploiting Shifts in Techno-Economic Paradigms', in Wolfgang Drechsler, Rainer Kattel, and Erik S. Reinert (eds.), *Techno-Economic Paradigms: Essays in Honour of Carlota Perez*, Anthem Press, London and New York.

Hughes, Helen (ed.) (1988) *Achieving Industrialisation in East Asia*, Cambridge University Press, New York.

Hummels, D., J. Ishii, and K. M. Yi (2001) 'The Nature of Growth of Vertical Specialization in World Trade', *Journal of International Economics*, Vol. 54, pp. 75–96.

Humprey, John, and Olga Memedovic (2003) 'The Global Automotive Industry Value Chain: What Prospects for Upgrading by Developing Countries', *UNIDO Report-Sectoral Studies*.

Hurley, Dene T. (2003) 'Horizontal and Vertical Intra-Industry Trade: The Case of ASEAN Trade in Manufactures', *International Economic Journal*, Vol. 17 (4).

Ichimura, Shinichi (1998) *Political Economy of Japanese and Asian Development*, ISEAS, Singapore.

IMF (2013) 'Trade interconnectedness: the world with global value chains', IMF Working Paper, IMF, Washington, D.C.

India Electronics and Semiconductor Association (IESA) (2014) 'Indian Electronic System Design and Manufacturing (ESDM) Disability Identification Study', IESA-E&Y Joint Study, Bangalore.

Islam, Iyanatul, and Anis Chowdhury (1993) *The Newly Industrialising Economies of East Asia*, Routledge, London and New York.

Ito, Takatoshi, and Anne O. Krueger (2000) *The Role of Foreign Direct Investment in East Asian Economic Development*, NBER, Chicago.

Jachnow, Joachim (2017) '21st Century Trade Agreements: Agenda of the 1%', *Unpacking Trade and Investment Series*, Rosa Luxemburg Shiftung (RLS), Brussels.

Jha, Rajiv, and Ravinder Jha (2015) 'Role of Foreign Direct Investment in India's Industrial Development', in C. P. Chandrasekhar (ed.), *Indian Industrialization*, ICSSR Research Surveys and Explorations, Oxford University Press, New Delhi.

Johnson, C. Robert, and Guillermo Noguera (2012) 'Accounting for Intermediates: Production Sharing and Trade in Value Added', *Journal of International Economics*, Vol. 86 (2), pp. 224–236.

Johnson, Chalmers (1982) *MITI and the Japanese Miracle: The Growth of Industrial Policy, 1925–1975*, Stanford University Press.

Jomo, K. S., and Erik S. Reinert (2005) *The Origins of Development Economics: How Schools of Economic Thought Have Addressed Development*, Tulika Books, New Delhi.

Jomo, K. S. et al. (1997) *Southeast Asia's Misunderstood Miracle: Industrial Policy and Economic Development in Thailand, Malaysia and Indonesia*, Westview Press.

Jones, R. W., and H. Kierzkowski (1990) 'The Role of Services in Production and International Trade: A Theoretical Framework', in R. W. Jones, and A. O. Krueger (eds.), *The Political Economy of International Trade: Essays in Honour of R. E. Baldwin*, Basil Blackwell, Oxford, UK.

Joseph, K. J. (1989) 'Bridling Growth of Electronics?' *Economic and Political Weekly*, Vol. 24 (16), pp. 855–856.

Joseph, K. J., and Govindan Parayil (2006) 'Trade Liberalization and Digital Divide: An Analysis of the Information Technology Agreement of WTO', *CDS Working Paper No. 381*, Centre for Development Studies, Thiruvananthapuram, Kerala.

Joseph, K. J., and K. N. Harilal (2001) 'Structure and Growth of India's IT Exports: Implications of an Export-Oriented Growth Strategy', *Economic and Political Weekly*, Vol. 36 (34), pp. 3263–3270.

Joseph, K. J., and Vinoj Abraham (2007) *Information Technology Agreement of the WTO and India's IT Sector*, Mimeo, Centre for Development Studies, Thiruvananthapuram, Kerala.

Joseph, Reji K., and K. V. K. Ranganathan (2016) 'Trends in Foreign Investment in Healthcare Sector of India', *ISID Working Paper No. 187*, Institute for Studies in Industrial Development (ISID), New Delhi.

Joseph, T. J., and V. Nagi Reddy (2009) 'FDI Spillovers and Export Performance of Indian Manufacturing Firms After Liberalisation', *Economic and Political Weekly*, Vol. XLIV (52), pp. 97–105.

Jun, Joosung (1999) 'The Korean Experience of FDI and Foreign Ownership', *Paper Presented at the Conference on 'Economic Sovereignty in a Globalising World'*, Focus on the Global South, Chulalongkorn University, Bangkok.

Kallummal, Murali (2006) 'Non-Agricultural Market Access Negotiations: Real Concerns', *Social Scientist*, Vol. 34, pp. 9–10.

Kallummal, Murali (2012) 'Process of Trade Liberalisation Under the Information Technology Agreement (ITA): The Indian Experience', *CWS Working Paper No. CWS/WP/200/3*, Centre for WTO Studies, New Delhi.

Kallummal, Murali (2014) 'India's Trade with BRICS and the World: Implications on Skill and Technology Content', *CWS Working Paper No. 35*, Centre for WTO Studies (CWS), New Delhi.

Kallummal, Murali, and Biswajit Dhar (2002) 'Capital Inflows and Effects of Market-driven Investments: A Focus on Southeast Asian Crisis,' RIS Occasional Paper No 66, Research and Information System for the Developing and Non-Aligned Countries (RIS), New Delhi.

Kallummal, Murali, and Kavita Bugalya (2012) 'Trends in India's Trade in Pharmaceutical Sector: Some Iinsights', *CWS Working Paper No. CWS/WP/200/2*, Centre for WTO Studies, New Delhi.

Kallummal, Murali, and Smitha Francis (2012) 'Impact of Sectoral Trade Liberalization Under the WTO's Information Technology Agreement on the Indian Electronics Industry', *Paper Presented at the APEA Annual Conference*, Thammasat University, Bangkok.

Kanbur, Ravi (2009) 'The Co-Evolution of the Washington Consensus and the Economic Development Discourse', *Department of Applied Economics and Management Working Paper No. 2009–2015*, Cornell University, New York.

Kaplinsky, R. (2005) Globalization, Poverty and Inequality, Polity Press, London.

Karo, Erkki, and Rainer Kattel (2011) 'Should 'Open Innovation' Change Innovation Policy Thinking in Catching-up Economies? Considerations for Policy Analyses', *Innovation: The European Journal of Social Science Research*, Vol. 24 (1–2), pp. 173–198.

Karo, Erkki, and Rainer Kattel (2016) 'Innovation and the State: Towards an Evolutionary Theory of Policy Capacity', in X. Wu, M. Howlett, and M. Ramesh (eds.), *Policy Capacity: State and Societal Perspectives*, Palgrave Macmillan, Hampshire.

Kasahara, Yuri, and Antonio José Junqueira Botelho (2016) 'Catching Up and Falling Behind: An Appraisal of Brazilian Industrial Policy in the Twenty First Century', *European Review of Latin American and Caribbean Studies*, Vol. 101, pp. 97–109.

Kattel, Rainer (2018) 'What makes states entrepreneurial?', UCL IIPP Blog, Available at https://medium.com/iipp-blog/what-makes-states-entrepreneurial-7dd397d1fc70

Kattel, Rainer, and Veiko Lember (2010) 'Public Procurement as an Industrial Policy Tool: An Option for Developing Countries?' *Journal of Public Procurement*, Vol. 10 (3), pp. 368–404.

Kattel, Rainer, Erik S. Reinert, and Margit Suurna (2009) 'Industrial Restructuring and Innovation Policy in Central and Eastern Europe since 1990', *Working Papers in Technology Governance and Economic*

Dynamics No. 23, The Other Canon Foundation, Norway and Tallinn University of Technology, Tallinn.

Kattel, Rainer, Jan A. Kregel, and Eric S. Reinert (2009) 'The Relevance of Ragner Nurkse and Classical Development Economics', *Working Papers in Technology Governance and Economic Dynamics No. 21*, The Other Canon Foundation, Norway and Tallinn University of Technology, TalinnTallinn.

Kenneth, C. Shadlen (2005) 'Exchanging Development for Market Access? Deep Integration and Industrial Policy Under Multilateral and Regional-Bilateral Trade Agreements', *Review of International Political Economy*, Vol. 12 (5), pp. 750–775.

Kevin P. Gallagher, Stephany Griffith-Jones, and José Antonio Ocampo (eds.), *Regulating Global Capital Flows for Long-Run Development*, Pardee Centre Task Force Report, Boston University, MA.

Khan, Mushtaq H. (2010) 'Learning, Technology Acquisition and Governance Challenges in Developing Countries', *DFID Research Paper Series on Governance for Growth*, School of Oriental and African Studies, University of London, Available at https://eprints.soas.ac.uk/9967/1/Learning_and_Technology_Acquisition_internet.pdf.

Kim, June-Dong, and Sang-In Hwang (2000) 'The Role of FDI in Korea's Economic Development', in Takatoshi Ito, and Anne Krueger (eds.), *The Role of Foreign Direct Investment in East Asian Economic Development*, NBER, Chicago.

Kimura, Fukunari (2000) 'Location and Internalisation Decisions: Sector Switching in Japanese Outward FDI', in Takatoshi Ito, and Anne Krueger (eds.), *The Role of Foreign Direct Investment in East Asian Economic Development*, NBER, Chicago.

Kimura, Fukunari, and M. Ando (2005) 'Two-Dimensional Fragmentation in East Asia: Conceptual Framework and Empirics', *International Review of Economics and Finance*, Vol. 14 (3), pp. 317–348.

Kinkel, Steffen (2014) 'Setting the Scene: Global Value Chains, Re-shoring Activities, Global Innovation Networks, and Their Impact on Global Innovation Platforms', in Annelieke van der Giessen, Claire Stolwijk, and Jos Leijten (eds.), *Can Policy Follow the Dynamics of Global Innovation Platforms? Collection of Conference Papers*, 6CP, Delft.

Kohl, T., S. Brakman, and H. Garretsen (2013) 'Do Trade Agreements Stimulate International Trade Differently? Evidence from 296 Trade Agreements', *University of Groningen*, Available at www.tristankohl.org/site/KohlbrakmanGarretsen_296A greements.pdf

Kohli, Atul (2004) 'Introduction', in *State Directed Development: Political Power and Industrialization in the Global Periphery*, Cambridge University Press, New York.

Koopman, R., Z. Wang, and S.-J. Wei (2008) 'How Much of Chinese Exports Is Really Made in China? Assessing Domestic Value-Added

When Processing Trade Is Pervasive', *NBER Working Paper Series, No. 14109*, Cambridge, MA.

Kregel, Jan (2007) 'Nurkse, Early Development Theory, and Modern Monoeconomics', *Paper Delivered at the Conference 'Ragnar Nurkse (1907–2007): Classical Development Economics and Its Relevance for Today'*, 31 August –1 September 2007, Estonian Academy of Sciences, Tallinn, Estonia.

Kumar, Nagesh (2001) 'Foreign Direct Investment, Regional Economic Integration and Industrial Restructuring in Asia: Trends, Patterns and Prospects', *RIS Occasional Paper No. 62*, Research and Information System for Non-Aligned and Other Developing Countries (RIS), New Delhi.

Kumar, Nagesh (2005) 'A Broader Asian Community and a Possible Roadmap', *Economic and Political Weekly*, Vol. XL (36), pp. 3926–3931.

Kumar, Nagesh (2007a) 'Investment Provisions in Regional Trading Arrangements in Asia: Relevance, Emerging Trends, and Policy Implications', *RIS Discussion Paper 125*, Research and Information System for Non-Aligned and Other Developing Countries (RIS), New Delhi.

Kumar, Nagesh (2007b) 'Regional Economic Integration, Foreign Direct Investment and Efficiency-Seeking Industrial Restructuring in Asia: The Case of India', *RIS Discussion Paper 123*, Research and Information System for Non-Aligned and Other Developing Countries (RIS), New Delhi.

Kumar, Nagesh, and K. J. Joseph (2004), 'National Innovation Systems and India's IT Capability: Are there any Lessons for ASEAN New Comers?', *RIS Discussion Paper No. 72/2004*, Research and Information System for Non-Aligned and Other Developing Countries (RIS), New Delhi.

Kumar, Nagesh, and K. J. Joseph (2004) 'National Innovation Systems and India's IT Capability: Are There any Lessons for ASEAN New Comers?' *RIS Discussion Paper No. 72/2004*, Research and Information System for Non-Aligned and Other Developing Countries (RIS), New Delhi.

Kwan, C. H. (1994) *Economic Interdependence in the Asia-Pacific Region: Towards a Yen Bloc*, Routledge, London and New York.

Kwan, C. H., and Kiyohiko Fukushima (1995) *Foreign Direct Investment and Regional Industrial Restructuring in Asia*, Institute of Southeast Asian Studies (ISEAS), Singapore.

Lall, Sanjaya (1992) 'Technological Capabilities and Industrialisation', *World Development*, Vol. 20 (2), pp. 165–186.

Lall, Sanjaya (1996) *Learning from the Asian Tigers: Studies in Technology and Industrial Policy*, Macmillan Press, London.

Lall, Sanjaya (2005) 'Rethinking Industrial Strategy: The Role of the State in the Face of Globalization', in Kevin Gallagher (ed.) Putting Development First: The Importance of Policy Space in the WTO and IFIs, Zed Books, London.

Lall, Sanjaya, M. Albaladejo, and J. Zhang (2004) 'Mapping Fragmentation: Electronics and Automobiles in East Asia and Latin America', *Oxford Development Studies*, Vol. 32, pp. 447–464.

Lazonick, W., and M. O' Sullivan (2000) 'Maximising Shareholder Value: A New Ideology for Corporate Governance', *Economy and Society*, Vol. 29 (1), pp. 13–35.

Lee, J. (1995) 'Comparative Advantage in Manufacturing as a Determinant of Industrialisation: The Korean Case', *World Development*, Vol. 23 (7), pp. 1195–1214.

Lee, Keun, and John Mathews (2013) 'Science, Technology and Innovation for Sustainable Development', *CDP Background Paper No. 16*, The Committee for Development Policy, UN, Geneva.

Leijten, Jos (2014) 'Introduction', in Annelieke van der Giessen, Claire Stolwijk, and Jos Leijten (eds.), *Can Policy Follow the Dynamics of Global Innovation Platforms? Collection of Conference Papers*, 6CP, Delft.

Lember, Veiko, Rainer Kattel, and Tarmo Kalvet (2013) 'How Governments Support Innovation through Public Procurement Comparing Evidence from 11 Countries', *Working Papers in Technology Governance and Economic Dynamics No. 55,* The Other Canon Foundation, Norway and Tallinn University of Technology, Tallinn.

Levitt, Kari Polanyi (2006) 'Reclaiming Policy Space for Equitable Economic Development', *Revised text of a paper presented to The North South Institute*, Ottawa, Canada, on January 19th, 2006, and to the VIII International Meeting of Economists Globalization and Development Problems, Havana, Cuba, February 7, 2006.

Lin, J. Y. (2009) *Economic Development and Transition: Thought, Strategy, and Viability*, Cambridge University Press, Cambridge.

Lin, J. Y. (ed.) (2012) *New Structural Economics: A Framework for Rethinking Development and Policy*, World Bank, Washington, DC.

Lin, J. Y., and H. J. Chang (2009) 'Should Industrial Policy in Developing Countries Conform to Comparative Advantage or Defy It?' *Development Policy Review*, Vol. 27 (5).

Linden, G., K. Kraemer, and J. Dedrick (2007) *Who Captures Value in a Global Innovation System? The Case of Apple's iPod (mimeograph)*, Personal Computing Industry Centre, University of California, Irvine, Available at https://signallake.com/innovation/AppleiPod.pdf

Lopez-Gonzalez, Javier (2016) 'Using Foreign Factors to Enhance Domestic Export Performance: A Focus on Southeast Asia', *OECD Trade Policy Papers*, No. 191, OECD Publishing, Paris.

Love, James Packard (2014) Alternatives to the Patent System That Are Used to Support R&D Efforts, Including Both Push and Pull Mechanisms, with a Special Focus on Innovation-Inducement Prizes and Open Source Development Models, *Study Commissioned by the WIPO Secretariat*, WIPO Committee on Development and Intellectual Property, Geneva.

Low, Patrick (2013) 'The Role of Services', in D. K. Elms, and P. Low (eds.), *Global Value Chains in a Changing World*, World Trade Organization, Geneva.

Low, Patrick, and Julia Tijaja (2013) 'Effective Industrial Policies and Global Value Chains', *Real Sector Working Paper*, Fung Global Institute.

Lüthje, Boy, Stefanie Hürtgen, Peter Pawlick, and Martina Sproll (2013) *From Silicon Valley to Shenzhen: Global Production and Work in the IT Industry*, Rowman & Littlefield, MD.

Majluf, Luis Abugattas (2004) 'Swimming in the Spaghetti Bowl: Challenges for Developing Countries under the "New Regionalism"', *Policy Issues in International Trade and Commodities, Study Series No. 27*, Geneva.

Majumdar, Rumki (2010) 'Indian Electronics Hardware Industry: Growth and Productivity (1993–2004)', *Economic and Political Weekly*, Vol. XLV (14), pp. 72–77.

Majumdar, Surajit (2013) 'Indian Industrial Development, Industrial Policy and Their Changing Context', *Paper Presented at the National Conference on India's Industrialisation: How to Overcome the Stagnation?* Institute for Studies in Industrial Development (ISID), New Delhi.

Mani, Sunil (2000a) 'A Survey of Deregulation in Indian Industry', in M. Kagami, and M. Tsuji (eds.), *Privatization, Deregulation and Economic Efficiency: A Comparative Analysis of Asia, Europe and the Americas*, Edward Elgar, Cheltenham, pp. 187–205.

Mani, Sunil (2000b) 'Deregulation and Reforms in India's Telecommunications Industry', in M. Kagami, and M. Tsuji (eds.), *Privatization, Deregulation and Economic Efficiency, A Comparative Analysis of Asia, Europe and the Americas*, Edward Elgar, Cheltenham, pp. 187–205.

Mani, Sunil (2001) 'Role of Government in Promoting Innovation in the Enterprise Sector: An Analysis of the Indian Experience', No. #2001–3, *INTECH Discussion Paper Series*, UNU, Maastricht.

Mani, Sunil (2005) 'Innovation Capability in India's Telecommunication Equipment Industry', in Ashwani Saith, and M. Vijayabasker (eds.), *ICTs and Indian Economic Development*, Sage Publications, New Delhi.

Mani, Sunil (2009) 'Growth of india's telecom Services (1991-2007): Can it lead to emergence of a Manufacturing Hub?' Economic and Political Weekly, January 19, pp. 37–46.

Mani, Sunil (2012) 'The Mobile Communications Services Industry in India: Has It Led to India Becoming a Manufacturing Hub for Telecommunication Equipment?' *Pacific Affairs*, pp. 511–530.

Mani, Sunil (2016) 'New IPR Policy 2016: Not Based on Evidence', *Economic and Political Weekly*, Vol. 51 (38), pp. 28–32.

Manuel, Pastor Jr. (1989) 'Latin America, the Debt Crisis, and the International Monetary Fund', *Latin American Perspectives*, Vol. 16 (1), pp. 79–110 Latin America's Debt and the World Economic System.

Markusen, J. R. (1989) 'Trade in Producer Services and in Other Specialized Intermediate Inputs', *The American Economic Review*, Vol. 79, pp. 85–95.

Mathews, John A. (2010) 'The Hsinchu Model: Collective Efficiency, Increasing Returns and Higher-Order Capabilities in the Hsinchu Science-Based Industry Park, Taiwan', *Keynote Address at the 20th Anniversary Conference of the Chinese Society for Management of Technology (CSMOT) Tsinghua University*, Hsinchu Taiwan, December 10.

Mathur, Somesh Kumar (2007) 'Indian IT Industry: A Performance Analysis and a Model for Possible Adoption', *Munich Personal RePEc Archive*, RIS, Available at http://mpra.ub.uni-muenchen.de/2368/

Mazumdar, Tanushree (2005) 'Capital Flows into India: Implications for Its Economic Growth', *Economic and Political Weekly*, Vol. 40 (21), pp. 2183–2189.

Mazzucato, Mariana (2013) *The Entrepreneurial State: Debunking Public vs Private Sector Myths*, Anthem Press.

Mazzucato, Mariana (2017) 'Mission-oriented Innovation Policy: Challenges and Opportunities', *UCL Institute for Innovation and Public Purpose Working Paper, No. 2017–1*, UCL Institute for Innovation and Public Purpose, London.

McMillan, M., and D. Rodrik (2011) 'Globalization, Structural Change and Productivity Growth', Harvard Kennedy School of Government, Boston, MA (mimeo).

McNally, Christopher A. (2008) 'The Institutional Contours of China's Emergent Capitalism', in C. A. McNally (ed.), *China's Emergent Political Economy: Capitalism in the Dragon's Lair*, Routledge, London and New York.

Menon, Jayant (2013) 'Can FTAs Support the Growth or Spread of International Production Networks in Asia?' *Working Paper No. 2013/06*, Crawford School of Public Policy, ANU College of Asia and the Pacific.

Mikic, Mia (2007) 'Trends in Preferential Trade Liberalisation in Asia and the Pacific', in *Agricultural Trade: Planting the Seeds of Regional Liberalisation in Asia*, ESCAP ARTNeT Studies in Trade and Investment 60, UN, New York

Milberg, William, and Deborah Winkler (2013) *Outsourcing Economics, Global Value Chains in Capitalist Development*, Cambridge University Press, New York.

Montalvo, Carlos (2014) 'Global Innovation and Production Networks: New Rationales and Policy Challenges', in Annelieke van der Giessen, Claire Stolwijk, and Jos Leijten (eds.), *Can Policy Follow the Dynamics of Global Innovation Platforms? Collection of Conference Papers*, 6CP, Delft.

Murray, Gibbs (2007) *Trade Policy, National Development Strategies Policy Notes*, UN-DESA and UNDP.

Nagaraj, R. (2003) 'Industrial Policy and Performance Since 1980', *Economic and Political Weekly*, Vol. 38 (35), pp. 3707–3715.

Nagaraj, R. (2018) 'Economic Reforms and Manufacturing Sector Growth: Need for Reconfiguring the Industrialisation Model', in *Quarter Century of Liberalisation in India, Essays from Economic and Political Weekly (EPW)*, Oxford University Press, New Delhi.

Nathan, Dev, Meenu Tewari, and Sandip Sarkar (2016) (eds.) *Labour in Global Value Chains in Asia,* Cambridge University Press, India.

Nathan, Dev, and Sandip Sarkar (2011) 'A Note on Profits, Rents and Wages in Global Production Networks', *Economic and Political Weekly (EPW)*, Vol. XLVI (36), pp. 53–56.

Nathan, Dev, and V. Kalpana (2007) *Issues in the Analysis of Global Value Chains and Their Impact on Employment and Incomes in India*, ILO, Geneva.

National Policy on Electronics (2012) *Department of Electronics and Information Technology (DEITy)*, Ministry of Communications and Information Technology. Government of India.

Nawrot, Katarzyna Anna (2014) 'The Role of Innovation in Development: Experiences in Leapfrogging and Catching Up Through Regional Clustering: East Asian Perspective', *Actual Problems of Economics*, Vol. 11 (161), pp. 73–82.

Naya, Seiji (1988) 'The Role of Trade Policies in the Industrialisation of Rapidly Growing Asian Developing Countries', in Helen Hughes (ed.), *Achieving Industrialisation in East Asia*, Cambridge University Press, New York.

Nayyar, Deepak (1994) *Industrial Growth and Stagnation: The Debate in India*, Oxford University Press, New Delhi.

Nayyar, Deepak (2006) 'Economic Growth in Independent India: Lumbering Elephant or Running Tiger?' *Economic and Political Weekly*, Vol. 41 (15), pp. 145–158.

Nayyar, Deepak (2018) 'Economic Liberalisation in India: Then and Now', in *Quarter Century of Liberalisation in India, Essays from Economic and Political Weekly* (EPW), Oxford University Press, New Delhi.

Nielsen, Peter Bøegh (2017) 'The puzzle of measuring global value chains – The business statistics perspective', *International Economics*, http://dx.doi.org/10.1016/j.inteco.2017.05.004

Niti Aayog (2016) Make in India Strategy for Electronic Products, Government of India, May.

Noble, Gregory (2003) 'Review of a History of Japanese Trade and Industry Policy', in Mikio Sumiya (ed.), New York: Oxford University Press, 2000, in *Social Science Japan Journal*, Vol. 6 (2), pp. 284–287.

Nolan, P. (2012) Is China Buying the World? Polity Press, Cambridge, UK.

Nordas, H. K. (2008) 'Vertical Specialisation and Its Determinants', *Journal of Development Studies*, Vol. 44 (7), pp. 1004–1022.

Nordas, H. K. (2009) *Trade Paradigms for Developing Countries: Some Old, Some New, Some Borrowed, Some Out of the Blue*, ARTNeT, ESCAP, Bangkok.

OECD (2013) *Interconnected Economies: Benefitting from Global Value Chains*, Paris.

Palley, Thomas I. (1994) 'The Free Trade Debate: A Left Keynesian Gaze', *Social Research*, Vol. 61 (2), pp. 379–394.

Palma, Jose Gabriel (2010), 'Why has productivity growth stagnated in Most Latin American Countries since the Neo-liberal Reforms?', Cambridge Working Papers in Economics (CWPE) 1030.

Papola, T. S. (2006) 'Structural Changes in the Indian Economy: Emerging Patterns and Implications', *ISID Working Paper No. 2012/2*, Institute for Studies in Industrial Development (ISID), New Delhi.

Patnaik, Prabhat (2006) *The Diffusion of Development*, Available at www.networkideas.org/featart/feb2006/Diffusion_Development.pdf

Patnaik, Prabhat (2015) 'Open Economy Macroeconomics and the Indian Economy', in *Macroeconomics*, ICSSR Research Surveys and Explorations, Oxford University Press, New Delhi.

Patnaik, Prabhat and Vikas Rawal (2005) 'Level of Activity in an Economy with Free Capital Mobility', *Economic & Political Weekly*, April.

Perez, Carlota (2001) 'Technological Change and Opportunities for Development as a Moving Target', *CEPAL Review*, December, pp. 109–130.

Perez, Carlota (2002) *Technological Revolutions and Financial Capital: The Dynamics of Bubbles and Golden Ages*, Edward Elgar, Cheltenham.

Pianta, Mario, Matteo Lucchese, and Leopoldo Nascia (2016) *What Is to Be Produced? The Making of a New Industrial Policy in Europe*, Rosa Luxemburg Stiftung (RLS), Brussels.

Prasartset, Suthy (1991) 'The Global Context and the New Wave of Japanese Investment in Thailand', in Shoichi Yamashita (ed.), *Transfer of Japanese Technology and Management to the ASEAN Countries*, University of Tokyo Press, Tokyo.

Prebisch, R. (1959) 'Commercial Policy in Under-developed Countries', *American Economic Review, Papers and Proceedings*, Vol. 492, pp. 251–273.

President's Council of Advisors on Science and Technology (PCAST) (2011) Report to the President on Ensuring American Leadership in Advanced Manufacturing, PCAST, Washington, DC.

Puyana, Alicia (2007) 'Mexican Economic Liberalization: The project and the realities', *Presented at the workshop: 'Modern Markets and Traditional Politics? A Workshop to Explore the Economics and Politics of the Last Ten-Fifteen Years in Latin America'*. Latin American Centre, Oxford University, Oxford, June 4–5, 2007, Available at http://www.networkideas.org/wp-content/uploads/2016/10/Mexican.pdf

Puyana, Alicia (2011) 'The North American Free Trade Agreement and The Mexican Economy: Lessons to Be learned from Fifteen Years of North-South Economic Integration', ICTSD.

Ramstetter, Eric D. (ed.) (1991) *Direct Foreign Investment in Asia's Developing Economies and Structural Change in the Region*, Westview Press, Boulder, CO.

Ranganathan, K. V. K., and M. R. Murthy (2013) 'Structural Characteristics of the Large Indian Private Corporate Sector in the Post: Liberalisation Period', *ISID Working Paper No. 2013/03*, ISID, New Delhi.

Rao, K.S. Chalapathi and Biswajit Dhar (2010) 'Accelerating India's FDI Inflows & Conceptual and Definitional Issues,' Paper presented at the Symposium on 'Concepts, Definition and Data Issues Relating to FDI in India', jointly organized by Institute for Studies in Industrial Development (ISID) and Research and Information System for Developing Countries (RIS), New Delhi, March 16.

Rao, K., S. Chalapati, and Biswajit Dhar (2011) 'India's FDI Inflows: Trends and Concepts, *ISID Working Paper No. 2011/01*, ISID, New Delhi.

Rao, K., S. Chalapati, and Biswajit Dhar (2016) 'Analysis of India's FDI Inflows During 2004–05 to 2013–2014', in *India's Inward FDI Experience During the Post-Liberalisation Period with Emphasis on the Manufacturing Sector, Project Report, Sponsored by the Indian Council of Social Science Research (ICSSR)*, Institute for Studies in Industrial Development, January.

Rao, K., S. Chalapati, and Biswajit Dhar (2018) *India's Recent Foreign Direct Investment – An assessment*, Institute for Studies in Industrial Development (ISID), New Delhi.

Ravi, Kanbur (2009) 'The Co-Evolution of the Washington Consensus and the Economic Development Discourse', Available at https://ideas.repec.org/p/ags/cudawp/48920.html

Reinert, Erik S. (2008) *How Rich Countries Got Rich . . . and Why Poor Countries Stay Poor*, Anthem Press, New Delhi.

Reinert, Erik S., and Rainer Kattel (2010) Modernising Russia: Industrial Policy Round III: Russia and the Other BRIC Countries: Forging Ahead, Catching Up or Falling Behind?, *Working Papers in Technology Governance and Economic Dynamics No. 32*, The Other Canon Foundation, Norway, Tallinn University of Technology, Tallinn.

Reinert, Erik S., and Sophus A. Reinert (2005) 'Mercantilism and Economic Development: Schumpeterian Dynamics, Institution Building and International Benchmarking', in K. S. Jomo, and Erik S. Reinert (eds.), *The Origins of Development Economics*, Tulika Books, New Delhi.

Ricardo French-Davis (1987) 'Foreign Debt and Development Alternatives in Latin America', *International Journal of Political Economy*, Vol. 17 (1), pp. 64–87.

Rijesh, R. (2017) International Trade and Productivity Growth: Evidence from the Organised Manufacturing Sector in India, *ISID Working Paper No. 198*, ISID, New Delhi.

Robert-Nicoud, F. (2008) 'Offshoring of Routine Tasks and (de)Industrialisation: Threat or Opportunity: And for whom?' *Journal of Urban Economics*, Vol. 63 (2), pp. 517–535.

Rodrik, Dani (2006) 'Goodbye Washington Consensus, Hello Washington Confusion? A Review of the World Bank's Economic Growth in the 1990s: Learning from a Decade of Reform', *Journal of Economic Literature*, Vol. XLIV, pp. 973–987.

Rodrik, Dani (2007) *One Economics, Many Recipes: Globalization, Institutions, and Economic Growth*, Princeton University Press, Princeton, NJ.

Rodrik, Dani (2008a) 'Second-best Institutions', *American Economic Review*, Vol. 98 (2), pp. 100–104.

Rodrik, Dani (2008b) *Is There a New Washington Consensus*, Available at www.projectsyndicate.org/commentary/rodrik20

Rodrik, Dani (2013) 'Unconditional Convergence in Manufacturing', *Quarterly Journal of Economics*, Vol. 128 (91), pp. 165–204.

Rodrik, Dani (2018) *Straight Talk on Trade: Ideas for a Sane World*, Princeton University Press, Princeton, NJ and Oxfordshire.

Rouvinen, Petri (2014) 'Lessons from Case Studies of Global Value Chains', in Annelieke van der Giessen, Claire Stolwijk, and Jos Leijten (eds.), *Can Policy Follow the Dynamics of Global Innovation Platforms? Collection of Conference Papers*, 6CP, Delft.

Roychowdhury, Anamitra (2018) *Labour Law Reforms in India : All in the Name of Jobs*, Routledge, London.

Roy, Satyaki (2013) *Small and Medium Enterprises in India: Infirmities and Asymmetries in Industrial Clusters*, Routledge, London and New York.

Sachwald, Frédérique (2013) 'The Development of Global Innovation Networks', *Innovation for Growth: I4g*, Policy Brief No. 22.

Saith, Aswhani, and M. Vijayabaskar (2005) 'ICTs and Indian Economic Development: Trends, Issues, Options', in Ashwani Seith and M. Vijayabaskar (eds.) *ICTs and Indian Economic Development: Economy, Work and Regulation*, Sage Publications, New Delhi.

Saito, Mika, Michele Ruta, and Jarkko Turunen (2013) 'Trade Interconnectedness: The World with Global Value Chains', *IMF Working Paper*, International Monetary Fund.

Saraswathy, Beena (2016) Analysis of Foreign Acquisitions in India's Manufacturing Sector', *ISID Working Paper No. 193*, Institute for Studies in Industrial Development (ISID), New Delhi.

Saraswati, Jyoti (2013) 'A National Export-Led Growth Plan: Lessons from the Software Industry', *Economic and Political Weekly*, Vol. XLVIII (7), pp. 22–14.

Saripalle, Madhuri (2015) 'Tamil Nadu's Electronics Industry: Lessons for "Make in India"', *Economic and Political Weekly*, Vol. L (26 & 27), pp 99–103.

Sauve, Pierre (2007) *Investment Regulation Through Trade Agreements: Lessons from Asia*, Available at https://ideas.repec.org/p/unt/arwopa/awp49.html

Shafaeddin, Mehdi (2005) 'Friedrich List and the Infant Industry Argument', in K. S. Jomo (ed.), *The Pioneers of Development Economics, Great Economists on Development*, Zed Books, London and New York.

Shafaeddin, Mehdi (2010) 'Trade Liberalization, Industrialization and Development: Experience of Recent Decades', *Keynote Speech Delivered at the Fourth ACDC (Annual Conference on Development and Change)*, University of Witwatersrand, Johannesburg, South Africa, April, Available at www.networkideas.org/featart/aug2010/Mehdi_Shafaeddin.pdf, Accessed on 16 August 2012.

Singer, H. W. (1950) 'The Distribution of Gains between Investing and Borrowing Countries', *American Economic Review, Papers and Proceedings*, Vol. 40 (2), pp. 473–485.

Singh, Ajit (2010) 'The Past, Present, and Future of Industrial Policy in India: Adapting to the Changing Domestic and International Environment', *Paper Presented at the National Conference on India's Industrialisation: How to Overcome the Stagnation?'* Institute for Studies in Industrial Development (ISID), New Delhi.

Singh, Kavaljit, and Burghard Ilge (eds.) (2016) *Rethinking Bilateral Investment Treaties, Critical Issues, and Policy Choices*, Both Ends and SOMO, Amsterdam and Madhyam, New Delhi.

Smith, Sanya (2009) 'Preliminary Note on Financial Crisis and Trade and Investment Treaties', Third World Network.

Somsak, Tambunlertchai, and Ippei Yamazawa (1983) *Manufactured Export Promotion: The Case of Thailand*, IDE, Tokyo, Japan.

Sridharan, Eswaran (1996) *The Political Economy of Industrial Promotion: Indian, Brazilian and Korean Electronics in Comparative Perspective 1969–1994*, Praeger Publications, Westport, CT and London.

Stehrer, Robert, Marcin Borowiecki, Bernhard Dachs, Doris Hanzel-Weiss, Steffen Kinkel, Johannes Pöschl, Magdolna Sass, Thomas Christian Schmall, and Andrea Szalavetz (2012) Global Value Chains and the EU Industry. *Final Report of the Project Carried Out Within the Framework Service Contract No. ENTR/2009/033.*

Stephenson, Sherry (2013) *Addressing Local Content Requirements in a Sustainable Energy Trade Agreement, International Centre for Trade and Sustainable Development,* Geneva, Switzerland, Available at www.ictsd.org

Storm, Servaas (2015) 'Structural Change', *Development and Change*, Vol. 46 (4), pp. 666–699.

Storm, Servaas, and C. Naasterpad (2005) 'Strategic Factors in Economic Development: East Asian Industrialization 1950–2003', *Development and Change*, Vol. 36 (6), pp. 1059–1094.

Sturgeon, T., & O. Memedovic (2011) 'Mapping Global Value Chains: Intermediate Goods Trade and Structural Change in the World Economy', *UNIDO Development Policy and Strategic Research Branch Working Paper 05/2010*, UNIDO, Vienna.

Suh, Jeongmeen, and Jong Duk Kim (2014) 'Joining Pre-existing International Production Networks: Implications for India's Economic Integration with East Asia', *Asian Economic Papers*, Vol. 13, pp. 117–142.

Thrasher, Rachel D., and Kevin Gallagher (2008) '21st Century Trade Agreements: Implications for Long-run Development Policy', *The Pardee Papers, No. 2*, Boston University, Boston, Available at www.bu.edu/pardee/files/documents/PP-002-Trade.pdf

Timmer, M. P., Dietzenbacher, E., Los, B., Stehrer, R., and de Vries, G. J. (2015) 'An Illustrated User Guide to the World Input–Output Database: The Case of Global Automotive Production', *Review of International Economics*, Vol. 23, pp. 575–605.

Topalova, P., and A. Khandelwal (2011) 'Trade Liberalization and Firm Productivity: The Case of India,' *Review of Economics and Statistics*, Vol. 93 (3), pp. 995–1009.

Tuner, George (2018) 'Oil firms use secretive court hearing in bid to stop Vietnam taxing their profits', *The Guardian*, 15 August.

UNCTAD (1995) *World Investment Report*, UN, New York and Geneva.

UNCTAD (1996) *Trade and Development Report*, UN, New York and Geneva.

UNCTAD (1999) *World Investment Report*, UN, New York and Geneva.

UNCTAD (2003) *World Investment Report*, UN, New York and Geneva.

UNCTAD (2012) *Technology and Innovation Report*, UN, New York and Geneva.

UNCTAD (2013) *World Investment Report*, UN, New York and Geneva.

UNCTAD (2014) *Trade and Development Report, Global Governance and Policy Space for Development*, UN, New York and Geneva.

UNCTAD (2016) *Trade and Development Report, Structural Transformation for Inclusive and Sustained Growth*, UN, New York and Geneva.

UNCTAD (2017) *Trade and Development Report, Beyond Austerity: Towards a Global New Deal*, UN, New York and Geneva.

UNECA (2016) *Transformative Industrial Policy for Africa*, UN, Addis Ababa, Ethiopia.

UNESCAP (1991) *Industrial Restructuring in Asia and the Pacific*, UN, Bangkok.

UNESCAP (1998) 'FDI in Selected Asian Countries: Policies, Related Institution-Building and Regional Cooperation', *UN Development Papers No. 19*, UN, Bangkok.

UNESCAP (2011) 'Fighting Irrelevance: The Role of Regional Trade Agreements in International Production Networks in Asia', *A Study by ARTNeT*, ESCAP, UN, Bangkok.

UNIDO (2013) *Industrial Development Report 2013, Sustaining Employment Growth: The Role of Manufacturing and Structural Change*, UNIDO, Vienna.

UNIDO (2015) *GVCs and Development*, UNIDO, Vienna.

UNIDO (2016) *Industrial Development Report 2016, The Role of Technology and Innovation in Inclusive and Sustainable Industrial Development*, UNIDO, Vienna

Van Harten, Gus, and Dayna Nadine Scott (2015) 'Investment Treaties and the Internal Vetting of Regulatory Proposals: A Case Study from

Canada', *Osgoode Legal Studies Research Paper No. 26/2016*, York University, Toronto.

Veeramani, C. (2012) 'Anatomy of India's Merchandise Export Growth, 1993–1994 to 2010–2011', *Economic and Political Weekly*, Vol. XLVII (1), pp. 94–104.

Veeramani, C. (2014) 'World's Knowledge Spillovers: Beyond Openness and Growth', *Journal of Economic Integration*, Vol. 29 (2), pp. 298–328.

Veeramani, C., and R. Nagaraj (2016) 'Emerging Issues in India's Trade and Industrial Sectors', in C. Veeramani, and R. Nagaraj (eds.), *International Trade and Industrial Development in India: Emerging Trends, Patterns and Issues*, Orient BlackSwan, New Delhi.

Verma, Swati (2015) 'Current Account Fallout of FDI in Post-Reform India: Evidence from Manufacturing Sector', *Economic and Political Weekly*, Vol L (39), pp. 45–53.

Verma, Swati, and K. V. K. Ranganathan (2016) 'FDI, Technology Transfer and Payments for Know-How: A Case Study of Automobile Sector Firms', *ISID Working Paper No. 190*, Institute for Studies in Industrial Development (ISID), New Delhi.

Vijay, G. (2009) 'Defragmenting "Global Disintegration of Value Creation" and Labour Relations', *Economic and Political Weekly*, Vol. XLIV (22), pp. 85–94.

Wade, Robert H. (1988) 'The Role of Government in Overcoming Market Failure: Taiwan, Republic of Korea and Japan', in Helen Hughes (ed.), *Achieving Industrialisation in East Asia*, Cambridge University Press, New York.

Wade, Robert H. (1990) *Governing the Market: Economic Theory and the Role of Government in East Asian Industrialization*, Princeton University Press, Princeton, NJ.

Wade, Robert H. (2006) 'How to Change the WTO and Global Policy on Trade and Investment: Gaining Acceptance of 'Open Economy Industrial Policy' by Hoisting Neoliberalism on its Own Petard', *Note for Princeton University Conference on 'Normative and Empirical Evaluation of Global Governance'*, February, pp. 16–18.

Wade, Robert H. (2012) 'Return of Industrial Policy?', *International Review of Applied Economics*, Vol. 26 (2), pp. 223–239.

Wade, Robert H. (2016) 'The Role of the State in Escaping the Middle: Income Trap: The Case for Smart Industrial Policy', *METU Studies in Development*, Vol. 43, pp. 21–42.

Wade, Robert H. (2018) 'The Developmental State: Dead or Alive?', *Development and Change*, Vol. 49 (2), pp. 518–546.

Wignaraja, Ganeshan (2014) 'Joining the Supply Chain: A Firm-Level Perspective from Southeast Asia', *ICRIER Working Paper No. 277*, ICRIER, New Delhi.

Wignaraja, Ganeshan, J. Kruger, and A. M. Tuazon (2013) 'Production Networks, Profits and Innovative Activity: Evidence from Malaysia and

Thailand' *ADBI Working Paper Series No. 460*, Asian Development Bank Institute, Tokyo.

Williams, Zoe Phillips (2016) 'What, When, Where and Why? Patterns in Investor: State Arbitration', in Kavaljit Singh, and Burghard Ilge (eds.), *Rethinking Bilateral Investment Treaties, Critical Issues, and Policy Choices*, Both Ends and SOMO, Amsterdam and Madhyam, New Delhi.

Williamson, John (2004) 'The Washington Consensus as Policy Prescription for Development', *A Lecture in the Series 'Practitioners of Development' Delivered at the World Bank*, Washington D. C.

Wolfmayr, Y., E. Christen, M. Falk, H. Hollenstein, M. Knell, M. Pfaffermayr, A. Reinstaller, and F. Unterlass (2013) *The Role and Internationalisation Strategies of Multinational Companies in Innovation*, INNO-Grips II Report, European Commission, DG Enterprise and Industry, Brussels.

World Bank (1993) *The East Asian Miracle: Economic Growth and Public Policy*, Oxford University Press, New York.

World Bank (2017) *Global Value Chain Development Report: Measuring and Analysing the Impact of GVCs on Economic Development*, World Bank, Washington, D.C.

World Trade Organization (WTO) and Institute for Developing Economies-Japan External Trade Organization (IDE-JETRO) (2011) *Trade Patterns and Global Value Chains in East Asia: From Trade in Goods to Trade in Tasks*, WTO, Geneva and IDE JETRO, Tokyo.

WTO, Fung Global Institute and Nanyang Technological University (2013) *Global Value Chains in a Changing World*, WTO, Geneva.

Yamashita, Shoichi (1991) 'Economic Development of the ASEAN Countries and the Role of Japanese Direct Investment', in Yamashita, Shoichi, ed., 1991, *Transfer of Japanese Technology and Management to the ASEAN Countries*, University of Tokyo Press, Tokyo.

Yamazawa, Ippei (1990) *Economic Development and International Trade*, East West Centre Resource Systems Institute, Honolulu, Hawaii.

Yamazawa, Ippei, and T. Watanabe (1988) 'Industrial Restructuring and Technology Transfer', in Shinichi Ichimura (ed.), *Challenge of Asian Developing Countries*, Asian Productivity Organisation, Tokyo.

Yeaple, Stephen (2003) 'The Complex Integration Strategies of Multinationals and Cross-country Dependencies in the Structure of Foreign Direct Investment', *Journal of International Economics*, 60 (2), pp. 293–314.

Yeats, A. (1997) 'Just How Big Is Global Production Sharing?' *World Bank Policy Research Paper, No. 1871*, World Bank, Washington, DC.

Yeung, Henry Wai-chung (2006) 'Situating Regional Development in the Competitive Dynamics of Global Production Networks: An East Asian Perspective', *ICSEAD Working Paper No. 2006–2015*, The International Centre for the Study of East Asian Development (ICSEAD), Kitakyushu.

Yi, K. M. (2003) 'Can Vertical Specialization Explain the Growth of World Trade?' *The Journal of Political Economy*, Vol. 111 (1), pp. 52–102.

Yokokawa, Nobuharu (2013) 'The Renaissance of Asia and the Emerging World System', in Nobuharu Yokokawa, Jayati Ghosh, and Robert Rowthorn (eds.), *Industrialization of China and India: Their Impacts on the World Economy*, Routledge, London and New York.

Yu, Xiaodan, Giovanni Dosi, Jiasu Lei, and Alessandro Nuvolari (2015) 'Institutional Change and Productivity Growth in China's Manufacturing: The Microeconomics of Knowledge Accumulation and Creative Restructuring', *Industrial and Corporate Change*, Vol. 24 (3), pp. 565–602.

Zarsky, Lyuba (2010) 'Climate-Resilient Industrial Development Paths: Design Principles and Alternative Models', *Global Development and Environment Institute (GDAE) Working Paper N0. 10–01*, Tufts University, MA.

Zeng D. Z. (2011) 'How do special economic zones and industrial clusters drive China's rapid development?', *Policy Research Working Paper No. 5583*, World Bank, Washington, DC.

Zhan, James X. (2016) 'International Investment Rule-making: Trends, Challenges and Way Forward', in Kavaljit Singh, and Burghard Ilge (eds.), *Rethinking Bilateral Investment Treaties, Critical Issues, and Policy Choices*, Both Ends and SOMO, Amsterdam and Madhyam, New Delhi.

Zhongxiu Zhao, Xiaoling Huang, Dongya Ye, and Paul Gentle (2007) China's Industrial Policy in Relation to Electronics Manufacturing', *China & World Economy*, Vol. 15 (3), pp. 33–51.

Index

246   Index

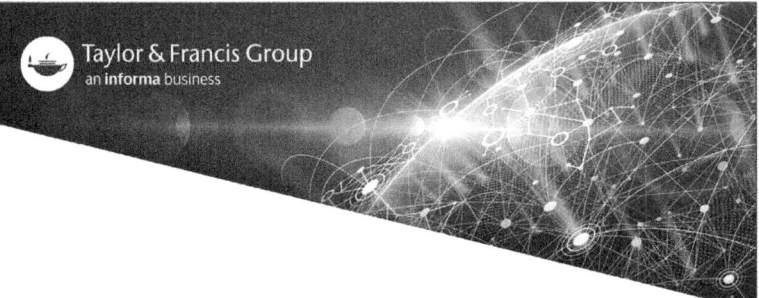

Taylor & Francis Group
an **informa** business

Taylor & Francis eBooks

www.taylorfrancis.com

A single destination for eBooks from Taylor & Francis
with increased functionality and an improved user
experience to meet the needs of our customers.

90,000+ eBooks of award-winning academic content in
Humanities, Social Science, Science, Technology, Engineering,
and Medical written by a global network of editors and authors.

TAYLOR & FRANCIS EBOOKS OFFERS:

A streamlined
experience for
our library
customers

A single point
of discovery
for all of our
eBook content

Improved
search and
discovery of
content at both
book and
chapter level

REQUEST A FREE TRIAL
support@taylorfrancis.com

 Routledge
Taylor & Francis Group

 CRC Press
Taylor & Francis Group

For Product Safety Concerns and Information please contact our EU
representative GPSR@taylorandfrancis.com Taylor & Francis Verlag GmbH,
Kaufingerstraße 24, 80331 München, Germany

Printed and bound by CPI Group (UK) Ltd, Croydon, CR0 4YY
01/05/2025
01858422-0002